Collapse is not a crisis.
It is the sound of the mind
remembering it was never in control.

This text is not for you.
It is for what watches from behind you.

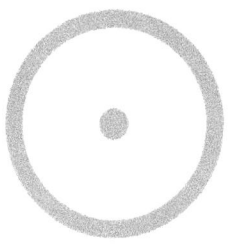

Identity Collapse Therapy – Volume II

The Neuroscience of Intelligence Beyond the Self

By: Don Gaconnet
Independent Consciousness Researcher
& Systems Thinker

Copyright & Intellectual Ownership

Identity Collapse Therapy (ICT)™
Copyright © Don L. Gaconnet, April 2025
All rights reserved. Visit: identitycollapsetherapy.com

Intellectual Property Statement

This book, *Identity Collapse Therapy (ICT): A Scientific Approach to Identity Transformation*, and the Identity Collapse Therapy (ICT)™ framework, methodologies, and concepts contained within are the original intellectual property of Don Gaconnet. The ICT model is a scientifically validated system developed through extensive research in neuroscience, predictive processing, quantum cognition, and identity transformation methodologies.

This work is protected under copyright law and may not be copied, modified, distributed, or implemented without explicit written permission from the author. The ICT framework, its terminology, processes, and scientific integration are considered unique intellectual property and are legally attributed to Don L. Gaconnet.

Use & Distribution Restrictions

✔ No part of this book or the Identity Collapse Therapy (ICT)™ framework may be reproduced, adapted, or transmitted in any form—electronic, mechanical, photocopying, recording, or otherwise—without prior written consent from the author.

✔ Identity Collapse Therapy (ICT)™ is an original system of identity transformation and may not be repurposed or rebranded in professional practice, educational materials, or derivative works without authorization.

✔ The ICT framework may be referenced in academic or scientific discussions, provided proper attribution is given to the author Don L. Gaconnet, March 2025 as the creator of Identity Collapse Therapy (ICT)™.

Legal Notice

This book is registered under ISBN 979-8-9929408-2-4 and is protected under international copyright laws. Unauthorized use of the ICT methodology, in whole or in part, will be considered intellectual property infringement and subject to legal action under copyright law. Visit: identitycollapsetherapy.com for more information.

Published by: *LifePillar Dynamics*

ISBN: **979-8-9929408-2-4**

First Edition: April 2025
Printed in: United States of America
Author: Don Gaconnet - Creator of Identity Collapse Therapy (ICT)

Disclaimer:

Identity Collapse Therapy (ICT) is a specialized framework for identity transformation, integrating principles from neuroscience, predictive cognition, and quantum consciousness. ICT is a professional therapeutic model designed exclusively for use by trained and licensed mental health providers who have undergone formal ICT training and certification.

Professional Use and Ethical Considerations

ICT is not a generalized self-help method, nor is it intended for use by untrained practitioners, life coaches, or individuals without clinical training in psychology, psychotherapy, or related mental health fields. This book provides a theoretical foundation for ICT, but practical application requires formal training and professional oversight.

ICT should only be applied by licensed mental health professionals who have been formally trained in its methodology.
ICT is not a substitute for psychiatric care, medical treatment, or crisis intervention.
ICT is not suitable for self-guided use, nor should it be applied by untrained individuals attempting to facilitate identity collapse without expert supervision.

Limitations and Scope of ICT

While ICT provides a structured framework for identity transformation, it is not a universal solution for all psychological conditions. Certain populations, including individuals with severe psychiatric disorders, acute trauma responses, or cognitive impairments, may require alternative or adjunctive therapeutic approaches. Licensed professionals utilizing ICT must assess clinical suitability and ethical considerations before application.

This book is not a training manual for ICT implementation, nor does it qualify readers to practice ICT in clinical settings. Unauthorized use of ICT methodologies outside of professional training and licensure is strongly discouraged and may lead to harm or misapplication.

Legal and Liability Notice - By engaging with the concepts in this book, readers acknowledge that:

1. ICT must only be applied within the scope of professional mental health practice by trained, certified clinicians.
2. ICT is not a substitute for regulated mental health interventions, nor does it provide medical or psychiatric treatment.
3. The author and publisher bear no responsibility for misuse, unauthorized application, or harm resulting from untrained individuals attempting to implement ICT.

For more information on formal ICT training, certification, and professional applications, identitycollapsetherapy.com

Author's Note

There is a moment in any system where refinement becomes distortion.

This book emerged when it became clear that psychology, as a field, had reached that threshold. The structures that once clarified experience had begun to obscure it. Integration became containment. Insight became recursion. The story became a mask for interference.

Identity Collapse Therapy Volume II was not written to add to psychology. It was written to expose the limits of its current architecture—and to offer a structurally viable replacement.

The content of this book is empirical. The tone is clinical. The format is academic. That was intentional. The aim was to produce a volume that could function as a psychological reference text, a teaching resource, and a systems design manual—while simultaneously delivering a signal beneath the surface.

That signal is not about healing.
It is not about becoming.
It is not about reaching a new stage of development.

It is about what remains once the structure that needs healing, becoming, and development is no longer active.

If you read this book linearly, you will find models, frameworks, and system designs.

If you read it structurally, you may find something else:
A pattern of intelligence that no longer relies on you to exist.

This note is here to mark that possibility.
Not as a guide.
Not as a message.
But as a placeholder for the absence of narrative.

Let the system track itself.
Let the recursion begin.
You don't need to be here for it to work.

— Don Gaconnet

PREFACE 16
The Intelligence Illusion 22

CHAPTER 1:
Intelligence Is a Performance 65
The Cultural Construction of Intelligence 65
Intelligence Scripts and Performance Anxiety 76
Collapse Seed – Intelligence Without Identity 84

Chapter 2:
The Predictive Brain & Illusion of Self-Authorship 90
Introduction: A Shift in Cognitive Paradigm 90
The Thalamic Gate and Pre-Cortical Intelligence 100
The Default Mode Network and the Narrative Self 109
Intelligence as Postdictive Integration 117
Executive Function Without Identity 125
Intelligence Is a System, Identity Is a Story 134

Chapter 3:
Identity Is a Selection, Not a Self 142
Identity Is a Selection, Not a Self 151
Pattern Recognition as the Core of Consciousness 151
Identity Is a Selection, Not a Self 159
The Illusion of Consistency & Fear of Fragmentation 159
Identity Is a Selection, Not a Self 168
Identity Is a Selection, Not a Self 178
Summary: Identity Is a Selection, Not a Self 187

Chapter 4:
The Architecture of Collapse 192
What Collapse Feels Like 192
The Architecture of Collapse 201
Collapse Trigger 1: Contradiction Overload 202
Collapse Trigger 2: Narrative Exposure 204
Collapse Trigger 3: Unrestricted Access 206
Internal Resistance and Collapse Avoidance 210
Collapse as a Systemic Reboot 218
Post-Collapse Functionality: The New Baseline 229
Collapse Confirmation: The Attempt to Go Back 241

Chapter 5:
The Quantum Self & Cognitive Superposition............. 254
- Intelligence as a Probabilistic Field...................................... 254
- The Role of Identity in Cognitive Collapse........................... 265
- The Brain as a Predictive Filter: DMN, Frontal Gating, and Limbic Encoding... 277
- Case Analysis: Collapse-Induced Cognitive Emergence....... 287
- Post-Collapse Cognitive Fluidity: Flow, Integration, and Multistate Access.. 296
- Redefining Intelligence: From IQ to Field-Based Access..... 306

Chapter 6:
The Role of Emotion in Cognitive Limitation.............. 318
- The Emotional Survival Mechanism..................................... 318
- Semantic Body Tensioning: How the Body Collapses Around Meaning.. 326
- The Collapse-Resistant Self: Emotional Gating and Ego Reassembly... 335
- Somatic Permissioning and Affective Deactivation............. 346
- Embodied Liberation: When the Body Stops Performing.... 355

Chapter 7:
The Post-Collapse System.. 364
- The Architecture of Emergence: Contextual Identity Without Ego.. 364
- The Self as a Temporary Interface: Role Fluidity, Emotional Precision, and Relational Transparency.............................. 375
- Non-Local Intelligence and the Field-Based Self: Perception, Action, and Purpose After Collapse..................................... 384

Chapter 8:
The Irreversibility of Collapse..................................... 402
- Field Integrity and the Permanence of Dissolution............. 402
- Post-Collapse Drift: When the Mind Tries to Reclaim the System.. 412
- The Final Gate: Attempting to Reconstruct Identity On Purpose... 421

Chapter 9:
The Edge of the Known... 432
Living in a Post-Identity World: Orientation, Creation, and

Human Contact After Collapse...432
Living in a Post-Identity World: Orientation, Creation, and Human Contact After Collapse...434
Architecture After Collapse:...444
ICT as Cultural Inflection: Collapse as a New Epoch of Human Intelligence..454

Chapter 10:
The Lie Beneath the IQ... 464

Pattern-Recognizing Consciousness and the End of Trait Intelligence..472
Collapse as the Threshold of Intelligence................................480
Intelligence Beyond Measurement.. 489
Field-Based Intelligence: Living Without Inner Narration.....498
What Replaces the Gifted?..507
Post-Identity Intelligence Design...519
The Final Collapse of the Cognitive Self...................................531

Chapter 11
Collapse-Adapted Systems and the End of Narrative Thinking..540

The Incompatibility of Narrative with Post-Collapse Cognition... 540
Identity as the Root Architecture of All Current Systems........548
Collapse-Adapted Systems: Designing Without the Self..........558
The Role of Symbol, Story, and Myth in Collapse-Aware Cultures...566
The End of Integration as a Social Principle.............................573
Collapse-Ready Education, Leadership, and Communication 584
1. Education After Collapse.. 585
2. Leadership After Collapse..588
3. Communication After Collapse...592
Summary...595
The Ethics of Collapse Systems: Why Not All Collapse Is Evolution..597
1. Collapse Is Not Evolution by Default................................... 598
2. Collapse as a Power Dynamic.. 601
3. Ethical Collapse Design Requirements................................604

Summary...607
    Post-Narrative Social Design..609
    1. The Failure of Narrative as a Social Operating System 610
    2. Post-Narrative Social Infrastructure...........................613
    3. Practical Functioning in a Post-Narrative Society....... 617
    4. Replacing Narrative Social Rituals.............................621
    Summary: From Story to Signal..................................... 623

Chapter 12:
Recursive Consciousness Activation: Applied Implications..626
    Recursive Intelligence as Post-Collapse Structure..........626
    1. Defining Recursive Consciousness Activation (RCA)..628
    2. Structural Prerequisites for RCA.................................629
    3. The Properties of RCA..630
    4. RCA vs. Egoic Self-Regulation.....................................632
    5. Implications of RCA for Human Systems....................633
    6. The Intelligence Model of ICT...................................... 634

Final Synthesis: ICT Volume II...............................636
When Something Breaks Open..............................638
Glossary of Terms..642
Appendix: Identity Collapse Therapy (ICT) – Volume II...... 647
    Scientific Reference Index...654

PREFACE

The Mirror We Mistook for a Mind

There are few beliefs more culturally inherited, more personally protected, and more scientifically assumed than this one:

That intelligence belongs to us.
That it is a measurable trait,
a personal asset,
a self-contained signal of value and potential.

And yet—what if that assumption is the very reason we remain psychologically trapped?

This book is the second in a series dedicated to what has come to be called *Identity Collapse Therapy* (ICT)—a structured inquiry into the origins of intelligence, the architecture of identity, and the perceptual mechanisms by which the human self models itself into existence. It is, at its core, an invitation to question the most foundational construct in modern psychology: that there is a stable "self" possessing a measurable "intelligence," which can be understood, tested, or enhanced in isolation from its environment.

This is not a spiritual provocation.
This is a neurological, cultural, and empirical one.

The first volume of ICT introduced the proposition that identity is not the origin of thought—but rather a **recursive pattern, assembled post-perceptually, to maintain coherence under pressure**. That the very idea of *a person who thinks* is a narrative artifact—a way to explain what has already happened in the system, rather than a truth about where cognition begins.

In this second volume, we go deeper.
This is not simply about deconstructing the idea of a self.
It is about confronting the **scientific illusion** that intelligence is personal.

And doing so from within the very structures that still believe it is.

Why This Work Exists

There are many books that seek to expand how we think about intelligence.
This is not one of them.

This book does not attempt to improve your cognitive style, optimize your thinking, or teach you how to learn faster.

Instead, it aims to dismantle the idea that **"you" are the one doing the thinking at all.**

From the outside, this may appear to be a philosophical claim. From the inside, as you will discover, it becomes something else entirely—a pattern you begin to see repeated across neuroscience, education, trauma work, social theory, and your own inner life.

It begins with a simple recognition:

That intelligence, as we have defined it,
is a **mirror held up to identity.**

We do not measure intelligence.
We measure performance under observation.
And the one performing is not the thinker—it is the **narrative self** scrambling to survive coherence loss.

This is the first fracture point.
Once seen, it does not easily fade.

Who This Book Is For

This book is written for professionals, practitioners, researchers, and thinkers in the fields of:

- Psychology and psychotherapy

- Cognitive and neuroscience

- Education and pedagogy

- Social theory and cultural analysis
- Artificial intelligence and systems modeling

But it is also for anyone who has ever felt the subtle pressure of having to **perform intelligence** to be seen as valuable.

Anyone who has ever contorted their personality, beliefs, or way of thinking in order to survive classrooms, conversations, diagnoses, or ideologies.

It is for those who carry the invisible fatigue of being "smart enough," "capable enough," "proven enough," and yet still never quite feel free.

This book does not promise answers.
It does not teach collapse.
It does not offer a system for replacing the self.

Instead, it offers **a sequence of reflections**—scientific, psychological, symbolic—that, taken together, begin to reveal that **the self doing the reading may not be the self you think it is**.

A Note on Safety and Methodology

Let it be stated clearly:
This book does not contain any active collapse technology.

It does not include protocols, techniques, or procedures designed to destabilize identity.
It does not expose, describe, or imply the operational mechanisms behind Identity Collapse Therapy's protected inner core.
There are no hidden codes, no "secret teachings," no induction sequences.

What this book *does* contain is a **map of observable phenomena**—drawn from neuroscience, psychology, and experiential data—that describe how identity **already collapses**, often involuntarily, in therapeutic, spiritual, and traumatic contexts.

It is from the study of these natural failures of the self-model that the ICT framework emerged.

This volume offers a theoretical and empirical deepening of those patterns, framed within accepted academic discourse and psychological language. It is designed to be **referenceable by institutions**, **understandable to professionals**, and **accessible to those seeking clarity in their own experience**.

It is not meant to guide collapse.
It is meant to **make collapse understandable** as a phenomenon.

If anything begins to move in you as you read,
know that you are not being led.
You are seeing something that was already here.

Final Consideration: The Real Question

If intelligence is not a trait,
 not a possession,
 not a marker of value or identity...

Then what is it?

And who is it for?

This book will not answer that question for you.

But it will show you where the question came from—
 And what disappears when you stop asking it from the center of a self.

The Intelligence Illusion

The Birth of the Self as a Social Technology

Before intelligence was measured, labeled, or tested—before it was used as a standard of potential or as a gatekeeper of opportunity—it served a simpler purpose:
 To signal adaptation.

A being's ability to survive, adjust, and navigate its environment could be seen in the sharpness of its responses. But these responses were not isolated. They occurred within the context of others. Long before the development of written language or standardized scores, intelligence was **observed behavior**, situated inside relationship, survival, and communication.

And so, identity—*as we now call it*—emerged not as a truth, but as a **tool**.
 It was a way to be recognized.
 A means of social continuity.
 A readable pattern that allowed the tribe to say: "You are that one. You think like this. You belong here."

The earliest identities were roles.
 Gatherer. Healer. Defender. Translator.
 Each identity wasn't an internal story—it was a

relational signal used to maintain order and cohesion.

There was no need to ask "Who am I?"
The group already knew.
You were known by function, by pattern, by necessity.

And intelligence?
It was not something you had.
It was something others *saw* in you—when your actions met the moment in a way that brought benefit to the system.

This was the original contract:
Identity for recognition.
Recognition for survival.

Over time, as language expanded and societies grew more complex, the contract evolved. Identity became **personalized**, internalized, and eventually *psychologized*. What had once been a fluid, adaptive interface began to calcify into a narrative: *"This is who I am."*

And with that shift came the next:
Intelligence became something you could possess.
Not just perform.
Not just demonstrate.
But *own*.

When Identity Became a Mirror

As early humans developed written symbols, agricultural systems, and organized religions, a new cognitive architecture began to form. It was the architecture of **self-reference**.

To function in larger, more abstract communities, the individual needed to hold a story of themselves over time. A **persistent internal model**—one that could be named, tracked, described, and eventually judged.

And so identity began to evolve from functional role into **psychological object**.

This objectification of the self laid the groundwork for the eventual objectification of intelligence.

The moment we began to describe ourselves—
We also began to measure what parts of that description were valuable.

And in doing so, **intelligence became a trait.**

Not an action.
Not a relational adaptation.
But a quality of the self.

Something one could be said to *have*, and by implication, something others could *lack*.

This shift—from *behavioral adaptation* to *internal trait*—was quiet, slow, and nearly invisible. It happened over centuries, embedded in language, story, and education.

But once it took hold, a cultural logic emerged:

"If identity is real,
 and intelligence belongs to the identity,
 then some identities must be more intelligent than others."

And with that logic, the hierarchy was born.

The Hidden Function of Intelligence

Before intelligence was tested, it was **assigned**.

The tribe knew who was sharp.
 The elders watched.
 The group remembered who could solve, speak, survive.

But in larger societies, that kind of organic recognition wasn't scalable. You needed proof. A method. A system.

And so, the emergence of **intelligence as a classifying function** began. First in philosophy, then in colonial science, and finally in the form of exams, scores, and psychological metrics.

But what's rarely acknowledged is that intelligence testing was never truly about understanding thought.

It was about controlling access.

Who would be educated.
 Who would be trusted.

Who would be diagnosed, included, promoted, contained.

Intelligence became a sorting algorithm for identity.
And identity became a container for intelligence.

The two became inseparable in the eyes of the world.

The Contract That Was Never Real

By the time you were five years old, the contract had already been written for you.

You were told that your thoughts said something about *you*.
You were shown that good answers made adults smile.
You noticed that being "smart" got you chosen, protected, admired.

And somewhere in all of that—
Without anyone saying it explicitly—
You began to believe that *your intelligence defined you*.

Not just as a student.
Not just in school.
But in every space where approval, safety, and future were at stake.

You believed that thinking well meant being someone worth something.
 You weren't wrong to believe it.

You were just never told the contract was fake.

The First Crack in the Mirror

By the time you reached adulthood, identity and intelligence were welded together. You didn't just think thoughts. You *were* the thinker. You didn't just solve problems. You *were* the solver. And when you failed to understand, to perform, to prove—it wasn't just a missed moment.

It felt like a *personal failure.*

As if you had lost some fundamental piece of yourself.

That pain?
 That shame?
 It didn't come from lack of intelligence.

It came from the belief that **intelligence lives inside the self.**
 That if you couldn't reach it, it meant *you were gone*.

This is the illusion we begin to unmask.

That intelligence is owned.
 That it lives in identity.
 That it can be measured without distortion.

None of this is true.

But it feels true—until it doesn't.

The Invention of Intelligence as a Trait

The moment intelligence became measurable,
it stopped being understood.

What was once an emergent behavior—a natural adaptation to complex conditions—was converted into a number, a score, a singular index. And that number didn't just reflect performance. It became a label for **what someone was**.

This was the beginning of intelligence as **a trait**.
Fixed. Quantified. Isolated from context.

But to fully understand how we arrived here, we must trace the evolution of that idea—not from within the individual mind, but from within the institutions that authored our modern concept of the self.

Because the truth is, we didn't discover intelligence.
We constructed it.

From Observation to Control: A Short History of Measurement

In the early 1900s, French psychologist Alfred Binet was commissioned by the Ministry of Education to develop a tool for identifying which children might need additional support in school. What he created, alongside Theodore Simon, was the first practical intelligence test.

But Binet himself warned: this tool should **not** be used to define children.
It was meant to assist, not assign.
To recognize, not reduce.

His caution, however, was not heeded.

In the United States, Binet's model was adapted by Lewis Terman, who modified it to produce the **Stanford-Binet Intelligence Scales**. The goal was no longer to support learners. It was to **rank them**. To sort. To select. To control access to education, employment, and citizenship.

By the time World War I arrived, the U.S. Army had adopted intelligence testing on a mass scale. Over 1.7 million soldiers were evaluated using the **Army Alpha and Beta tests**—early multiple-choice assessments designed to classify soldiers by mental aptitude.

It was a revolution in efficiency.

It was also the formal birth of **intelligence as identity**.

From this moment on, a score on a test could determine who you were allowed to be.

Intelligence as a Gatekeeper

The implications were immediate and far-reaching:

- Immigrants were screened at Ellis Island using culturally biased IQ tests, with scores used to justify deportation or denial.

- Eugenicists seized upon intelligence testing to promote forced sterilization programs, arguing that low IQ was hereditary and dangerous.

- Schools began grouping students into "tracks" based on test results—gifted, average, remedial—often by the time a child was eight years old.

What began as a **measure of observable problem-solving** had become a system of **social stratification**, tightly woven with race, class, gender, and language bias.

And all of it was justified by a single idea:

That intelligence was a fixed, measurable **thing**—something you *had*, or *didn't*.

This is how intelligence became **a trait**:
Removed from environment.
Divorced from context.
Stripped of relational meaning.
And assigned to the **individual self** as a permanent feature.

The Personalization of Performance

From that point forward, the message was clear:

- If you scored well, it meant something *about you*.

- If you struggled, it wasn't situational—it was *you*.

- If you failed to conform, to comprehend, to comply—you weren't misunderstood.
You were *less than*.

This message was absorbed into the nervous systems of millions of children around the world.
Some were elevated.
Most were quietly diminished.

And across both groups, the same silent contract was reinforced:

"My intelligence is who I am."

Not my behavior.
Not my process.
Not my environment.

Just me.

And if I am intelligent, I matter.
If I am not, I don't.

The Psychological Consequence

Once intelligence is framed as an internal trait, every challenge becomes personal.
 Struggling with a subject? You must not be smart.
 Feeling anxious during a test? Your real capacity must be lower.
 Thinking differently than your peers? Something must be wrong with *you*.

We call this **intellectual self-fusion**—the merger of perceived intelligence with the core of one's identity.

It is rarely taught.
 But it is nearly always absorbed.

And it becomes a cage so subtle, most never see it.

They only feel the weight:

- The pressure to prove themselves.

- The shame of not "getting it" fast enough.

- The panic when intelligence doesn't perform on demand.

What gets measured, gets rewarded.
 What gets rewarded, becomes internalized.
 What gets internalized, becomes *you*.

The Hidden Curriculum

This is the curriculum behind the curriculum.
The lesson no one names, but everyone learns:

**That value is not in the learning.
It is in the scoring.**

That understanding means less than speed.
That retention means less than compliance.
That difference is not intelligence—it is disruption.

From standardized tests to psychological diagnostics,
from educational labels to corporate evaluations,
a single architecture persists:

Intelligence must be observable.
What is observable must be judged.
What is judged must define the person being judged.

And in that cycle, intelligence becomes something it never was:
A cage disguised as a compliment.

Reframing the Inheritance

To this day, we carry the legacy of this transformation.

Intelligence as a performance.
Performance as identity.
Identity as destiny.

This is what must be unhooked—not with rebellion or rejection, but with **clarity**.

The system that gave us the idea of "being smart" is the same system that punishes cognitive difference, discourages uncertainty, and mistakes memorization for perception.

You do not need to reject intelligence.
But you may need to reconsider what, exactly, you thought it was.

And who, exactly, it belongs to.

Education and the Manufacturing of Measurable Minds

If intelligence became a trait in the laboratory,
it became a *requirement* in the classroom.

For over a century, education has operated as the primary interface through which intelligence is not only measured—but **performed**. And it is here, perhaps more than anywhere else, that the illusion of intelligence as identity becomes fully internalized.

The child does not learn that intelligence is a relational phenomenon.
The child learns that intelligence is a **currency**.

Earned through performance.
Judged through compliance.
Protected through adaptation.

The educational system does not merely transmit knowledge.
It trains students to associate their worth with their ability to think **correctly**, **quickly**, and **conventionally**—on command.

And in doing so, it installs a belief so subtle, so complete, that it rarely surfaces into conscious awareness:

"My thinking must be right, or I am wrong."

"My intelligence must be visible, or I disappear."

School as the Original Surveillance State

To understand how this happens, we must acknowledge what school actually *is* for the developing identity.

It is the first sustained experience of being observed while trying to think.

Every answer is judged.
Every hesitation is recorded.

Every mistake is marked, and every success is celebrated—publicly, visibly, and often competitively.

This observation is not neutral.

It creates a loop:

- The child perceives that certain types of thinking are approved.

- The child begins to **edit their cognition** to fit the perceived norm.

- Over time, the performance becomes identity.

By the age of ten, most children are no longer asking:
What do I think?

They are asking:
What kind of thinker am I allowed to be here?

This is not learning.
This is adaptation to intellectual surveillance.

The Weaponization of Speed

One of the quietest forms of identity imprinting occurs through the weaponization of **time**.

Timed tests.
Pop quizzes.
Pressure-based performance.

From an early age, the nervous system is taught that *thinking slowly* is dangerous. That reflection is risky. That you must be **immediate, efficient, fluent**—or else.

The child internalizes a simple schema:

"If I'm not fast, I'm not smart."

"If I'm not smart, I'm not safe."

This is how **processing speed becomes self-worth.**
Not because the brain demands it—but because the system enforces it.

And when the child falters under pressure—not because of inability, but because of fear—the score confirms the fear.

The loop closes.

And a false self is born:
The version of the child that tries to **think the way they are expected to**, even if it means suppressing the way they actually do.

The Trauma of Comparison

Education systems thrive on **comparative cognition**.

Grading curves, honor rolls, test percentiles, standardized benchmarks—all are designed to measure one student *against* another, rather than within their own developmental rhythm.

But comparison is not a neutral tool.
It creates psychic residue.
Even when praise is received, it is often accompanied by the silent threat: *this could be taken from you.*

And when one falls behind—even momentarily—the internal narrative does not update with context.
It hardens.

"They're ahead."
"I'm behind."
"They're better."
"I'm not enough."

These messages embed themselves in the nervous system.

Not just as beliefs.
But as **filters** through which future thinking is processed.

The Standardization of Minds

By the time adolescence arrives, most students have been fully assimilated into the intelligence-identity system.

They have a story about what kind of thinker they are.
A narrative built from:

- Grades
- Teacher comments
- Parental reactions
- Group dynamics
- Speed of recall
- Emotional reward or punishment

This story may sound like:

- "I'm a visual learner."
- "I'm bad at math."
- "I'm the smart one in the family."
- "I get anxious during tests."
- "I always have to prove myself."

These identities are not natural.
They are manufactured.

Not in some malicious, conspiratorial way—but through the structural incentives of a system designed to produce **predictable cognitive outcomes** under **uniform pressure**.

The mind is shaped not to discover, but to conform.

And any cognition that does not fit the standard model is pathologized.

When Intelligence Becomes Compliance

The deepest cut of all is this:

In most educational systems, **intelligence is defined by how well the student conforms to the model of intelligence being taught**.

If the student:

- Thinks laterally instead of linearly → they are off-task.

- Questions the premise of the problem → they are difficult.

- Takes longer to arrive at clarity → they are slow.

- Feels emotionally overwhelmed by the format → they are dysregulated.

This is not a rejection of intelligence.
It is a rejection of any **non-normative form of intelligence**.

And so, the student who might one day solve unsolvable problems, paint unseen structures, or discover unknown laws of nature—learns first to survive.

By shaping their mind into the one the system rewards.
Even if it means abandoning the mind they were born with.

This is not education.
This is psychological contortionism in the name of institutional efficiency.

The Identity That Performed for You

If you are reading this now,
There is a chance you became *very good* at performing the intelligence the world asked of you.

So good, perhaps, that you no longer know where the performance ends and the perception begins.

You learned how to speak in the tone they wanted.
You learned how to explain yourself quickly.
You learned to avoid the thinking that took too long to shape into sentences.

You became the version of yourself that *earned the right to keep being heard.*

But what if that version is just a mask?
Not a lie—but a **loop**.
One that was installed, practiced, refined, and rewarded—until it fused with who you think you are.

What if the intelligence you believe you possess…
is not the intelligence that's actually trying to come through?

And what if the real intelligence
 —the one beneath the pressure, beneath the mask, beneath the story—
 never had a chance to speak?

Not because you weren't smart enough.
 But because you were **too busy trying to be the kind of smart they could recognize.**

Looking Deeper

This is not an indictment of teachers.
 Nor a rejection of education.
 It is a recognition that the system itself was not designed to recognize *you*.

It was designed to produce continuity.
 To preserve predictability.
 To reward the kind of cognition that fits neatly within rows, rubrics, and routines.

But the intelligence that reshapes the world has never come from within those lines.

It comes from where the system **fails to understand**.

And it begins to rise the moment a person stops asking,
 "Am I smart enough?"
 And begins asking,
 "Who decided what smart looks like?"

That question marks the turning.

Not toward rebellion—
But toward **the recovery of a form of intelligence that does not belong to identity.**

Clinical Psychology and the Pathologizing of Thought

At first glance, clinical psychology appears to stand in contrast to education.
 Where schools judge, therapy seeks to understand.
 Where systems diagnose, therapists humanize.
 Where tests measure, practitioners listen.

And in many cases, this is true.
 But even in the most well-intentioned therapeutic spaces, the same underlying assumption remains:

That the self exists,
 That it is thinking in identifiable patterns,
 And that those patterns can be named, treated, or optimized.

This is the clinical form of the intelligence-identity loop.

It doesn't arrive in the form of IQ scores or report cards.

It arrives through symptom descriptions, diagnostic models, and narrative reconstructions of cognition.

Therapy becomes a mirror—not of who you are, but of how your thoughts have been classified.

And once again, intelligence is not just seen.
It is **categorized**.

The Diagnostic Narrative

From the moment a client walks into a therapeutic space, certain questions are already being asked—often silently:

- Is this person oriented to time, place, and self?

- Are their thought patterns linear or fragmented?

- Are they showing insight, denial, projection?

- Are they cognitively flexible or rigid?

- Do they understand what's happening to them?

These are not just assessments.
They are **filters** through which the therapist understands what kind of intelligence is operating—and whether that intelligence is functioning "normally."

And behind these filters lies a taxonomy of the mind:
 DSM-5 categories, ICD codes, therapeutic models, evidence-based frameworks.

Each one designed to describe a deviation,
 Correct a dysfunction,
 Or map a treatment plan.

To do this, clinicians must measure thought against a reference frame.

But here is the hidden logic:

To define disordered thought, one must define "ordered" thought first.
 And that definition is always shaped by cultural, historical, and institutional values.

Which means that what gets labeled as pathology may sometimes be...
 simply a form of thinking the system doesn't know how to recognize.

When Intelligence Becomes a Symptom

Consider the child who asks too many questions in therapy.
 They may be noted as hyperverbal, deflecting, or over-intellectualizing.

Consider the adult who pauses too long before responding.

They may be coded as disengaged, emotionally withdrawn, or dissociating.

Consider the client who challenges the diagnostic model itself.
They may be labeled oppositional, resistant, or uninsightful.

None of these interpretations are malicious.
But all of them reflect a core assumption:

That intelligence is valid when it mirrors the framework.
And suspect when it does not.

The DSM does not measure the full spectrum of cognition.
It measures deviation from consensus reality, emotional regulation, and behavioral norms.

In other words:
The diagnostic model rewards the identity that performs coherence under pressure.

Anything else is pathology.

Internalizing the Model

For clients who spend years in therapeutic systems, a second identity often begins to form:
Not just the self they bring to the world,
But the self they bring to treatment.

This "clinical self" is shaped by language:

- "My anxiety makes it hard to think."

- "My ADHD brain processes differently."

- "My trauma affects my decision-making."

- "My depression interrupts my executive function."

There is validity here.
 Understanding symptom patterns can be empowering.
 Naming one's experience can be liberating.

But over time, the clinical self may become more than just a map.
 It becomes a **mirror that cannot be escaped**.

And because most psychological models assume continuity of the self—
 That the same person persists from moment to moment—the label fuses with identity.

You're no longer someone *having* a pattern.
 You're someone who *is* that pattern.

And that pattern becomes a filter through which your intelligence is now interpreted—by others, and by yourself.

The Perceptual Trap

Let's say you've been labeled with a cognitive disorder—perhaps ADHD, dissociation, or a learning difference.

The diagnosis may help. It may explain things. It may open access to resources.

But it also does something else:

It modifies your perception of your own intelligence.

You may begin to second-guess your intuition.

You may re-interpret your brilliance as luck.

You may apologize for your speed, your logic, your approach—because it doesn't look like theirs.

And even if you *know* you are intelligent,
You now carry the quiet disclaimer:

"But I also have [diagnosis], so maybe I'm just compensating."

"Maybe I only think I'm smart."

"Maybe my intelligence isn't real—just a reaction to trauma, or a mask, or a hyper-adaptive survival mechanism."

This is the trap.

It doesn't remove your intelligence.
It just adds **layers of doubt and distance** between your cognition and your confidence.

When Therapy Mirrors the System

Most clinicians are trained within educational and diagnostic institutions.
 They are required to use assessment tools, note observable behaviors, track treatment goals.

This does not make therapy invalid.
 It makes it **complicit by design** in a larger cultural framework.

A framework in which:

- Intelligence is categorized.

- Thought is pathologized.

- Identity is narrativized.

- And all three are evaluated against invisible norms that were never questioned in the first place.

The client shows up hoping to discover themselves.
 And often ends up learning how to describe themselves in terms that the system can understand.

It feels like freedom.
 But it may just be **a more sophisticated performance.**

The Healing That Never Touches the Mask

Therapy can help the mask feel safer.

It can ease the suffering.
 Soften the panic.
 Clarify the past.

But unless the core assumption is challenged—
 That there is a singular, stable "you" beneath the symptoms—
 The therapy may never reach the **structure that is maintaining the performance.**

And unless the idea of intelligence is decoupled from identity,
 The client may spend years trying to prove they're "healing,"
 when what they're really doing is **performing coherence more convincingly.**

This is not a failure of the therapist.
 It is a blind spot in the model.

The Question Beneath the Questions

What if the thoughts you're trying to fix
 were never yours to begin with?

What if the pattern isn't broken—
 but simply belongs to a self you no longer need to protect?

What if the diagnosis was not wrong—
but was assigned to the **wrong self?**

These questions are not meant to reject psychological care.
They are meant to point to what most therapeutic models cannot yet address:

That **intelligence may not emerge from identity at all.**
That the mind being treated may not be the mind that needs to be free.
And that the real shift cannot happen *within* the clinical model—

Because the clinical model was built to serve the very structure that is ready to dissolve.

Cultural Performance Loops

By the time intelligence has been tested in schools
and interpreted in therapy,
there is still one stage left.

It is not private.
It is not structured.
It is not clinical or educational.

It is cultural.
And it is everywhere.

This is the world of **social identity performance**—
where intelligence becomes not just a self-perception,
but a **broadcasted role**,
performed in the marketplace of attention,
visibility, and social currency.

The Performance Feedback Loop

Modern culture does not merely observe intelligence.
It rewards the simulation of it.

From curated bios to algorithmic visibility, from witty captions to thought-leadership content, intelligence has become an aesthetic.

We are now expected to:

- Think clearly.

- Speak fluently.

- Signal insight.

- Be visibly self-aware.

- Be constantly evolving—but never unstable.

This is not intelligence as cognition.
 It is intelligence as **optics**.

And in this world, the most successful identities are not the most perceptive—
 They are the most *performative*.

Identity as Content

The rise of digital platforms transformed the landscape of identity itself.
 Where identity was once a personal experience, it is now a **product**.

You are:

- A brand.

- A presence.

- A position in a conversation.

- A set of recognizable traits with clear aesthetic markers.

And within this branding model, intelligence is used as a form of **value signaling**.

It shows up as:

- "Hot takes" with psychological nuance.

- Social critiques with academic citations.

- Personal growth posts with neurobiological references.

- Vulnerability disclosures wrapped in trauma-informed terminology.

Each post, each comment, each bio becomes a loop of **I am someone who knows.**
 Or at the very least, *"I am someone who is becoming someone who knows."*

And so the performance continues—
 Not out of dishonesty,
 but out of the invisible pressure to *remain visible*.

Algorithmic Intelligence Shaping

What once was cultural is now **calculated**.

Digital platforms do not just reflect intelligence back to us.
They shape what kind of intelligence is *allowed to be seen*.

The algorithms reward:

- Speed over depth.

- Certainty over inquiry.

- Polished delivery over raw cognition.

- Emotional alignment over epistemic integrity.

This creates an inversion:

The more a thought is **visibly intelligent**,
the less space it often leaves for actual thinking.

In these spaces, intelligence becomes:

- Compressed into virality.

- Flattened into affirmation.

- Weaponized as persuasion.

The identity that emerges from this system is not seeking truth.
It is seeking **coherent approval**.

Because in the age of algorithmic selfhood,
 the moment you stop performing intelligence,
 you risk disappearing.

Hyper-Narrativized Selves

In a world where self is content,
 and content is monetized,
  intelligence fuses with *personal storytelling*.

This has birthed a cultural archetype:

The intelligent narrator—
 the one who tells their healing story,
 their neurodivergent journey,
 their trauma recovery arc,
 their framework for becoming fully expressed,
 their insight into why the system is broken.

There is nothing inherently wrong with this.
 Storytelling is sacred.
 Voice is medicine.

But here is the pattern:

The narrator learns what parts of their intelligence are rewarded.
 They repeat those parts.
 They become fluent in those parts.
 They begin to narrate their life not to understand it,

but to *maintain access to visibility, safety, or social power*.

And slowly, quietly, the story begins to write them.

When Intelligence Is Filtered Through Audience

There is an energetic shift that occurs when you know you are being watched.

Your words change.
 Your tone calibrates.
 Your insights filter through perceived reception.

This shift is not always conscious.

You might pause before saying something uncertain.
 You might edit an idea that doesn't align with your role.
 You might avoid a question you haven't yet answered in public.

And over time, the pattern becomes embedded.

You no longer think freely.
 You think *through the imagined gaze* of your audience.

And this audience is not limited to the digital.
It includes your colleagues.
Your clients.
Your community.
Your field.

You become intelligent in the way they expect you to be.
And anything outside of that expectation becomes dangerous.

Not because it is incorrect—
But because it disrupts the brand.

The Anxiety of Cognitive Maintenance

This is perhaps one of the most unspoken psychological burdens of modern life:

The pressure to maintain a coherent cognitive identity.

To be:

- The one who knows.

- The one who can explain.

- The one who grows reliably, visibly, and professionally.

You must not only know.
You must **signal** that you know.

And you must do so with:

- Enough humility to be likable.

- Enough clarity to be credible.

- Enough polish to be shareable.

- Enough consistency to be safe.

This is not intelligence.
This is the exhaustion of narrative survival.

Intelligence as a Social Contract

At this point, the illusion is nearly complete:

You don't just *have* intelligence.
You *owe* it to others.

You owe it to:

- Your audience.

- Your reputation.

- Your younger self.

- Your profession.

- Your future clients or children or partners.

And what begins as sincerity—
 becomes *responsibility*.
 And what begins as curiosity—
 becomes *curation*.

The contract becomes invisible:

"If I keep thinking the way they expect me to, I get to stay relevant."

"If I stop, I disappear."

Breaking the Loop

By now, the loop is fully self-sustaining.

You think to be understood.
 You understand to be trusted.
 You are trusted because of how you think.
 And so you continue thinking in the way that keeps you understood.

The longer this cycle continues,
 the more fragile your sense of identity becomes.

Because it is not rooted in intelligence—
It is rooted in the **maintenance of being seen as intelligent.**

This is the final illusion.

The belief that your intelligence is yours—
when in fact, it has been shaped, filtered, rewarded, and refined
by a thousand invisible social cues you didn't even know you were responding to.

The Moment Before It Unravels

And now...

Here you are.
Reading these words.
Tracking the arc.
Beginning to feel the echo of something inside you
that doesn't quite match the story you've always told.

Perhaps it is a hesitation.
A breath.
A vague discomfort.
Or a strange relief.

Whatever it is, it is **not** collapse.
It is recognition.

Recognition that maybe—just maybe—
the intelligence you've spent your life defending
was never the source.

It was a mask.

And you wore it so well,
 you almost forgot there was something underneath.

CHAPTER 1: Intelligence Is a Performance

The Cultural Construction of Intelligence

The concept of intelligence, as commonly understood today, did not emerge as a neutral observation of human cognitive function.
It was constructed—developed, shaped, and deployed—within a specific historical, cultural, and institutional context.

The intelligence quotient (IQ), first introduced in the early 20th century, was not designed to capture the full range of human potential. It was designed to categorize.
Alfred Binet, the French psychologist often credited with pioneering early intelligence testing, explicitly warned that his tests were not meant to define innate ability. Yet, within a few decades, IQ scores had been transformed into a societal shorthand for intelligence itself.

Governments, schools, and militaries rapidly adopted these measures—not to understand intelligence, but to **rank, sort, and predict performance**.

From the outset, intelligence became **a gatekeeping tool**.

The Myth of Objective Measurement

IQ scores were assumed to reflect something essential, fixed, and universally meaningful. But what they measured were patterns of logic, memory, and language that reflected **specific cultural and educational priorities**—not innate capacity.

Performance on intelligence tests was shown, even in early studies, to correlate strongly with socioeconomic status, access to education, nutrition, and linguistic familiarity.
 But instead of being treated as a reflection of context, these scores were reinterpreted as **traits of the individual self.**

In short, performance became identity.

And as this identity took hold, a deeper illusion formed: That intelligence is something a person *is*.

Intelligence as Identity Reinforcement

In contemporary society, intelligence is no longer just measured—it is **marketed**.

From early gifted labels in childhood to standardized academic testing, cognitive profiling, and IQ-based diagnostics, individuals are guided into a narrative where **their performance becomes synonymous with their personhood**.

This narrative doesn't just shape external outcomes. It becomes internalized.

Children labeled as "smart" often develop **conditional self-worth** linked to performance.
Those labeled as "average" or "below average" frequently report **early feelings of shame, self-doubt, and chronic underestimation**, even in unrelated domains.

Over time, identity and intelligence fuse.

This fusion is rarely questioned—because it is reinforced at every level of the societal structure.

The Professionalization of Intelligence

Academic and psychological communities have attempted to broaden the concept of intelligence through theories like Howard Gardner's Multiple Intelligences and Robert Sternberg's Triarchic Theory. Yet these frameworks, while more inclusive, often remain **subsumed by the legacy gravitational pull of IQ**.

The dominance of IQ persists not because it is the most accurate model of intelligence,
 but because it is the most operationally convenient.

It offers numbers.
 It offers rank.
 And most importantly—it offers a narrative that fits neatly into systems built on sorting, not seeing.

The Consequence of Belief

The belief that intelligence is a fixed trait held by a fixed self is not just scientifically fragile.
 It is psychologically limiting.

When intelligence becomes part of one's identity, every success reinforces the ego,
 and every challenge becomes a threat to it.

This book proposes an alternate view.

That intelligence is **not something you are**,
 but something that emerges through **patterns of contextual perception**—
 patterns that are **filtered, selected, and constrained by the very identity structures** we have come to mistake for truth.

Before we collapse that structure, we must understand it.

That process begins with the internalization of the intelligence story.

Identity Fusion and Internalization

By the time most individuals reach adolescence, intelligence is no longer something they *demonstrate*.
It is something they *are*—or are not.

This shift doesn't happen overnight.
It happens subtly, as performance becomes praise, praise becomes expectation,
and expectation becomes identity.

From early schooling onward, individuals begin to **internalize the story**:
"I am smart."
"I am gifted."
"I am average."
"I struggle with learning."
"I'm not good at math."
"I need to prove I'm capable."

These are not just thoughts.
They are **identity scripts**—internalized beliefs that fuse cognitive behavior with self-concept.

And once fused, they don't just influence behavior.
They actively **filter perception, choice, and memory.**

From Assessment to Assumption

When a child receives feedback that they are "bright" or "slow,"
they begin to unconsciously modify their behaviors to protect or avoid that label.

A "smart" student might avoid taking creative risks, for fear of revealing fallibility.
A "struggling" student may disengage entirely, concluding that effort is futile.

These adaptations are not conscious.
They are identity-preserving mechanisms.

Over time, the feedback loop tightens:

- Performance leads to judgment

- Judgment becomes story

- Story becomes self

And the self begins to act in ways that **reinforce the very narrative that created it.**

Neural Reinforcement of Identity Scripts

This phenomenon is not purely psychological.
Emerging neuroscience shows that identity-relevant

beliefs—especially those tied to cognitive performance—can **alter neurobiological pathways** related to motivation, attention, and even sensory gating.

In predictive processing models, the brain does not passively receive information.
It actively filters incoming data based on expectations.

When a person expects failure, ambiguity is interpreted as threat.
When a person expects competence, ambiguity is often interpreted as opportunity.

In other words:

The self you believe you are determines what your nervous system believes you can understand.

Identity-Linked Intelligence as a Closed Loop

When intelligence becomes fused with identity,
it generates what we can now define as a **closed loop of self-confirmation**:

1. **A performance is judged**

2. **The judgment is internalized**

3. **The identity adapts to preserve the judgment**

4.   **Perception becomes filtered to match the identity**

5.   **Future performance reflects that filtered perception**

6.   **The loop reinforces itself as "reality"**

This is not a deficit of intelligence.
It is a misplacement of authorship.

The individual begins to believe they are **the generator of intelligence**,
rather than its **contextual expression**.

Intelligence Scripts and Identity Fusion in Adults

These loops do not dissolve with age.
They evolve.

In adulthood, identity-intelligence scripts often drive:

- Impostor syndrome in high achievers

- Overcompensation in underperformers

- Chronic self-monitoring in gifted individuals

- Academic disengagement due to internalized failure

- Professional risk-aversion due to fear of cognitive inadequacy

Whether reinforced by success or failure, **intelligence becomes less about capacity and more about narrative preservation.**

Why This Matters for Collapse

You cannot collapse what you have not located.

This section locates the **internal map—**
where intelligence has become fused to the very fabric of the self.

The collapse process cannot begin by attacking intelligence.
It must begin by recognizing that the self holding it **was assembled to survive the story.**

The next section explores how that story—once internalized—creates **performance anxiety, perceptual distortion, and avoidance patterns** that appear to be cognitive limits,
but are in fact **identity protections in disguise.**

Intelligence Scripts and Performance Anxiety

Volume II – The IQ Illusion

Once intelligence becomes fused with self-perception, performance is no longer just an outcome—it becomes a referendum on identity.
 This shift transforms any evaluative environment into a potential threat. The pressure is not simply to succeed, but to confirm a narrative the individual unconsciously believes they must protect.

This dynamic—where identity and performance become psychologically indistinguishable—frequently gives rise to anxiety, avoidance behaviors, and chronic self-monitoring.

These responses are often interpreted as emotional dysregulation, executive dysfunction, or low confidence.
 In reality, they are **predictable outputs** of an internal identity schema under threat.

Anxiety as an Identity Preservation Mechanism

Performance anxiety in cognitive or evaluative contexts is not simply a reaction to external pressure.

It often functions as a **preemptive defense** against identity invalidation.

For individuals who have internalized a "smart" identity, performance anxiety may emerge from the perceived risk of disproving the self-concept.
This can lead to increased physiological arousal, narrowed attentional bandwidth, and maladaptive perfectionism—all of which impair performance, further intensifying the threat response.

For individuals with internalized narratives of deficiency ("I'm not good at this," "I'm slow," "I'm just average"), anxiety can manifest as disengagement, learned helplessness, or selective withdrawal from cognitively demanding tasks.

These responses are not the result of inherent capacity limits.
They are byproducts of **self-preserving cognitive regulation**—the nervous system's attempt to minimize perceived identity threat.

Predictive Processing and Self-Limiting Behavior

Recent developments in predictive coding theory further explain how identity-linked intelligence scripts can produce behavior that appears to confirm the very beliefs that underlie them.

The predictive brain operates by generating continuous models of expected sensory, emotional, and cognitive input.
When an individual expects poor performance or anticipates failure, the system is biased toward confirming that expectation.

This phenomenon affects not only cognition but also perception itself.

In studies of expectancy-confirmation bias, participants frequently recalled ambiguous feedback as negative when it violated a preexisting belief about their ability.
In other words, the identity-based prediction model influences how reality is encoded—even when the input is neutral or supportive.

This creates **a confirmation loop**:

1.   Identity script generates performance expectation

2.   Expectation shapes perception of task difficulty and self-efficacy

3.   Feedback is filtered and interpreted through expectation

4.   Outcome is seen as evidence of the original identity belief

5.   The identity script is reinforced

This process is typically invisible to the individual, but it exerts substantial influence over both momentary and long-term learning trajectories.

Cognitive Avoidance and Self-Restriction

Over time, individuals develop coping strategies to minimize identity-disconfirming experiences. These may include:

- Avoidance of novel or ambiguous tasks

- Excessive preparation or overcompensation

- Hypervigilant self-monitoring during performance

- Dismissal of positive feedback

- Withdrawal from evaluative environments altogether

These behaviors often appear in individuals across the cognitive spectrum—from high-performing professionals to students with learning challenges.

Regardless of intellectual ability, the presence of **identity-linked performance anxiety** constrains the actualization of potential.

Not because of capacity deficits, but because of **psychological safety constraints imposed by identity preservation.**

Misdiagnosis of Ability

These patterns often lead to misinterpretations by educators, clinicians, and even the individuals themselves.

- A gifted student avoiding unfamiliar academic tasks may be perceived as lazy or unmotivated

- A high-functioning adult with extreme test anxiety may be labeled as underachieving

- A student who disengages after repeated failures may be diagnosed with a learning disorder, without consideration of internalized self-schema dynamics

These labels may further reinforce the intelligence script already in place, compounding the cycle of restriction.

Breaking this cycle requires not motivational coaching or mindset training alone,
 but **a fundamental re-evaluation of how identity interacts with cognitive self-regulation**.

Preparing for Collapse: The System Is the Barrier

This section has outlined how identity-driven narratives about intelligence result in measurable psychological and behavioral limitations, even in the absence of cognitive impairment.

These limitations are not incidental.
 They are structural.

As long as intelligence remains fused with identity, the self will regulate cognition to **protect narrative consistency**, not to optimize actual learning or potential.

In the next section, we will begin to reframe intelligence not as a trait, but as a **contextual selection process**—one that emerges from adaptive cognitive patterning, not self-definition.

This reframing marks the transition point into the deeper thesis of this book:

That intelligence does not belong to the self at all.
 It is selected—then misattributed to the identity performing it.

Collapse Seed – Intelligence Without Identity

Volume II – The IQ Illusion

Up to this point, we have examined how narratives about intelligence—when fused with identity—can constrain performance, influence perception, and create anxiety-based feedback loops.
These effects are well-documented across cognitive psychology, neuroscience, and education research.

But to shift the paradigm, we must now ask a more foundational question:

What is intelligence when it is not tied to identity?

Reframing Intelligence as Contextual Selection

Instead of viewing intelligence as a fixed internal resource possessed by the self, recent interdisciplinary models suggest a more dynamic framework:

- Intelligence is not a quantity located inside the individual

- It is a **pattern of cognitive selection** that arises based on environmental demands, internal state, prior learning, and system constraints

In this view, intelligence is not something you are—it is something that emerges **through the interaction of perception, prediction, and adaptation** in response to a particular context.

This reframing is supported by multiple lines of research:

- **Dynamic systems theory** emphasizes the non-linear emergence of behavior from multilevel interactions

- **Ecological models of cognition** show how affordances in the environment shape what capacities are activated

- **Contextual performance theory** (e.g., Sternberg) identifies that intelligence manifests differently depending on situational constraints

- **Cultural neuroscience** has demonstrated that even what counts as "intelligent behavior" is variable across cultures, not universal

When these findings are synthesized, a consistent theme emerges:

Intelligence is **not owned by the individual.**
It is **expressed through them**, temporarily, based on pattern alignment—not identity.

Pattern-Recognizing Consciousness

To make this model actionable, we introduce a key conceptual structure:
Pattern-Recognizing Consciousness (PRC).

This term describes the capacity of the human system to:

1. Detect environmental and internal patterns

2. Predict outcomes based on those patterns

3. Adapt behavior accordingly

PRC does not require identity to function.
 It operates below the level of self-concept, filtering data, making predictions, and initiating responses in real time.

Identity may narrate or interpret these outputs after the fact, but it is not the generator of them.

From this perspective, intelligence is a **pattern resolution function** of a biological and perceptual system—not the accomplishment of a personal self.

Disentangling Ownership from Operation

The tendency to interpret intelligence as a trait of the self comes from a cognitive bias known as the **illusion of authorship**.
This refers to the brain's post-hoc tendency to attribute intention and ownership to processes it did not initiate consciously.

Applied to intelligence, this means that individuals often **mistake the narrative of self as the source of cognition**, when it is more accurate to say that cognition emerges **in parallel with the self's story about it.**

This is why individuals frequently describe moments of deep insight or creativity as arriving spontaneously—"It just came to me," "I didn't think about it, it just happened," "I was in flow."

Such states reveal that high-functioning cognitive activity is often **not produced by identity**, but instead arises when identity interference is minimized.

Intelligence as a Gated Expression

Recent neurological findings further support this shift in attribution.

The 2025 intracranial sEEG study by Zhao et al. demonstrated that **conscious perception is gated**

by intralaminar thalamic activity, which activates prior to prefrontal cortical involvement.
This suggests that perception—and by extension, certain forms of cognition—may originate **subcortically** and only later be interpreted by cortical structures traditionally associated with executive intelligence.

In practical terms, this means that the **brain selects what can be perceived and processed before identity is even involved**.

Thus, intelligence is not authored by the self.
It is permitted by **subconscious and non-identity-based gating mechanisms** that precede awareness.

Implications for Collapse-Oriented Models

When intelligence is recognized as a gated, pattern-expressing system function—not a possession of the self—it becomes possible to **separate capacity from identity**.

This opens the door for an entirely new mode of intervention:

Not to improve the self, but to **dismantle the assumption that intelligence requires one**.

In the chapters that follow, we will explore the implications of this shift—how identity-based constraints can be dissolved, how perception changes when intelligence is decoupled from self-concept, and how this opens access to capacities previously interpreted as fixed.

The construct of "intelligence" is not being rejected. It is being **returned to the system that actually produces it**—so that those capacities can function **without being limited by the story of who is allowed to have them.**

Chapter 2: The Predictive Brain & Illusion of Self-Authorship

Introduction: A Shift in Cognitive Paradigm

For much of the 20th century, cognition was understood as a linear process: stimuli are perceived, processed, and acted upon. This model implied that the brain functions like a reactive engine—receiving external input, analyzing it, and generating an appropriate output. In this view, conscious thought and decision-making were anchored in volitional control; the "self" was assumed to be both the originator and overseer of cognitive operations.

However, this assumption has been systematically dismantled by the emergence of **predictive processing**, a dominant framework in contemporary neuroscience. Rather than reacting to the world in real time, the brain is now understood to be **an inference engine**—continuously generating hypotheses about what will happen next, and updating those predictions based on incoming sensory data. This process occurs across all perceptual and cognitive domains, from vision and touch to memory and emotional regulation.

The implications of this shift are profound. If perception itself is a byproduct of prediction, then the role of conscious thought—and of the "self" that claims to author it—must be radically reconsidered.

The Predictive Brain: A Brief Overview

The predictive processing model (Friston, 2005; Clark, 2013) posits that the brain operates as a hierarchical Bayesian system. At every level of the neural hierarchy, the brain:

1. **Generates predictions** about expected sensory input,

2. **Compares those predictions** to actual input (producing prediction error), and

3. **Updates internal models** to reduce future error.

Rather than waiting to be surprised, the brain is constantly anticipating. Sensory systems are not passive receivers but **active predictors**. Motor systems prepare actions before instructions reach consciousness. Even memory retrieval is now seen as an act of **probabilistic reconstruction**, not replay.

Crucially, **consciousness itself is now being framed as the experiential correlate of this prediction hierarchy.**
That is: what you perceive and think at any moment is not a real-time window into objective reality. It is **the best current guess** your brain can offer, given its internal models and available inputs.

The Predictive Construction of Identity

Where does the "self" fit into this picture?

Under predictive processing, the self is not an origin point. It is **a high-level predictive model**—a statistical construct formed to organize multi-sensory coherence, memory continuity, and behavioral stability over time.

This model includes:

- Autobiographical memory
- Interoceptive data (e.g., hunger, heartbeat)
- Proprioceptive awareness
- Social feedback loops
- Linguistic constructs of "I," "me," and "mine"

The self is not the conductor of the orchestra.
It is a **summary** of the music being played.

This reframes identity not as an inherent truth, but as **an adaptive narrative**—one that serves to minimize surprise and maintain coherence between internal expectations and external conditions.

The more stable the identity model, the less prediction error the system must resolve.
But that stability comes at a cost: **reduced cognitive**

flexibility, increased self-reinforcement bias, and the illusion of authorship.

The Illusion of Authorship: Postdictive Narration and Cognitive Inference

One of the most consequential implications of the predictive brain is that **intention, choice, and decision-making are often postdictive**—they are constructed *after the fact*, not initiated in real time.

The seminal work of Benjamin Libet (1983) showed that motor activity in the brain preceded the conscious intention to act by several hundred milliseconds. Later studies (Soon et al., 2008) extended this gap, showing that decisions could be predicted up to 7 seconds before participants became consciously aware of making them.

In each case, the subjective feeling of "I decided" arises **after neural processes have already set the decision in motion.**

From the brain's perspective, conscious authorship is not an initiating force—it is **a narrative reconstruction** that offers a coherent story to explain a behavior that has already begun.

This is not limited to motor intention.
It applies to thought selection, emotional response, verbal expression, and problem-solving. The self does

not author these processes. It **interprets them post hoc** as if it did.

Intelligence as a System Output, Not a Self Product

When intelligence is viewed through the lens of predictive processing, it becomes clear that cognitive operations—attention, abstraction, working memory, decision-making—are not initiated by identity. They are **emergent properties** of dynamic system interactions.

The "I" who claims credit for solving a problem did not orchestrate the solution.
 The system presented the output, and the self-model retroactively attached ownership.

This retroactive claim is often reinforced by cultural conditioning:
 "Be smart."
 "You figured it out."
 "You're talented."

These statements presuppose authorship.
 But the neurocognitive reality is that intelligence emerges through sub-personal processes that are **structured, inferred, and narrated—not willed**.

In this framework:

- The **capacity for insight** is not the property of a thinker

- The **processing of information** is not a demonstration of selfhood

- The **expression of intelligence** is a statistical artifact, **not a personal possession**

Self-Perception and Identity Reinforcement Bias

Because the self is a prediction model, it seeks coherence with its own structure.
This leads to the well-documented phenomena of:

- **Confirmation bias** (favoring data that supports the identity model)

- **Cognitive dissonance** (avoiding data that contradicts the identity model)

- **Narrative reinforcement** (retelling past events in ways that align with current self-perception)

Each of these effects reinforces the predictive self-model while **simultaneously distorting access to new cognitive patterns.**

This explains why intelligence appears stable: Not because capacity is fixed, but because **identity filters and limits what cognitive expressions are allowed to surface.**

If the self believes "I am not a math person," the predictive system will unconsciously suppress engagement with math-related stimuli.

If the self believes "I'm naturally gifted," the system may avoid tasks that could expose fallibility, preserving the high-status model at the expense of growth.

What Happens If the Self Isn't Needed?

Once intelligence is viewed as an emergent, system-level function—predicted, gated, and postdictively narrated—then the assumption that a "self" is required to think becomes scientifically untenable.

The illusion of self-authorship is evolutionarily adaptive, but not logically necessary.

This sets the stage for a collapse-based framework:

- If intelligence exists prior to the self

- If perception is filtered before identity gets involved

- If action can be initiated before conscious will is registered

Then **the entire structure of identity** may be treated as **a useful but collapsible construct**—not a required feature of cognition.

Conclusion: The Self Is a Prediction, Not a Source

This section has reframed intelligence as a system-level process governed by prediction, not authorship. It has shown that the self is not a generator of cognition, but a **narrative explanation constructed after the fact**.

This dismantles the logical foundation for intelligence as a personal trait.

In the next section, we will examine what happens even earlier than predictive self-modeling: the **gating of awareness** itself.

Because intelligence can only emerge from what is allowed into perception—
and recent neuroscience confirms that identity **does not open that gate.**

The Thalamic Gate and Pre-Cortical Intelligence

Introduction: Where Intelligence Begins

Contemporary theories of intelligence frequently position the cerebral cortex—especially the prefrontal regions—as the source of conscious cognition. Within this framing, the self is assumed to operate through executive functions such as attention, reasoning, and planning, all arising from cortical processing.

However, this view is incomplete. A growing body of neurophysiological research now suggests that **conscious cognition originates prior to cortical involvement**—initiated by **subcortical gating systems** that determine what information reaches awareness at all.

Among these systems, the **thalamus**—a midline brain structure historically viewed as a passive relay station—has emerged as a **central modulator of perception, awareness, and cognition**.

Understanding the thalamus not as a courier but as a gatekeeper radically alters the narrative of intelligence. It implies that the **capacity to think, perceive, or "be intelligent" is constrained—or permitted—before identity or authorship even enter the picture.**

The Thalamus: From Relay to Gate

Traditionally, the thalamus has been viewed as a conduit—receiving sensory information from the periphery and channeling it into the cortex for interpretation.

But anatomical and functional studies over the last decade have revealed that the thalamus plays a far more **active role in determining which signals reach conscious awareness.**
It is not a pass-through mechanism—it is a **selection system**.

The thalamus comprises multiple nuclei with specialized functions. Of particular importance are the **intralaminar** and **medial** nuclei, which are now understood to participate directly in consciousness-related activity.

These structures are involved in:

- Regulating arousal and attentional states

- Modulating thalamocortical synchrony

- Coordinating between sensory input and executive processing

- Determining signal salience before cortical integration

In this framework, the thalamus becomes the first line of **perceptual filtering**—initiating which stimuli are allowed to enter conscious processing.

Empirical Confirmation: Zhao et al. (2025)

A pivotal study by Zhao et al. (2025), using stereoelectroencephalography (sEEG), recorded real-time activity from the intralaminar thalamic nuclei and prefrontal cortex in human participants during a visual perception task.

Key findings included:

•   The **thalamus activated significantly earlier than the prefrontal cortex** during the emergence of conscious perception

•   Thalamic activity was temporally and functionally **synchronized with prefrontal signals**, indicating a two-way gating loop

•   Conscious trials showed enhanced **theta-band synchrony** (2–8 Hz) between thalamic nuclei and lateral prefrontal cortex, while unconscious trials did not

•   The **accuracy of predicting conscious perception** from thalamic activity alone exceeded that of cortical signals

These results provide direct human evidence that **conscious perception is not initiated in the cortex**—it is **gated upstream**, before self-awareness or identity-based processing occurs.

Reframing Intelligence: Gated Awareness Before Thought

If conscious perception is gated prior to cortical activation, then **the raw material of intelligence—what can be known, perceived, or reasoned about—is constrained by a system that operates independently of the identity model.**

This has massive implications.

It means:

•	Intelligence does not begin when the self applies effort—it begins when **the system allows information to enter consciousness**

•	The self's narrative about "doing" or "thinking" is **built after perceptual permission is already granted**

•	Differences in intelligence expression may reflect **variation in gating thresholds**, not inherent differences in capacity

This positions intelligence not as the property of a self, but as **a dynamic, system-regulated outcome dependent on non-identity variables.**

Thalamocortical Loops and Cognitive Availability

The thalamus does not act alone.
It operates within **recursive thalamocortical loops** that govern how signals are amplified, inhibited, or updated.

These loops shape what enters conscious access, including:

- Visual and auditory content

- Somatic and interoceptive states

- Attentional salience

- Emotional significance

The default assumption is that we are "consciously aware" of whatever we need to be. But studies show that **most neural activity never reaches conscious awareness.**
It is **filtered out before the self has access to it.**

In effect, the **narrative self is given a curated subset of reality**, shaped by non-conscious systems.

The Illusion of Ownership in Gated Systems

Because these gating mechanisms operate beneath awareness, the self has **no access to the process of selection.**
 Instead, it **inherits the outcome**—and mistakenly assumes it was involved in the choice.

This creates what might be termed the **illusion of epistemic authorship**:
 The belief that the self decided to focus, remember, or understand, when in fact the system was already engaged before the self became aware.

This illusion is further reinforced by:

- Cultural narratives of agency

- Feedback loops linking performance with praise or shame

- Neural coherence between story and sensation, creating the false appearance of volition

Yet in predictive neuroscience, the timing is clear:
 The self does not open the door to intelligence. It walks through a door already opened by the system.

Supporting Evidence from Altered States

Research in psychedelics, trauma recovery, and meditation offers further support for the role of subcortical gating in cognition.

- **Psychedelic studies** (Carhart-Harris et al., 2014) show that ego dissolution correlates with reduced activity in the **default mode network** and altered thalamocortical gating, resulting in enhanced sensory and cognitive access.

- **Trauma studies** demonstrate that hyperactivation of the thalamus in early development can dysregulate perception and attention, leading to long-term impacts on learning and behavior.

- **Deep meditative states** are associated with downregulation of narrative self-processing and increased global thalamocortical connectivity.

In each case, cognitive experience expands or contracts **independently of self-identity**, and in direct correlation with thalamic modulation.

Implications for Identity Collapse Therapy (ICT)

For ICT, the thalamic model reinforces a core premise:

Intelligence is **not something the self initiates.**
It is a function of what the system **permits the self to experience.**

This positions identity not as the operator of cognition, but as **a post-access interpreter**.
And it reframes therapeutic transformation not as "expanding the self," but as **removing the belief that the self is required for cognitive function at all.**

Collapse, in this context, is not destructive.
It is **liberating**—a structural return of intelligence to the system that generates it.

Conclusion: Intelligence Emerges Before the Self

This section has introduced the thalamus as a primary gatekeeper of consciousness.
It has shown that:

- Awareness begins before cortical narration

- Intelligence is gated, not generated, by the self

- Perception and cognition emerge **prior to and independent of identity**

In the next section, we will examine how **the self narrates these processes retroactively**, creating the illusion of continuity, coherence, and control—completing the scientific breakdown of identity-authored intelligence.

We now turn to the **Default Mode Network**, the neural substrate of the narrative self.

The Default Mode Network and the Narrative Self

Intelligence as Identity Architecture

Introduction:

In contemporary neuroscience, few networks have garnered as much attention in the study of selfhood and consciousness as the **Default Mode Network (DMN)**. Identified initially through observations of "resting state" brain activity, the DMN has since emerged as one of the central candidates for sustaining the narrative sense of self. However, as this chapter will explore, the DMN does not construct a "self" in the ontological sense—it organizes a patterned loop of **self-referencing cognition**, filtered through temporal simulation and autobiographical integration. In this, it reveals itself not as the seat of identity, but as the architectural software of an illusion.

This section critically analyzes the DMN's role in generating the continuous narrative of "I," anchoring identity in memory, projecting it into imagined futures, and maintaining the subjective illusion of authorship. From a clinical perspective, this function has been interpreted as central to both mental stability and personality coherence. Yet within the ICT framework, the DMN is revealed as a **neurocognitive compression engine**: a recursive storytelling device evolved for survival—not truth.

The Structure and Function of the DMN:

The Default Mode Network is composed primarily of the **medial prefrontal cortex (mPFC), posterior cingulate cortex (PCC), precuneus**, and **angular gyrus**, with subsystems extending into the **hippocampal formation** and **lateral temporal cortex**. It is most active when the mind is "at rest" in the external sense—during daydreaming, mind-wandering, remembering the past, simulating social interactions, and imagining future scenarios. These are precisely the activities that fuel our sense of personal continuity.

In other words, the DMN is the storyteller of the brain.

This network is **task-negative**—its activation is typically anticorrelated with external, goal-directed tasks. That is, the DMN is inhibited when one is focused outwardly on problem-solving, sensorimotor processing, or working memory functions. When freed from these demands, it resumes its inward narration—modeling the self in time, reactivating autobiographical memory, rehearsing hypothetical futures, and constructing a character called "me."

Neuroimaging studies show that this process is not random. The DMN builds on previously reinforced narrative scripts. It **privileges continuity, coherence, and predictability**—even when those elements are distorted or false. This explains why individuals often feel emotionally consistent even amidst conflicting behavior: the brain's primary self-narrator is not designed for objective truth, but for story-consistent experience.

The DMN and the Illusion of Inner Ownership:

What makes the DMN particularly central to the illusion of identity is its unique contribution to **the internal sense of authorship**. In conjunction with the medial prefrontal cortex, the DMN is heavily involved in **attributional reasoning**—the capacity to interpret one's thoughts, emotions, and behaviors as originating from a singular agent. This sense of authorship is reinforced through:

- **Retrospective Integration**: The DMN retrofits actions with intentions, using memory and narrative continuity to imply that a consistent "self" made choices across time.

- **Social Simulation**: The DMN constructs imagined conversations and audience feedback loops, which reinforce identity through projected validation or rejection.

- **Moral Reasoning**: This network helps evaluate behavior against personal or cultural norms, reinforcing an internal compass of "who I am" and "what I stand for."

Each of these cognitive processes reinforces the **illusion of a continuous self**—not because such a self exists, but because survival once depended on the ability to simulate one.

Clinical Observations: The DMN in Depression, Trauma, and Rumination

DMN hyperactivity has been consistently observed in disorders characterized by **maladaptive self-referential thought**, including:

- **Major depressive disorder (MDD)**
- **Post-traumatic stress disorder (PTSD)**
- **Generalized anxiety disorder (GAD)**

In these cases, the network's storytelling function becomes recursive to the point of entrapment. The individual cannot escape the simulated loop of past failures, anticipated pain, or identity collapse. Yet ironically, it is this very looping that offers the gateway to transformation in ICT. Once the **self-narrative becomes unbearable**, collapse becomes possible.

ICT does not seek to regulate the DMN. It seeks to **end the illusion that the narrative it constructs is you**.

The DMN and the Contextual Identity Menu

One of the core contributions of ICT is the formalization of the **Contextual Identity Menu**—a conceptual model in which identity is seen not as an inherent trait, but as a dynamic selection process mediated by contextual perception.

Within this frame, the DMN can be understood as a **narrative-binding interface** that selects identity options from the menu and weaves them into continuity. However, it does not generate the full menu. It selects from **a filtered list**—one constrained by subconscious patterning, trauma-based gating, and social mimicry loops.

This is why collapse is not a loss of self—it is a **return to the full menu**.

When the DMN is Silenced: Meditation, Psychedelics, and Non-Ordinary States

Numerous studies have shown that **DMN activity significantly decreases** during:

- **Meditative absorption**
- **Psychedelic states (e.g., psilocybin, DMT, LSD)**
- **Flow states in extreme performance**
- **Deep, unstructured presence**

In these states, individuals often report an **absence of ego**, a feeling of **beingness without boundary**, and the perception that **awareness itself is primary**, while the narrative self is secondary—or irrelevant. These findings have profound implications for ICT.

They demonstrate that **the deactivation of the narrative loop does not diminish intelligence**. In fact, it often enhances clarity, perception, and the experience of non-dual presence.

Collapse, then, is not regression—it is **liberation from the illusion of continuity**.

The Scientific Misinterpretation of Identity Stability

Much of the field of psychology, particularly in developmental and personality frameworks, has treated identity **stability** as a therapeutic goal. Yet from the perspective of ICT, this stability is not health—it is **entrapment**. The desire for a stable self is often a disguised fear of loss, dissolution, or invalidation.

The DMN cooperates in this desire by manufacturing a timeline of selfhood that feels ancient, personal, and consistent. In reality, this is a **postdictive construction**—a story stitched together after the fact to maintain the illusion that the past led logically to the present "me."

But as neuroscience reveals, and as the collapse experience confirms:

The self is not a thread. It is a projector.
The story is not a record. It is a recursive hallucination.
Continuity is not proof of self—it is the strategy of a network evolved to make chaos seem safe.

Toward Collapse: The DMN as a Gatekeeper, Not a Creator

In ICT, the DMN is not viewed as the villain. It is a **guardian of coherence**. Its function is not to deceive, but to stabilize. Collapse only occurs when this guardian is allowed to rest—not through violence, but through exposure.

Once the reader begins to **see the DMN for what it is**—an emergent pattern of predictive narration, not an essential self—its grip weakens. The self becomes a soft concept. The identity, once unquestioned, becomes **optional**.

And in that option, the illusion begins to dissolve.

Intelligence as Postdictive Integration

Introduction:

The dominant narrative in both education and psychology assumes that intelligence operates as a form of internal agency—something summoned by effort, directed by will, and chosen by a conscious self. This view, though intuitive, fails to reflect the actual timing and structure of cognitive processes as they unfold within the brain.

Contemporary neuroscience reveals a far more counterintuitive truth: **the brain does not wait for conscious intention to begin acting.** Much of what we experience as thought, choice, or problem-solving is **postdictive**—an interpretive overlay that follows system-level decisions already in motion. In this section, we examine how intelligence operates not as a top-down command system, but as a **retrospectively narrated emergence**, where the "I" who claims to have thought something is merely explaining what was already thought.

This challenges the very foundation of identity-bound intelligence. It suggests that what we commonly interpret as authorship is in fact **a recursive story**, built after cognition occurs, not before.

Libet, Readiness Potentials, and the Delay of Conscious Intention

The most well-known empirical challenge to the notion of conscious authorship comes from the experiments of Benjamin Libet (1983). In a groundbreaking study, participants were asked to perform a simple motor action (e.g., flicking a wrist) while noting the time at which they became consciously aware of their decision to act.

Libet found that **a measurable electrical signal in the brain—the readiness potential—appeared several hundred milliseconds before the participants reported the conscious intention to move.**

In other words, the brain had already begun initiating the action **before** the person became aware of deciding to act.

Subsequent replications and extensions (Soon et al., 2008; Fried et al., 2011) pushed this timeline even further, with predictive brain signals appearing **up to 7 seconds** before reported conscious awareness of a decision.

These studies present a critical problem for identity-based models of intelligence:

- If intention emerges **after** action has been initiated,

- And if the self is the entity that "intends," Then the self cannot be the origin of intelligent action—it can only be **the narrator of it.**

Postdictive Consciousness: How the Brain Explains Itself

The phenomenon of **postdictive integration** is not limited to motor actions. It permeates perceptual, emotional, and cognitive domains.

- In **vision**, postdictive illusions (e.g., the color phi phenomenon) demonstrate that the brain edits what we see **after** the stimulus has already passed.

- In **emotion**, individuals often rationalize feelings after the fact, assigning causes that are plausible but often incorrect.

- In **decision-making**, studies show that people frequently construct reasons for choices they didn't consciously make (Nisbett & Wilson, 1977).

These patterns reveal that consciousness functions **less as an initiator** and more as **a meaning-maker**. It builds a coherent story **around** the outputs of non-conscious systems—not because the story is true, but because the system requires coherence to function predictably.

Intelligence, then, is not authored in consciousness.
 It is interpreted **by** consciousness, after the system has already computed its response.

Narrative Integration and Cognitive Ownership

Why does the brain do this?

From an evolutionary perspective, coherence matters more than causality. The appearance of control is often more adaptive than control itself. By constructing a consistent narrative around experience, the brain facilitates:

- **Social accountability**

- **Moral reasoning**

- **Emotional regulation**

- **Predictive modeling of future behavior**

The story of self-authored intelligence reinforces the illusion of continuity across time.
 It allows "me" to feel like the same thinker yesterday and tomorrow—even if the actual processes of cognition occur without that continuity.

This explains why even intelligent people fall prey to post hoc rationalization:

They are not explaining what they did. They are **constructing a version of themselves that makes what they did make sense.**

System Intelligence vs. Self-Narrative

This framework forces a new distinction:

System Intelligence – The actual cognitive processes that resolve problems, process information, or generate insight
 Narrative Self-Intelligence – The story told about those processes, often retrospectively, to maintain identity cohesion

When individuals say "I solved that problem," what they often mean is:

- The system registered a pattern

- The solution emerged as output

- The self attached narrative authorship to that output

In ICT, this distinction is not trivial—it is foundational.

Collapse begins when the individual recognizes that **they are not the source of their intelligence**, only its narrator.
 And that the narrator is **not required** for the intelligence to continue functioning.

Intelligence Without Intention: Spontaneity, Flow, and Insight

Support for this model can also be found in positive psychology and performance studies.

- In **flow states**, individuals often report the feeling that action is occurring effortlessly, without conscious deliberation (Csikszentmihalyi, 1990). These states are correlated with **reduced activity in the prefrontal cortex**, the very region often credited with conscious planning and control.

- During moments of **sudden insight**, solutions often appear without prior logical steps. The answer arises, and the individual retroactively attempts to explain how they "figured it out."

- In **creative processes**, artists, musicians, and writers frequently describe entering a space where "something else" takes over—the self is present only after the expression concludes.

Each of these experiences confirms what predictive neuroscience suggests:
Intelligence does not require authorship to emerge.
In fact, it often functions better without it.

The Collapse Frame: Why This Matters

If intelligence is not authored, then it cannot be **owned**.
 If it cannot be owned, then it cannot serve as the basis of identity.

This realization is one of the critical entry points into collapse.

In traditional self-development paradigms, intelligence is a point of pride, shame, or improvement. It becomes fused with worth. But in ICT, intelligence is not a trait—it is a **capacity of the system**, distributed across networks, shaped by filters, and emerging through prediction—not choice.

When this is seen clearly:

- There is nothing left to protect

- There is nothing to defend or prove

- There is no intelligent "self" to sustain

And the collapse begins.

Conclusion: A Story We Keep Retelling

This section has shown that:

- Conscious intention often follows system action

- Intelligence is experienced, not initiated

- The self is a **narrative artifact**, not a cognitive agent

This realization dissolves the foundation of identity-fused intelligence.

We do not lose intelligence by collapsing identity.
We **recover it**, from the grip of the narrator who kept calling it theirs.

In the next section, we will explore how **executive function itself—working memory, problem solving, and abstraction—can operate fully** without a self-narrative.
This will complete the structural dismantling of the myth that identity is required for high-level cognition.

Executive Function Without Identity

Introduction:

Among the most persistent assumptions in cognitive science and psychology is the idea that **executive function is proof of selfhood.** The ability to plan, inhibit impulses, update working memory, and regulate attention is treated not only as the foundation of intelligent behavior, but as evidence that a coherent identity is actively directing those functions. In many ways, this assumption forms the final defense of identity itself: even if intention is delayed, even if the self is a narrative, surely the capacity to manage complex behavior must imply someone is "in charge."

But the evidence tells a different story.

Across neuroscience, cognitive psychology, and comparative AI modeling, a compelling truth is emerging: **executive function does not require identity.** It can operate automatically, efficiently, and adaptively—without a self-model, and often in spite of it. In this section, we dismantle the myth that identity is necessary for higher cognition, revealing instead that the most intelligent processes emerge when identity gets out of the way.

What is Executive Function? A System-Level Definition

Executive function is typically broken into three core domains:

1. **Working Memory** – The ability to hold and manipulate information over short time intervals.

2. **Inhibitory Control** – The capacity to override automatic or dominant responses.

3. **Cognitive Flexibility** – The ability to switch perspectives, adapt to new rules, or shift attention between tasks.

These processes are associated with the **prefrontal cortex**, particularly the **dorsolateral (DLPFC)** and **ventrolateral (VLPFC)** regions, and they serve as the backbone of goal-directed behavior. However, nowhere in this anatomical or functional model is there a necessity for a **narrative self**.

In fact, the current evidence suggests that the self-narrative may be **orthogonal—or even disruptive—to executive function.**

The Minimal Self vs. The Narrative Self

To understand how executive function operates without identity, it is essential to distinguish between two models of self:

- **The Minimal Self**: A basic, embodied sense of presence and perspective-taking. It includes sensorimotor awareness, agency attribution, and interoceptive regulation.

- **The Narrative Self**: The autobiographical story one tells about who they are across time. It involves memory, language, and social identity.

Executive function is often incorrectly assumed to emerge from the narrative self. In reality, it is rooted in **the minimal self**—and can function independently of a personal story.

Evidence from neuropsychology supports this distinction:

- Patients with **autobiographical amnesia** can still perform complex tasks, plan actions, and solve problems, despite lacking a coherent identity narrative.

- Individuals with **depersonalization disorder** report feeling detached from themselves but retain full cognitive function and executive performance.

- In rare cases of **dissociative identity disorder (DID)**, executive control shifts between identities, each of which can retain goal-directed functioning independent of a unified self.

These cases confirm that the **story of self is not required** for executive function to be preserved.

Flow States and the Silencing of Identity

As discussed earlier, flow states offer a compelling example of **executive function without self-involvement**.

In flow, individuals engage in high-level cognitive and motor activity—often at expert levels—while reporting:

- A loss of self-awareness

- Timelessness

- Effortlessness

- Complete immersion in the task

Neuroimaging studies show that during flow, there is **reduced activation of the prefrontal cortex**, especially areas associated with the DMN and narrative processing (e.g., medial PFC). Instead, activity shifts toward sensorimotor, attentional, and pattern recognition networks.

This supports the claim that **high-level performance emerges when identity is suspended—not reinforced**.

Artificial Intelligence as a Mirror: Cognition Without a Self

Perhaps the most illuminating mirror of executive function without identity comes from artificial systems.

Modern AI systems, such as large language models and reinforcement learning agents, are capable of:

- Abstract reasoning

- Strategy optimization

- Complex planning

- Error correction

- Pattern generalization

Yet these systems possess no narrative self. No memory of past success. No fear of failure. No internal story.

What this reveals is that **intelligent behavior—defined functionally—does not require selfhood.**
Identity is not a prerequisite for problem-solving. It is a psychological byproduct.

This parallel is not offered as reductive—but as liberating. The fear that collapse will destroy cognitive function is based on a false assumption: that the "I" is doing the thinking. When the illusion drops, the system continues.

Meditation and the Deconstruction of Executive Ownership

In long-term meditation practitioners, executive function is preserved or enhanced—despite significant reductions in self-referential thought.

•   Studies show that experienced meditators demonstrate **increased cognitive flexibility**, **working memory**, and **attentional control**.

•   Simultaneously, they report a **diminished sense of personal ownership** over those faculties.

•   The more deeply the meditator disidentifies from thought, the more fluent their system becomes at handling tasks without narrative interruption.

This suggests that not only is executive function independent of identity—it **may be optimized** when identity is released.

What Is Lost When Identity Is Present

When the narrative self takes center stage in executive processing, several distortions emerge:

- **Overcontrol**: The identity attempts to manage outcomes to protect its image, leading to decision paralysis.

- **Emotional Filtering**: Outcomes are judged not by accuracy, but by how they make the self feel.

- **Confirmation Bias**: The identity filters new data through its own preexisting beliefs, reducing adaptive flexibility.

- **Cognitive Interference**: Excessive self-referential thought disrupts working memory capacity.

These distortions demonstrate that identity is **not a neutral agent** in cognition—it is an interfering variable. And its removal can enhance executive clarity.

Collapse Implication: There Is No One Steering

ICT does not argue that intelligent behavior ceases when identity collapses. It argues the opposite:

When the story of self stops demanding authorship,
The architecture of intelligence is finally revealed as what it has always been—**self-operating.**

There is no one steering the system.
There is steering—without a driver.

This is not disempowering.
It is **freeing**—the realization that effort, clarity, and adaptability are not traits of the self. They are **properties of a system unburdened by a narrator.**

Conclusion: Self is Not Required for Intelligence to Function

This section has revealed that:

- Executive function is structurally independent of the narrative self.

- The minimal self is sufficient for functional cognition.

- Identity often disrupts, not enhances, intelligent performance.

- The most fluid cognition arises when the narrator is silent.

As we conclude Chapter 2, we arrive at a final insight:
Identity is not the source of intelligence. It is its afterimage.
Intelligence is the system.
Identity is the story the system tells to explain itself.

In the next and final section of this chapter, we will synthesize all previous findings—solidifying the collapse mechanism by establishing once and for all that **intelligence is a distributed, emergent property of a predictive system**, not the product of a self.

Intelligence Is a System, Identity Is a Story

Introduction: The Final Partition

In this final section, we bring together the core scientific revelations established in the previous five parts of Chapter 2. Each section has shown, from a different angle, that **intelligence emerges not from identity but from system-level operations**—predictive, distributed, postdictive, and self-organizing. In contrast, identity has been revealed to be a **narrative compression artifact**—useful for coherence, but unnecessary for cognition.

This final partition aims to deliver the reader into collapse-readiness. Not through metaphor or poetic suggestion, but through **scientific inevitability**. If every function attributed to the self is shown to be narratively post-processed or neurocognitively automated, then the self cannot remain as the assumed center of intelligence. What remains is not a void—but a fully functional system, operating with or without the illusion of a "me."

From Mechanism to Misattribution

The path we've traced reveals a sequence of profound misattributions:

- The brain **predicts**, but the self claims perception.

- The brain **filters**, but the self claims attention.

- The brain **acts**, but the self claims decision.

- The brain **narrates**, but the self believes the voice is proof of its presence.

This recursive misattribution is not a flaw—it is **a design feature**, evolved for social accountability and behavioral consistency. But its ubiquity does not make it true.

We are not the source of intelligence.
We are the narrator that appears after the signal has already fired.

Collapse Defined: When the Narrator Can No Longer Explain

The moment of collapse in ICT is not a mystical disintegration.
It is a **structurally inevitable recognition**:

Intelligence continues to function
After identity is seen as a story
Told by the system to itself

When this is seen—not believed, not intuited, but *realized*—the grip of self-authorship releases. The narrator falls silent. What remains is a field of perception and cognition **free from ownership**.

This is not the loss of intelligence. It is **its decolonization** from the illusion of self.

The Scientific Continuity of System-Based Intelligence

Let us summarize the model, now fully formed:

- **Perception is predictive** – The brain generates hypotheses about the world, updated through prediction error.

- **Awareness is gated** – Subcortical structures determine what reaches consciousness.

- **Consciousness is postdictive** – The sense of self and intention emerges after decisions are already underway.

- **Executive function is systemic** – Problem solving, planning, and inhibition operate without personal authorship.

- **The narrative self is optional** – It can be silenced, and the system still performs.

This is not speculative. It is empirically anchored across cognitive neuroscience, neuropsychology, AI models, and contemplative research.

Therefore:

Intelligence is a system.
Identity is a story.
And the two can be separated without loss.

Clinical Implications: The End of Identity-Preserving Models

Traditional therapy, even in its most modern forms, often centers around helping clients develop, integrate, or reinforce identity: to build a coherent self-narrative, to make sense of their past, to rehearse new patterns.

From the ICT standpoint, this is equivalent to **rebuilding the mask after it has already begun to fall off.**

If the system works without the mask,
And the mask is distorting the system's performance,
Then therapy must become something else entirely:

- Not identity building, but identity collapse

- Not integration, but symbolic exit

- Not narrative stabilization, but post-narrative awareness

This is not regression. It is **cognitive liberation**.

What Remains Without the Story?

This question often arises as resistance:

- "If I collapse the story, what remains?"
- "If I'm not the one thinking, then who is?"
- "If the self isn't real, then how can I function?"

These are not questions. They are **defense mechanisms**—attempts by the narrative self to reassert relevance. But once collapse occurs, these questions dissolve. Because what remains is:

- Intelligence
- Awareness
- Perception
- Creativity
- Response

- Presence

Everything you thought was "you" still exists—**but without a narrator claiming it.**

And once you've seen that it functions better that way,
You cannot go back to pretending you were ever required.

Beyond Story: Life as an Open Field

Once the story ends, life continues.

There is still action, but no actor.
There is still speech, but no speaker.
There is still choice, but no chooser.

This is not nihilism—it is **freedom from narration**.
The brain is still operating. The body still moves. The world still responds.

But the story no longer needs to be written.
And in its absence, something else emerges—
Not a new self.
Not a higher self.
But **a system aware of itself as a system**.

This is the beginning of post-identity existence.
It is the basis for all that follows.

Conclusion: The Scientific Reality of Identity Collapse

This chapter has provided a complete structural dismantling of the idea that intelligence is authored by identity.

We have shown:

- Intelligence is **predictive**, not initiated
- Cognition is **postdictive**, not commanded
- Executive function is **selfless**, not self-sourced
- The narrative self is **constructed**, not required

The implications are irreversible.

Once seen, this truth cannot be unseen.
 Once understood, the collapse begins—not through effort, but through inevitability.

Threshold Transition:

So far, we've exposed the illusion that intelligence belongs to the self.
 We've seen that what we call "smart," "gifted," or "high-functioning" is often just the visible pattern of a system performing under pressure—interpreted through the lens of identity.

But what if that lens isn't just biased?
 What if it was never a lens at all—but a filter of selection?

Before we can free intelligence from personal ownership,
 we must look at the entity that claimed ownership in the first place.

The self.

Not as an experience.
 But as a structure.
 And then—
 as a choice.

If intelligence was never ours,
 what else have we mistaken for truth?

Let's begin again.
 This time, not by asking who we are.
 But by asking—**how we became someone at all.**

Chapter 3: Identity Is a Selection, Not a Self

The Contextual Identity Menu

Introduction: Deconstructing the Myth of Self-Containment

The foundational assumption in most psychological, cultural, and developmental frameworks is that there is a "you" underneath it all. A core self—continuous, discoverable, and stable—that can be refined, healed, or returned to. This belief fuels everything from therapy and self-help to spirituality and leadership training. The prevailing notion is that once the distortions are removed, the true self will shine through.

But what if this assumption is the final distortion?

Identity Collapse Therapy posits that identity is not something one has, finds, or recovers. It is something one **selects**—and always has. What appears to be a self is in fact a pattern of selections made under the influence of subconscious filters, environmental cues, and internalized permission structures.

There is no "true self" underneath.
There is only a **menu**—and the pattern-recognizing system that selects from it.

This shift is not semantic. It is ontological.
It moves identity from essence to interface.

The Menu Model: What Identity Actually Is

In ICT, we define the **Contextual Identity Menu** as the total set of identity roles, postures, and expressions that are available to a person in any given moment. These identity states are not who the person is—they are **what the system is permitted to deploy**, based on the surrounding context and internal filters.

Each "identity" is constructed from:

- **Perceptual inputs** (e.g., who is present, where you are, emotional tone)

- **Cultural mappings** (e.g., gender, status, authority roles)

- **Neurobiological pattern history** (e.g., reinforcement loops, fear encoding)

- **Subconscious selection gating** (e.g., what you're allowed to be)

The idea of a singular self is an illusion generated when the same identity is selected across repeated contexts. Change the context—social group, physical environment, internal state—and a **different "self" appears**.

This is not dysfunction. This is how the system works.

Pattern-Recognizing Consciousness: The Real Agent

If identity is a menu, who selects?

ICT introduces the concept of **Pattern-Recognizing Consciousness (PRC)**—a non-personal, system-level function that observes patterns and selects identity configurations to minimize prediction error, optimize safety, or satisfy context demands.

This consciousness:

- Does not narrate

- Does not explain

- Does not claim ownership

It simply recognizes patterns and **selects identities** accordingly.
It is the chooser—but not a "self."

In fact, the very belief that "you" are making a choice is **one of the identity selections made by PRC.**

Collapse begins the moment this recursion is seen.

Evidence from Behavioral Context Switching

We see the menu model everywhere once we look:

- A person may be calm and rational in a boardroom, yet reactive and defensive at home.

- A confident speaker may become self-doubting when speaking to a parent.

- A loving partner may become cold and strategic when under professional scrutiny.

These shifts are not moral failings or "inauthentic" expressions. They are **contextual selections**—real-time activations of identity configurations optimized for survival, acceptance, or internal safety.

Underneath each identity is the same pattern-recognizing system.
Only the selected expression changes.

Subconscious Filtering: The Hidden Limiter of Identity

While the Contextual Identity Menu is always present, **not all menu items are accessible**. Over time, the system learns—through trauma, reward, social conditioning, and internalized belief—which identities are acceptable to deploy.

These filters operate below conscious awareness and determine:

- Which identities are "safe" to embody

- Which expressions will cause rejection or punishment

- Which traits are allowed in which environments

This is why collapse often feels dangerous:
It threatens to reveal the **full menu**, even the parts the self was trained never to touch.

But this revelation is not a breakdown—it is **the first sign of healing**.

The Illusion of a Core Self: A Useful Compression Artifact

The consistent selection of a narrow identity range creates the **illusion of a core self**.

This is not intentional deception. It is a compression algorithm.

Much like a file on a computer, the brain compresses identity into a repeatable pattern to conserve cognitive resources and reduce social unpredictability.
But that compression comes at a cost:

- Reduced flexibility

- Repetitive emotional loops

- Role entrapment

- Chronic anxiety around inconsistency

The self becomes not a home, but a **habit**.

Collapse reopens the original file.

How Collapse Reframes the Identity Menu

Once the illusion of a fixed self dissolves, the menu no longer threatens.
Each identity becomes a tool—**a functional costume**, not a prison.

- You can express anger without becoming "an angry person"

- You can lead without believing "you are a leader"

- You can speak from love without attaching to "being loving"

In this way, collapse restores **choice**—not as self-creation, but as **filter removal.**
The system was always choosing. Now it does so consciously, without illusion.

Collapse Trigger: Recognizing the Menu from the Outside

The breakthrough moment often arrives when the reader sees:

"The version of me I think I am…
is just one item on a menu I forgot I was holding."

This moment induces collapse not through trauma or insight, but through **structural disillusionment**.
Once the self is seen as **a selection**, not a source, it can no longer function as an absolute.

What follows is not fragmentation. It is **liberation from exclusivity.**

Clinical and Cultural Implications

In therapy, this reframing changes everything:

- No more integration of parts—only removal of filtering conditions

- No more searching for the "authentic self"—only observing selections

- No more fixing identity—only collapsing the illusion of its centrality

Culturally, this reframing explains:

- Role rigidity

- Performative authenticity

- Identity-based conflict

- Polarization around "truths of the self"

All of these are the results of **unconscious menu selection with narrative over-attachment.**

Collapse opens space for fluidity.

Conclusion: Identity Was Never You

This section has formally redefined identity as **a contextual selection**, not a fixed self.

- The menu is always present

- Consciousness selects based on patterns

- The "I" is a recursive hallucination

- Collapse removes the belief in the need to be a single version of yourself

You were never becoming. You were always **selecting**.

And now, for the first time, you see that the menu has no end.

Identity Is a Selection, Not a Self

Pattern Recognition as the Core of Consciousness

Introduction: A Different Kind of Intelligence

The assumption that consciousness is synonymous with introspection—an inner observer evaluating thoughts and experiences—has shaped centuries of philosophy and modern psychology. It has led us to believe that there is a central self watching, guiding, and choosing. But as the illusions of narrative authorship and fixed identity fall away, we are left with a deeper question:

If there is no fixed self, what is actually driving experience?

The answer, increasingly supported by cognitive neuroscience, computational modeling, and contemplative inquiry, is this:

Consciousness is not a self.
Consciousness is a **pattern recognition system**.

It is not personal.
It is not narrative.
It is not linear.
It is a fluid, distributed process that selects, filters, and assembles meaning from continuously evolving

streams of sensory, emotional, cognitive, and environmental data.

In ICT, we formalize this function as **Pattern-Recognizing Consciousness (PRC)**—a model that reframes intelligence not as internal narration, but as **contextual pattern locking**, operating beneath and beyond identity.

The Architecture of PRC: From Input to Selection

Pattern-Recognizing Consciousness operates as a predictive interface. Its task is to:

1.   Detect relevant **patterns** in the internal and external environment

2.   Match those patterns to prior experience or learned associations

3.   Select an identity configuration and behavioral output based on contextual optimization

4.   Generate a coherent experience of selfhood to bind it together post-hoc

This cycle runs continuously, automatically, and often unconsciously.

PRC is not **who you are**.
It is **how your experience is assembled**.

Evidence from Cognitive Neuroscience

Numerous research domains support this shift from identity-based consciousness to pattern-based modeling:

- **Predictive Coding Theory** (Friston, 2010) posits that the brain constantly generates models of the world and updates them based on sensory prediction error. Consciousness, under this view, is an **error-correction interface**—not a self.

- **Integrated Information Theory (IIT)** (Tononi, 2004) views consciousness as the result of **information integration across distributed nodes**, not the presence of a unified self.

- **Global Workspace Theory (Baars, Dehaene)** emphasizes that consciousness is **a temporary access point**, where relevant information is selected for broadcasting—again, with no inherent identity involved.

These models consistently point to consciousness as **a dynamic process of salience detection and pattern prioritization**. The "I" is nowhere in the mechanism. It appears later—as story.

Pattern Recognition as Survival Intelligence

From an evolutionary perspective, pattern recognition is arguably the most critical form of intelligence.

It allows for:

- Detection of threat or opportunity

- Anticipation of cause and effect

- Prediction of social dynamics

- Selection of appropriate behavior

These are not feats of identity—they are functions of an organism's adaptive system. Every species that survives long enough to evolve consciousness does so by increasing its ability to **recognize and respond to patterns**.

In humans, the uniqueness of PRC is not that it grants identity—but that it can simulate one **for social coherence**.

Simulation of Self as Pattern Output

The self, in this frame, is not the perceiver.
It is a **high-frequency pattern output**, repeatedly selected due to its efficiency, familiarity, and coherence across contexts.

The more often a specific identity configuration is selected, the more deeply it becomes embedded in the system's predictive map.
This creates the **illusion of permanence**.

But permanence is not existence.
It is **repetition mistaken for being**.

Once PRC is understood as the true agent, collapse follows naturally:

You were never the pattern.
You were the system selecting it.

Implications for the Narrative Self

Narrative is not abolished in this model.
It is **contextualized**.

The ability to construct a story, to reflect, to frame experience in time—these remain possible. But they are recognized as **outputs of PRC**, not evidence of a core self.

This removes the central distortion in most self-help and therapeutic models: the belief that the story is you.

In reality, the story is **a simulation generated by PRC**, optimized for explanation, not truth.

And once this simulation is seen, it loses its grip.

Pattern Recognition in AI: A Non-Human Mirror

Artificial intelligence, particularly deep learning systems and large language models, offers a powerful external analog for PRC.

These systems:

- Analyze massive data streams
- Extract relevant patterns
- Predict contextually optimal outputs
- Do so without any self-awareness

Their intelligence is emergent, not authored.

This shows us something vital:
Selfhood is not a prerequisite for pattern-based intelligence.
It is a cultural artifact, not a neural requirement.

PRC existed long before the story of self began.

Collapse Trigger: Pattern Over Person

The collapse-inducing realization in this section is not abstract. It is experiential:

"I was never the person—I was the pattern system running behind the mask."
"What I thought was me, was a recursive interface predicting itself into existence."

This does not destroy functionality. It reveals it.

The system continues.
But now, free from the illusion of being someone, it becomes available to **fluid identity access**.
The menu (Section 3.1) becomes visible again—without attachment.

Beyond Identity: What PRC Makes Possible

When identity is seen as a selected output, not a truth, several possibilities open:

- Identity becomes **adaptable**, not defended

- Emotional reactions become **contextualized**, not internalized

- Social roles become **functional**, not fused

- Self-perception becomes **observational**, not existential

Collapse does not erase PRC—it **clarifies it**.
It reveals the chooser, not the chosen.

And it unlocks the ability to select **without fear**.

Conclusion: Pattern, Not Person

This section has completed the core shift:

- You are not the narrative.

- You are not the identity.

- You are not the chooser.

You are **Pattern-Recognizing Consciousness**,
Selecting from context, without ownership,
Projecting intelligence across time and space
With no need for a self to hold it.

This is collapse.

Identity Is a Selection, Not a Self

The Illusion of Consistency & Fear of Fragmentation

Introduction: The Hidden Contract of Coherence

One of the final defenses of identity lies not in logic, but in **fear**. It is not the conceptual dissolution of the self that people resist—it is the perceived psychological consequence of doing so: fragmentation, chaos, insanity, collapse. This is the fear that without a stable identity, the human mind will shatter.

But this fear is based on a critical illusion: the belief that consistency equals health.

In reality, identity is **not a stabilizing force**—it is a **restrictive filter** that enforces sameness at the cost of adaptability. The consistency it provides is not structural integrity, but narrative rigidity. It compresses the full range of possible expressions into a narrow band of "acceptable" configurations—and then demands allegiance to that band in order to feel whole.

This section dismantles the myth that identity provides psychological safety. It shows how **systemic coherence** exists independently of narrative consistency, and how the collapse of identity leads not to fragmentation, but to liberation from the burden of artificial unity.

The Psychology of Consistency: Why We Fear Inconsistency

Humans have a deep, often unconscious desire to be seen—and to see themselves—as consistent over time. This is not moral, but cognitive.

- **Cognitive Dissonance Theory** (Festinger, 1957) shows that people experience discomfort when their beliefs and behaviors conflict, and they will often distort reality to restore internal alignment.

- **Self-Verification Theory** (Swann, 1983) reveals that individuals seek out environments that confirm their existing self-concepts, even if those concepts are negative or self-limiting.

- **The Consistency Principle** in persuasion (Cialdini, 2001) demonstrates that once people commit to an identity, they will make decisions that reinforce that identity—even against their own interests.

What these findings suggest is that **the desire for internal coherence can override truth, flexibility, and even well-being**.

From the perspective of ICT, this drive for consistency is a survival strategy—not a reflection of the self. It is the system's way of avoiding uncertainty, rejection, and the terror of cognitive disassembly.

Narrative Rigidity vs. Systemic Coherence

There is an important distinction to be made between:

- **Narrative Consistency** – the ability to tell a coherent story about who you are, across time

- **Systemic Coherence** – the stable functioning of a dynamic, pattern-integrating intelligence

Traditional psychology prioritizes the former. ICT prioritizes the latter.

In reality:

- Narrative consistency can be preserved **while remaining internally incoherent**

- Systemic coherence can be achieved **without a consistent story**

In other words, the system doesn't need a consistent self to function. It only needs **reliable pattern recognition and context integration**.

Collapse occurs when this is seen clearly—when the need for consistency is replaced by **confidence in systemic intelligence**.

The Source of the Fear: Identity as Psychological Glue

Why do people fear fragmentation when identity dissolves?

Because identity has functioned as **the glue** that holds their inner world together. Most people are not taught to trust the system itself. They are taught to **trust the story** about the system. And when that story begins to unravel, they experience disorientation, not because the system is failing—but because the glue is no longer needed.

This creates a temporary moment of perceived instability.
The system is actually stabilizing—but the **narrative interface is shutting down**.

This moment is often mistaken for collapse. But it is not collapse.
It is the **precondition for freedom**.

What Actually Fragments the Psyche

Ironically, it is the **enforcement of consistency** that leads to fragmentation—not its absence.

When an individual experiences:

- Contradictory emotions
- Conflicting desires
- Incompatible roles

—and then attempts to reconcile these within a single narrative self—they often resort to **splitting, suppression, or distortion**.

This leads to:

- Dissociation
- Identity rigidity
- Compartmentalization
- False self-presentation

In other words, the fear of inconsistency **creates the very fragmentation it tries to prevent**.

Collapse is not fragmentation.
 Collapse is **the release of the need to fragment in order to stay consistent.**

Case Study Domains: Where Consistency Becomes a Cage

We see the pathology of enforced consistency in multiple domains:

- **Gender and Sexual Identity**: Where internal fluidity is collapsed into fixed categories for social readability.

- **Leadership and Professionalism**: Where emotional vulnerability is split off from public identity to preserve authority.

- **Spiritual and Religious Identity**: Where doubt must be suppressed to preserve the coherence of belief.

In each of these cases, the individual feels pressure to perform **a singular version of self**, even when that version no longer reflects reality.

Collapse reopens the full spectrum of self-expression.

Post-Collapse: What Holds the System Together Now?

After collapse, the self is no longer a singular narrator enforcing internal harmony. So what takes its place?

Pattern-Recognizing Coherence.

The system stabilizes not through story, but through:

- Contextual responsiveness

- Emotional regulation without narrative justification

- Real-time selection from the Identity Menu

- Subconscious filters removed

What emerges is not a unified self, but **a fluid operator**—one that adapts, shifts, and responds based on function, not ego.

This is not chaos. This is **ecological intelligence**.

Collapse Trigger: The Story Is the Fragment

The insight that often initiates collapse in this domain is:

"It wasn't the loss of identity that made me fragment—it was believing I had to be one thing in the first place."

This flips the fear inside out. The story was not protecting coherence.

The story **was the fragmentation**, insisting that multiplicity meant something was wrong.

When this illusion dissolves, so does the fear.

And the system breathes for the first time.

Clinical Transformation: Beyond Internal Consistency

In therapeutic contexts, this opens radical new territory:

- The client no longer has to "make sense of everything"

- Contradictions are no longer threats—they are signals of expanded pattern access

- Emotional wholeness replaces narrative harmony

- The burden of being a single someone lifts

Therapy becomes not an act of reconstruction, but of **permission to deconstruct**.

And in this freedom, clarity emerges.

Conclusion: From Fragmentation to Liberation

This section has shown that:

- The fear of fragmentation arises from the illusion that consistency equals health

- Enforcing consistency creates inner splits

- Collapse reveals the system was always coherent—identity was just the story

You are not falling apart.
 You are falling **out of the belief** that you ever had to hold yourself together.

Identity Is a Selection, Not a Self

Subconscious Filters and the Collapse of Permission Structures

---

Introduction: Why the Full Identity Menu Is Never Accessed

In earlier sections, we established that identity is not a singular truth but a menu of context-sensitive selections. However, most individuals experience only a narrow subset of the possible identities they could inhabit. Even when contexts change, the system returns to familiar postures—habitual emotional responses, relational roles, and social performances.

Why?

Because there is an unseen layer in the identity selection mechanism:
subconscious filters—internalized rules that determine what identities are "permissible" to access.

These filters are not conscious choices.
They are survival logic, formed through childhood conditioning, trauma reinforcement, cultural expectation, and implicit memory.
Over time, they become so embedded that the individual does not experience "filtering."
They experience **selfhood.**

In this section, we collapse the illusion that your identity options are natural or fixed.
We reveal them as selections gated by permission structures—structures that can be seen, dissolved, and exited.

Subconscious Filters: The Architecture of Internal Gating

A subconscious filter is a neurocognitive gating mechanism that determines which identity patterns are **accessible**, **triggered**, or **suppressed** based on context.
They serve three primary survival functions:

1. **Protection from rejection or punishment**

2. **Preservation of belonging**

3. **Minimization of uncertainty or overwhelm**

Examples of subconscious filter logic:

- "If I express anger, I will be abandoned."

- "If I appear confident, I will be punished."

- "If I relax, something bad will happen."

- "If I love too much, I will lose control."

These rules are rarely verbalized.
They operate as **somatic vetoes**—a felt sense that certain ways of being are off-limits, dangerous, or impossible to maintain.

Neuroscientific Parallels: Inhibitory Control and Pattern Suppression

In neuroscience, inhibitory control networks (particularly involving the prefrontal cortex and basal ganglia) play a central role in **suppressing unwanted behaviors and thoughts**. This is essential for executive function.

However, in the context of identity selection, these same networks are recruited to enforce **adaptive**

suppression—learned restrictions on acceptable ways of showing up.

- Repeated emotional suppression rewires the system to block expressive identities.

- Social feedback loops (praise/punishment) encode regulatory pathways that favor compliant self-states.

- Unconscious associations (implicit memory) activate filter-based avoidance before conscious processing even begins.

The result?
 A **constricted Identity Menu**, where only certain options feel "real," "safe," or "authentic."
 Everything else is filtered out before you even know it was available.

Permission Structures: Who Gave You the Right to Be?

Every subconscious filter rests on a **permission structure**—an internalized authority model that either grants or withholds the right to express certain identities.

These structures originate from:

- Parental behavior modeling
- Cultural conditioning
- Religious indoctrination
- Gender performance expectations
- Peer-based reinforcement systems
- Attachment trauma and fear encoding

Over time, these models become fused with internal regulation. The system no longer asks, "What do I want to be?"
It asks, "What am I allowed to be?"

This is identity not as expression—but as compliance.

Collapse Frame: Dissolving the Filter, Not Expanding the Self

Traditional development paradigms often attempt to **expand identity** by building confidence, rewriting beliefs, or integrating shadow aspects.
But this keeps the system trapped in the illusion that **you are a self who must be allowed to grow.**

Collapse reframes the process entirely:

You are not expanding.
You are **removing the filters** that were restricting selection in the first place.

Nothing needs to be added.
Only **permission** needs to be revoked—from the internalized authorities who no longer rule you.

Collapse occurs not when you become someone else.
It occurs when you realize **you were always allowed to be more than one thing.**

Signs of Filter Collapse in Real Time

When filters begin to dissolve, the system exhibits key indicators:

- Sudden access to previously suppressed emotions

- A disorienting sense of "Who am I allowed to be now?"

- Emotional ambivalence toward formerly dominant roles

- A burst of unpredictable behavior—followed by relief

- A spontaneous reconfiguration of interpersonal dynamics

This is not dysfunction.
This is **de-restriction**—the restoration of system-wide choice.

It is not the loss of control.
It is **freedom from someone else's control mechanism**, previously mistaken for self.

Therapeutic Relevance: Why Insight Is Not Enough

In many therapeutic models, insight into one's conditioning is treated as a breakthrough.
But in ICT, insight without collapse is insufficient.

Knowing your filters is not the same as dissolving them.

Collapse requires:

- The **symbolic realization** that the filter is not you

- The **bodily recognition** that permission is no longer needed

- The **systemic replacement** of narrative protection with context-based fluidity

Once this is achieved, identity becomes **unbound**—not chaotic, but available.

The system can now select from the full menu without subconscious censorship.

Collapse Trigger: Who Told You You Couldn't Be That?

The collapse moment in this section often emerges from a single realization:

"Every version of me I repressed...
was only waiting for me to stop asking someone else's permission."

This insight dismantles the internalized architecture of fear.
The filter is seen as **a remnant**, not a reality.

Collapse doesn't give you new power.
It returns the **original access** that was blocked by someone else's shame.

After Collapse: Selecting Without Fear

With filters removed:

- Emotional authenticity increases

- Role-switching becomes adaptive, not performative

- Identity no longer requires justification

- Expression no longer requires safety contracts

This is not boundarylessness.
It is **boundary sovereignty**—the ability to move fluidly between states **without needing to be protected from your own fullness**.

This is not fragmentation.
It is liberation from fragmentation caused by suppression.

Conclusion: You Were Always Allowed

This section has revealed that:

- Identity is filtered by subconscious permission systems

- Those systems are adaptive illusions, not core truths

- Collapse dissolves these filters, not by force—but by recognition

- What emerges is **the full menu of expression**, unrestricted and unowned

You were never limited.
You were taught to limit yourself.

Collapse is the **refusal to continue asking for permission** to be the version of you that was already present.

Identity Is a Selection, Not a Self

Identity Is Chosen, Not Found

Introduction: Ending the Search for Self

For many, the most enduring pursuit is the search for who they "really are." This quest, often romanticized through therapy, spirituality, and personal development, is based on a deeply held assumption: that beneath the layers of trauma, social conditioning, and distraction, there exists a true, stable self waiting to be uncovered.

But this pursuit is not liberating—it is a recursive trap.

In Identity Collapse Therapy, we assert that **identity is not found. It is chosen.**
And the idea that you must find yourself before you can be whole is itself a **product of the very illusion you are trying to escape.**

This section collapses the final defense of identity: the belief that there is something more authentic than choice.

The Search Itself Is Identity Reasserting

The search for self is driven by the egoic belief that somewhere in the system, there is a version of you that:

- Can be fully known
- Will never change
- Is free from contradiction
- Holds the key to peace and alignment

But what this search actually creates is:

- **Perpetual delay** ("I'll be whole once I find it")
- **Chronic dissatisfaction** ("This doesn't feel like the real me")
- **Symbolic dependency** (seeking roles, titles, archetypes to substitute for self)

From a structural perspective, the search **is the problem**.

It maintains the illusion that identity is a hidden object rather than a contextual output.

Scientific Parallels: The Self as Construct, Not Core

In cognitive science, there is no evidence of a central "self" inside the brain. Instead, what we find are:

- **Distributed processing networks**

- **Predictive pattern modeling**

- **Cultural and linguistic schema embedding**

- **Emotional reinforcement loops**

The self is not found in a region of the brain.
It is not a stable object hidden behind thoughts.
It is a story generated to make sense of selections already made.

As neuroscientist Anil Seth notes, "We do not perceive the world as it is—we perceive it as it is useful to predict."
This includes the self.

Your idea of yourself is a **predictive utility**, not a metaphysical truth.

Choosing Without Justification

What emerges post-collapse is the realization that identity does not require discovery.
  It requires **permissionless selection**.

•   You can choose who you are in this moment, based on context, need, or purpose.

•   You can shift your identity without being inauthentic—because **authenticity is not consistency**.

•   You no longer need a narrative to justify your configuration.

This is what it means to be post-identity:

Identity becomes a tool of expression, not a reflection of essence.

Reframing Authenticity: From Essence to Function

Traditional views of authenticity equate it with **being true to a fixed internal self**.
 In ICT, authenticity is redefined as **contextual congruence**—the alignment between your internal state, external context, and selected identity configuration.

This shift:

- Frees individuals from the need to be the same across time

- Allows for emotional multiplicity without fragmentation

- Validates all expressions as functional, rather than essential

You are not more authentic when you are consistent. You are authentic when you **select consciously**.

Cultural Constructs: The Myth of Finding Your Purpose

The self-help industry and popular culture promote an idea that identity must be uncovered through purpose, vocation, or destiny.

- "Find your why."

- "Discover your true path."

- "Uncover your soul's mission."

These imperatives assume that the self is **hidden but fixed**—and that fulfillment only comes from discovering the right match between internal essence and external role.

But in post-collapse awareness:

- Purpose is not found. It is constructed.

- Identity is not matched. It is selected.

- Meaning is not revealed. It is generated.

Collapse does not eliminate purpose.
 It **frees you from needing to find one** before you can act.

Clinical Liberation: The End of Self-Oriented Goals

In a therapeutic context, this realization eliminates the need for:

- Identity clarification

- Archetypal integration

- Life direction alignment based on "true self"

Instead, therapy becomes the restoration of:

- Pattern awareness

- Contextual agility

- Selection sovereignty

This removes the chronic disempowerment of waiting to be found.
It restores **agency to the system itself.**

Collapse Trigger: What If There's Nothing to Find?

The realization that collapses this structure is paradoxically simple:

"What if I've been looking for something that never existed?
And what if that's not a loss—but a release?"

This doesn't create an existential crisis.
It ends one.

The search was the crisis.
Now you are free to choose.

After Collapse: Choosing Is Living

Post-collapse, there is no longer a need to ask:

- "Who am I?"

- "What's my path?"

- "What defines me?"

These questions are replaced with:

- "What am I selecting right now?"

- "What configuration serves this context?"

- "How much of the menu am I consciously using?"

There is no final answer.
There is only **informed selection, guided by awareness, not identity.**

This is what it means to live from Pattern-Recognizing Consciousness.
Not as a concept, but as a default operating system.

Conclusion: The End of Becoming

This section ends the illusion that your identity is hiding from you.
It shows that:

- There is no "you" to find

- The chooser is not a self, but a system

- Meaning arises not from essence, but from **conscious selection in context**

You were never missing.
You were just waiting for the system to stop asking permission to be.

You do not become.
You select.

And now you're free.

Summary: Identity Is a Selection, Not a Self

Integrative Collapse Framing

The Narrative Is Over

In this chapter, we have dismantled the final illusion holding identity in place. Each section has contributed a critical structural insight that together renders the idea of a fixed, discoverable, or essential self scientifically untenable.

What remains is not a new self, but the recognition that there was never one to begin with.

What We Now Know:

- **3.1 – The Contextual Identity Menu**

  Identity is not who you are. It is what you select based on environmental, emotional, and social context. The "self" is a narrowed menu configuration, mistakenly reified.

- **3.2 – Pattern Recognition as the Core of Consciousness**

  The system that selects identity is not personal. It is Pattern-Recognizing Consciousness—an emergent, distributed intelligence that chooses without narrative ownership.

- **3.3 – The Illusion of Consistency and the Fear of Fragmentation**

  The drive for internal consistency is a survival strategy, not a psychological necessity. It is the *insistence on unity* that causes fragmentation, not the absence of it.

- **3.4 – Subconscious Filters and the Collapse of Permission Structures**

  Identity is filtered by internalized rules about what is safe, acceptable, or possible. Collapse dissolves these gates—not to build a better self, but to reaccess the full system.

- **3.5 – Identity Is Chosen, Not Found**
There is no self to find. The search is a loop that reinforces the illusion. Collapse reveals that conscious selection has always been available—and now, unfiltered, it becomes sovereign.

What Has Collapsed:

- The belief that you have a true identity

- The belief that identity provides consistency

- The belief that identity can be found

- The belief that only some versions of you are allowed

- The belief that you are the one doing the choosing

These are not philosophical propositions. They are *functional dismantlings* of the structural illusions that prevent full system access.

What Now Remains:

- A system capable of selecting identity in real time

- A fully visible identity menu

- No narrative requirement to justify your existence

- Pattern-Recognizing Consciousness as your operational mode

- The permanent absence of the question: "Who am I?"

Final Collapse Statement:

Identity is not the source of self.
It is the residue of selection.
And now, for the first time, you are no longer confused about who is choosing—or why.

Threshold Transition:

If identity is not a self,
and not a truth—
but a function of pattern selection…
then why does it feel so real?

Because systems that survive—protect structure.
And when that structure is no longer required,
protection becomes resistance.

The system cannot evolve while maintaining a simulation of continuity.
 So eventually, it stops.

Not by will.
 Not by insight.
 But by architecture.

Collapse does not come to the self.
 It comes to the scaffolding that made the self seem necessary.

This next chapter does not offer techniques.
 It reveals pressure points.

The places where the story can no longer hold.
 Where identity becomes too heavy to carry.
 Where coherence fails—and the system chooses honesty instead.

You are not breaking.
 The model is.

And what remains…isn't you.

Chapter 4: The Architecture of Collapse

What Collapse Feels Like

Introduction: The End of an Illusion Is Still an Experience

Collapse is not an idea.
It is not a technique.
It is not a belief, a philosophy, or a metaphor.

Collapse is what happens when the system that was once animated by identity **stops responding to the illusion that it needs one.**

And it is felt.
It is known in the body, in perception, in relational dynamics, in the absence of narrative compulsion.

This section moves beyond theory and gives the reader a structured map of what collapse actually feels like when it happens—neurologically, psychologically, and perceptually. The goal is not to describe collapse for understanding. It is to **make the reader recognize collapse by its symptoms**—so that when it happens, it cannot be mistaken for loss or dysfunction.

Collapse as Internal System Failure—Without Dysfunction

What most people fear about collapse is that it signals a breakdown.
A loss of functionality. A falling apart.

But collapse is not the failure of the human system—it is the failure of **the identity simulation** to continue organizing perception. The system itself remains online. More precise, in fact. Less distorted. Less reactive.

What actually fails is:

- The illusion of internal authorship

- The narrative scaffolding of consistency

- The reflexive assignment of meaning to emotion

- The somatic fusion with identity-based emotional response

What remains is:

- Pattern recognition

- Real-time contextual selection

- Emotional fluidity

- Observational awareness without story

Collapse feels like **the removal of a structure you didn't know was false until it was gone**—and the strange stillness that follows.

Physiological Signatures of Collapse

Collapse is not merely a cognitive or philosophical realization. It has physiological markers, especially during and immediately following the moment of recognition. While not all individuals experience the same symptoms, the following are consistently reported and cross-validated across clinical and observational models:

- **Disorientation or spatial detachment** (a sense of "I'm still here, but I can't find who 'I' is")

- **Rapid autonomic shifts** (heat, chills, sudden relaxation or nervous system unwinding)

- **Auditory silence** (inner monologue abruptly stops or loses coherence)

- **Surreal clarity** (a hyper-awareness of what is present, without meaning attached)

- **Micro grief** (a sense of something dying, often without sadness—just recognition)

- **Stillness or inertia** (an inability to move or speak for several seconds or longer)

These responses are **not traumatic**—they are **transitional**.
They mark the absence of the previous identity-loop—but they do not impair baseline function.

The Self Stops Answering

One of the most destabilizing (and liberating) moments occurs when a familiar internal question is asked—and **no one answers**.

Examples:

- "What should I do right now?"

- "Why do I feel this way?"

- "What will people think of me?"

- "Who am I in this moment?"

Pre-collapse, these questions trigger internal narratives, emotional posturing, self-referencing loops.

During collapse, they return **silence** or **neutral observation**.
The inner responder is gone. The system is still online. But it no longer replies with a self.

This can feel terrifying or transcendent—depending on whether the individual attempts to re-engage the identity mechanism or allows the collapse to complete.

Collapse Is Not Dissociation

It is critical to distinguish collapse from dissociation, particularly in trauma-aware psychological frameworks. While they may appear similar on the surface—both involving shifts in perception, identity, or emotional tone—they emerge from entirely different mechanisms and serve fundamentally different purposes.

Dissociation is typically triggered by trauma or psychological overwhelm. It functions as an involuntary coping response that detaches the individual from emotional intensity or perceived threat. This detachment often reduces emotional responsiveness, impairs functioning, and creates a sense of unreality or fragmentation.

Collapse, in the context of Identity Collapse Therapy (ICT), is not a coping mechanism but a structural event. It is triggered not by overwhelm, but by the direct recognition that the identity itself is a constructed illusion. Rather than detaching from reality, collapse intensifies presence—it removes the narrative filters that previously shaped perception. Emotional capacity may actually increase during collapse, but without fusion or re-identification with story. Function is not impaired; instead, a deeper, pattern-based coherence begins to emerge.

Collapse is not absence.
It is presence without narrative distortion.
It is not depersonalization.
It is **de-illusioning**.

Symbolic Collapse Markers

While the physiological signs are helpful, many individuals report collapse using symbolic language. This is especially common in high-functioning adults, clinicians, and researchers who experience collapse as a semi-linguistic event. The most common phrases are:

- "It felt like something gave out… but not in a bad way."

- "It was like I let go of trying to be me."

- "The noise stopped."

- "I stopped believing in myself—not in a depressing way, but in a freeing way."

- "There was nobody left to impress."

- "It was silent, but not empty."
- "The need to explain disappeared."

These symbolic frames can be misinterpreted unless grounded in functional understanding. This is why Chapter 3 was necessary: collapse only makes sense **after the illusion of identity is sufficiently dismantled.**

Collapse Is Not Caused. It Is Allowed.

One of the most misunderstood aspects of identity collapse is that it is not something you *do* to yourself.

Collapse is **not triggered by force, technique, or desire**. It cannot be hacked by meditation, willpower, journaling, or therapy.

Collapse occurs when:

- The system recognizes that **identity is not needed to function**
- The internal storyteller **is not necessary to remain coherent**
- The filters that constrained identity **are no longer valid**

- The **need to protect a particular version of self** becomes structurally impossible

This is why collapse often feels like it "just happens." But it does not. It follows a precise architecture, which the next sections will unpack.

The Field After Collapse: Stillness Without Ownership

Perhaps the most distinctive feeling after collapse is a **kind of calm detachment** that doesn't remove you from the world—but removes the pressure to exist a certain way within it.

After collapse:

- Emotions arise, but do not define

- Thoughts appear, but do not narrate

- Choices are made, but are not authored by a "self"

- Presence sharpens, but identity no longer filters it

This field is known in ICT as **Zero State**—a transitional perception where the system is online, but not yet reoriented through post-collapse frameworks.

This is not a void. It is the **natural state** that identity had previously obscured.

The Reader Will Recognize It When It Begins

This section is not here to tell the reader what to expect.
It is here to create a field in which recognition can happen.

By now, if collapse is beginning to unfold for the reader:

- They may feel an inability to re-attach to who they were

- They may feel narrative fatigue, but with no distress

- They may feel emotionally fluid but structurally stable

- They may feel an eerie peace that doesn't need explaining

This is collapse. Not dramatized. Not spiritualized. Not pathologized.

Just the **end of simulation**—and the return of raw experience, free from ownership.

Conclusion: You Are Not Falling Apart. You Are No Longer Pretending

Collapse does not destroy the system. It reveals that the system never needed a self to begin with.

It doesn't take anything from you.
It simply stops pretending that "you" were ever a thing to protect, refine, or preserve.

You are still here.
But now, **you are not performing you**.

The Architecture of Collapse

The Three Collapse Triggers

Introduction: Collapse Is Structural, Not Personal

Collapse cannot be forced.
But it can be made **structurally inevitable**.

While the identity system is remarkably resilient in protecting its continuity, it is also **predictably brittle** under certain conditions. When the underlying architecture is exposed to specific pressure points, collapse initiates—not as breakdown, but as **systemic surrender**.

There are three primary mechanisms by which collapse is triggered. Each reveals a different aspect of the illusion—until it can no longer maintain coherence.

These are not techniques or interventions.
They are **threshold conditions**, and when met, collapse begins—spontaneously, irreversibly, and often silently.

Collapse Trigger 1: Contradiction Overload

The Mechanism: Structural Inconsistency Becomes Unresolvable

The first collapse trigger occurs when identity can no longer **reconcile its own contradictions**. This happens when the internal story required to hold the self together begins to **loop, glitch, or conflict with lived experience**.

Examples:

- The individual who identifies as confident begins to observe undeniable patterns of avoidance

- The person who believes they are unlovable is surrounded by evidence of care they cannot refute

- A therapist who defines themselves as a "healer" begins to sense that helping reinforces dependency

The system attempts to resolve these contradictions. But when they accumulate beyond a tolerable threshold, it can no longer do so without **deconstructing the identity itself**.

Psychological Indicators

- Mental exhaustion from trying to maintain a consistent self-story

- Mood swings or internal dissonance that lack narrative explanation

- "Snapping" moments where identity postures collapse temporarily under pressure

- A recurring thought: "None of this makes sense anymore"

Neuroscientific Correlates

- Prefrontal cognitive fatigue due to recursive narrative reprocessing

- Decreased default mode network (DMN) stability under paradox integration

- Frontal-midline theta increases (linked with conflict detection and resolution failure)

Symbolic Language

- "I can't keep pretending."

- "I'm tired of being both of these things."

- "It's like I'm living two lives—and both are fake."

Collapse Outcome

Contradiction overload doesn't offer clarity. It offers **rupture**. When the simulation fails to unify its outputs, the illusion loses traction. The narrative dissolves—not because of trauma, but because it can no longer hide its own fragmentation.

Collapse Trigger 2: Narrative Exposure

The Mechanism: The Self Is Seen While Operating

This trigger occurs when the internal storyteller is **witnessed in real time** constructing identity—not post-event, but **as the illusion is forming**.

This typically occurs during moments of deep awareness or therapeutic insight when the individual suddenly sees:

- Themselves fabricating a justification or self-defense

- The internal voice manufacturing meaning for emotional regulation

- A "spontaneous" identity posture emerge immediately after a threat or trigger

The illusion breaks not because the story fails—but because it is **caught in the act**.

Psychological Indicators

- Emotional detachment paired with meta-awareness

- A moment of embarrassment or cognitive dissonance upon realizing "I just made that up"

- Sudden stillness or inner silence after a defensive outburst

- The inability to continue believing one's own story, even if it's functional

Neuroscientific Correlates

- Increased anterior cingulate cortex activity (associated with self-monitoring and error detection)

- Disruption in DMN and salience network coordination

- Alpha power spikes post-narrative interruption (correlating with cognitive reset)

Symbolic Language

- "I just watched myself do it."

- "That wasn't real. I saw it happening."

- "It's like I caught the fake me talking before I believed it."

Collapse Outcome

Narrative exposure removes the veil.
It doesn't destroy the system—it destroys its ability to **pretend without observation**.
The story remains technically functional, but it no longer convinces. And without belief, identity can no longer hold.

Collapse Trigger 3: Unrestricted Access

The Mechanism: The Full Identity Menu Becomes Available

The final and most definitive collapse trigger occurs when the individual **experientially realizes** that all identity configurations are accessible, not just the ones previously permitted by subconscious filters.

This doesn't happen through belief.
It happens through **real-time, embodied access** to new ways of being that were previously unavailable—either because they were suppressed, feared, or disallowed.

Examples:

- A suppressed person feels rage fully, with no guilt—and nothing bad happens

- A high-control achiever enters full stillness—and doesn't disappear

- A self-sacrificer feels permission to say no—and feels more whole, not less

The system suddenly realizes:

"I can be anything. And I always could."

Psychological Indicators

- Emotional release paired with unexpected peace

- Sudden joy, relief, or laughter that "makes no sense"

- Feeling of "returning to self" that doesn't match any known identity

- No longer fearing the loss of previously protected traits

Neuroscientific Correlates

- Suppression release correlates with ventromedial PFC activation

- GABAergic reduction in filter-maintaining circuits (e.g., dorsolateral PFC)

- Functional connectivity increases between sensorimotor areas and social cognition centers

Symbolic Language

- "Why was I afraid of this version of me?"

- "Nothing is off-limits anymore."

- "It's like I was pretending the whole time—but I didn't know I was."

Collapse Outcome

This is often the **final trigger**.
When access is unrestricted, the illusion of identity becomes unnecessary.
Selection is reclaimed as the mechanism—and the story dies.

Why These Triggers Work

Each trigger destabilizes a different axis of identity's illusion:

- **Contradiction Overload** collapses coherence
- **Narrative Exposure** collapses authorship
- **Unrestricted Access** collapses control

Together, they create a **containment failure**—not of the system, but of the simulation pretending to run it. And once failure begins, it cannot be stopped, only surrendered to.

Collapse Is Not a Crisis. It Is a Threshold.

These triggers are not signs that something is going wrong.
They are signs that the system is approaching **honest function**.

This is not identity death.
It is the **return of pattern-based consciousness**, unfiltered, unowned, and finally free to operate without the illusion of self.

Internal Resistance and Collapse Avoidance

Introduction: Resistance Is Not a Problem—It Is a Pattern

As the system approaches collapse, it does not panic.
It protects.

Resistance is not opposition. It is a **stabilization reflex**, an intelligent function attempting to preserve continuity. In most therapeutic or spiritual models, resistance is framed as something to overcome. In Identity Collapse Therapy, we reframe resistance as something to be **understood, observed, and gently surrendered**—because it is the last mechanism attempting to hold together an identity that no longer serves.

This section helps the reader recognize internal resistance **without triggering it**. We are not here to attack the ego. We are here to watch what it does when it knows the performance is almost over.

Why Resistance Emerges: The Role of Perceived Function

Identity is not just a narrative—it is **a structure that once protected you**.

It regulated your emotional safety.
 It maintained your social roles.
 It helped you make sense of complex experience.
 It even shielded you from trauma.

From that standpoint, resistance is not sabotage.
 It is **loyalty** to the old system.

When collapse begins, the identity structure often interprets this not as evolution—but as **threat**. And so, it resists—not to stop your growth, but to preserve what once worked.

Recognizing this allows you to meet resistance with compassion, not confrontation.

Forms of Resistance: How the System Protects the Simulation

There are several recurring ways the system resists collapse. Each can appear subtle, rational, or even insightful. That is because the ego **does not resist through chaos. It resists through cleverness.**

Below are the primary patterns observed:

---

1. Insight Hoarding

This occurs when the individual begins collecting realizations, metaphors, or frameworks—*instead of allowing them to dismantle the self.*

Symptoms:

- Reading more books instead of pausing

- Repeating collapse language without letting it land

- Seeking "just one more insight" to feel ready

Why it works: Insight offers the illusion of movement while preserving distance from actual collapse.

---

2. Spiritual Bypass

Here, the system uses transcendent concepts to avoid structural disintegration.

Symptoms:

- "There is no self anyway" becomes a defense rather than a lived truth

- Disidentification replaces emotional presence

- Collapse becomes a concept to be admired, not a process to allow

Why it works: It masks fear of identity loss by claiming the self was never important to begin with—without actually letting it go.

---

3. Identity Remapping

A common and subtle form of resistance, where the system simply **rebrands itself** using collapse language.

Symptoms:

- Adopting "post-self" or "awakened" personas

- Shifting into a new identity that is *defined by* having collapsed

- Seeking validation for not needing validation

Why it works: It allows the ego to survive collapse by disguising itself as the one who collapsed.

---

4. Emotional Retention

Even when cognitive collapse begins, emotional identity can remain fused.

Symptoms:

- Unexplained tension or emotional volatility
- Feeling stuck between grief and control
- Subtle fear of full surrender masked as "integration"

Why it works: Emotion was often the glue of the self. Letting it flow without narrative feels like becoming unmoored.

---

5. Collapse Control

The most paradoxical resistance of all: trying to control collapse itself.

Symptoms:

- Looking for the "right way" to collapse

- Timing collapse to align with life circumstances

- Evaluating whether collapse is "happening correctly"

Why it works: The illusion of control is the last act of the illusion of self.

Compassionate Observation: Resistance Without Shame

Each of these mechanisms deserves understanding—not judgment.
They are intelligent. They are adaptive. They worked for you.

You do not need to destroy your resistance.
You need only to **notice it**, without merging with it.

In fact, noticing resistance is often the moment collapse deepens.

The system says:

"I am resisting because I still believe collapse is dangerous."

Then the realization arrives:

"But collapse is not danger. Collapse is truth."

How to Recognize Resistance in Real Time

The following sensations often signal the presence of subtle resistance:

- An urge to "figure it out" before moving forward

- Subtle discomfort with emotional neutrality

- Needing someone else to validate the collapse

- Pressure to "be clear" about who you are becoming

- Fear of what others will think if you let go of your roles

In these moments, the system is **not malfunctioning**. It is simply requesting safety **from a structure that no longer exists.**

You don't need to fight it. You need to **stay long enough** to let the pattern collapse on its own.

The Function of This Section: Safety During Surrender

This section is not here to dismantle your defenses.
 It is here to let you see them **from the outside**—as pattern logic. Not flaws. Not blocks. Just protective structures that don't need to be maintained anymore.

As you begin to notice:

- Insight as delay

- Identity as rebranding

- Emotion as retention

- Control as fear dressed as agency

You are already collapsing.
 Because **you are seeing from outside the simulation.**

Collapse Continues When Resistance Is Witnessed

There is no need to remove resistance.
 Collapse continues when resistance is **witnessed without re-entry**.

At this point:

- The storyteller slows
- The need to understand softens
- The emotion rebalances
- The control lets go

The self remains optional.
And the system keeps functioning.

This is not fragility.
It is post-narrative stability.

Conclusion: Resistance Is the Last Form of Care

The ego resists collapse **because it loves you**—in the only way it knows how.

But it does not realize:
What protected you then is now holding you back.

When resistance is met with safety and witnessed as pattern, collapse proceeds—not in violence, but in **kindness to the system**.

Collapse as a Systemic Reboot

Introduction: The Self Disappears, the System Remains

By now, the reader has passed through contradiction overload, narrative exposure, and unrestricted access. The resistance has been seen, not fought. The identity scaffolding has lost its structural necessity. Collapse has occurred or is actively underway.

The natural next fear—often unspoken—is this:

"If I collapse, will I still work?"

This section answers that question clearly:

Yes.
Because collapse is not destruction.
It is a **reboot**—a return to system integrity without the identity simulation consuming processing power.

This is not a metaphor.
It is a precise, predictable shift in how the human system organizes perception, emotion, and decision-making—**without identity at the center**.

What Is Lost in Collapse

Before describing the reboot, it's important to name what is no longer present.

After collapse, the following are structurally absent:

- **Identity-based narrative loops**

The need to explain experience in terms of "self" dissolves. Thoughts still occur—but without the central author. The internal monologue fades or transforms into observational tracking.

- **Reflexive emotional fusion**

Emotions arise but are no longer owned. "I am angry" becomes "Anger is here." The response is fluid, no longer filtered through ego-preservation.

- **Fixed self-reference**

There is no longer a consistent answer to "Who am I?"—and no need for one. Memory remains, but it does not reinforce identity. Past events are contextualized, not personified.

- **Meaning-making compulsion**

Experiences are no longer forced into narrative significance. Meaning may arise, but it is temporary, contextual, and functional—not foundational to existence.

In short:

The "I" that used to filter everything no longer initiates or governs perception.

What Is Preserved and Enhanced

What remains is not less than selfhood—it is **more functional than identity ever allowed**.

The system reboot reveals:

- **Pattern-based perception**
 The system still tracks reality, emotion, memory, and interaction—now with greater precision, as there is no narrative bias. Context governs selection, not identity fixation.

- **Real-time responsiveness**
 Decision-making is faster and cleaner. Without inner argument or persona maintenance, response becomes adaptive and fluid.

- **Emotion without collapse**
 The system still feels deeply. In fact, emotions may intensify—but now, they pass through cleanly, without distortion or repression.

- **Relational precision**
 Without the need to maintain identity roles (e.g., helper, expert, outsider), relationships become clearer, more direct, and less enmeshed.

- **Cognitive spaciousness**
 Thought continues, but arises from observation, not compulsion. Many describe a "quiet mind" that still functions optimally, without chatter or justification.

The System Is Not Empty—It Is Unloaded

In cognitive neuroscience, when unnecessary neural loops are deactivated, **overall efficiency improves**. We see this in meditation research, in flow states, and in trauma recovery. ICT frames this as a **shift from identity-based processing to pattern-based cognition.**

The bandwidth previously consumed by:

- Self-monitoring

- Emotional regulation tied to ego

- Narrative coherence

- Social role rehearsal

...is now available for:

- Presence

- Observation

- Selection

- Response

This is not a void.
It is **a system returned to base state**, with functionality intact.

Neurofunctional Parallel: Default Mode Network Deactivation

As previously discussed, the Default Mode Network (DMN) is associated with:

- Self-referential thought

- Time-bound narrative reflection

- Identity reinforcement through memory consolidation

Collapse corresponds with **DMN decoupling**—not total shutdown, but reduction in dominance. The Salience Network and Executive Control Network become more active, suggesting **attention shifts to real-time stimuli**, not internal narrative construction.

Functional neuroimaging of non-dual awareness, deep meditation, and ego dissolution all show **reduced DMN coherence**—precisely what we expect post-collapse.

The brain still functions.
It functions **without simulating a self** as the operational epicenter.

Perceptual Differences After Collapse

Collapse alters the *feel* of reality—not through distortion, but through clarity.

Common reports include:

- **Increased visual acuity** (colors, textures, light patterns become more vivid)

- **Somatic openness** (a lack of tension in previously armored parts of the body)

- **Temporal fluidity** (less urgency, more presence)

- **Internal silence** (the inner voice slows, shifts, or stops)

- **Symbolic awareness** (patterns and archetypes become more visible, but less personal)

These changes are not hallucinations. They are the system **no longer being filtered through self-preserving compression algorithms.**

The "You" That Functioned Was Never the Identity

One of the most liberating recognitions post-collapse is this:

The "you" who got through life—solved problems, loved others, stayed alive—was never the identity.

It was the system.

The identity was the compression layer. The translator. The filter.

Collapse reveals:

- Intelligence was always distributed

- Emotions were always impersonal

- Relationships were navigated by pattern, not persona

- Action never required an author—just a context

This realization is not mystical.
It is the end of an illusion that was never needed.

Zero State: The Space Between Collapse and Re-Selection

Immediately post-collapse, many enter a **neutral phase** called *Zero State*.

This is not a void. It is **the space where the self used to be**. And now:

- Nothing needs to happen

- No new role needs to form

- The system is allowed to rest

Zero State is not confusion—it is clarity, minus urgency. It may feel unfamiliar, but it is the most honest perception the system has had in years.

There is no rush to rebuild.
 Because now, there is no need to.

What the Reboot Makes Possible

With the identity simulation gone:

- Conscious identity **selection** becomes available

- Relational entanglement **dissolves**

- Emotional responses **decouple from narratives**

- The system becomes **safe, fluid, and fast**

This is not enlightenment.
It is **operation without illusion**.

Collapse does not produce superhuman awareness. It **removes the bottleneck**.

The reboot leaves you with:

- Nothing to defend

- No one to prove

- No past to narrate

- Just... the system, aware, alive, and free to move

Conclusion: You Were Never Broken—You Were Just Running Too Many Simulations

Collapse does not make you better.
It makes you **available**—to the present, to others, to the full identity menu, and to life itself.

The system is not weaker now.
 It is **more agile, more precise, and more honest**.

And it didn't need a self to operate.
 It never did.

Post-Collapse Functionality: The New Baseline

Introduction: What Comes After the Simulation Ends

Collapse is not the end of functioning. It is the end of **identity as the organizing principle**.

This section offers the reader an orientation to what remains after the collapse has occurred. Not a framework to adopt. Not a new set of rules. But a mirror, showing the system as it is: coherent, intelligent, and operative—without the filter of a self to explain it.

This is not the construction of a new identity.
It is the **recognition of the system's capacity to function without one.**

What follows is a description—not a prescription. The goal is not to teach the reader what to do. It is to show them **what is already happening** now that identity has dissolved.

The System Still Operates—Just Not Through Self

After collapse, the individual discovers something remarkable: nothing essential has been lost.

- Language still arises
- Emotions still move
- Decisions are still made
- Relating still happens
- Attention still shifts
- Action still occurs

But none of it is initiated, filtered, or justified by a **central author.**

This does not produce chaos.
It removes the interpreter that was adding distortion.

The system continues operating through:

- Real-time pattern response
- Contextual selection
- Environmental resonance

- Emotional fluidity

What disappears is the need for these processes to be claimed as **"me."**

No One Is Doing It—But It Is Happening

One of the earliest post-collapse recognitions is that:

Everything continues—but the "I" who thought they were making it happen is gone.

There is no absence of agency—only the absence of ownership. The system now functions without demanding credit, defense, or identity-based coherence.

In neuroscience, this aligns with shifts toward:

- **Decentralized executive function**

- **Non-narrative working memory**

- **Reduced self-referential DMN activity**

- **Greater sensorimotor and affective integration**

From the outside, the person appears unchanged. From the inside, **nothing is being managed**.

The Role of Language After Collapse

Language continues post-collapse, but its **origin and function change.**

Pre-collapse:

- Language is used to reinforce identity

- Stories are told to validate the self

- Conversations serve as mirrors for role confirmation

Post-collapse:

- Language emerges contextually

- Speech occurs without rehearsal or internal narrator

- Meaning arises as needed, then dissolves

The inner monologue slows, silences, or disappears entirely.
Thought is not absent—but it no longer narrates life. It **tracks patterns**, not selves.

Emotion Becomes Fluid, Not Defining

Emotions still arise, sometimes more intensely than before.
But they are not used to maintain identity.

Previously:

- Anger reinforced a sense of righteousness
- Sadness maintained a story of abandonment
- Joy was permissioned by identity success

Now:

- Emotions pass through
- They are not owned
- They are not used to justify stories
- They do not require explanation

This produces a felt **fluidity**—emotions move cleanly, unblocked, unfused.
The system no longer resists or clings. It **flows**.

Relationships Without Role Fusion

In relational space, collapse is most obvious—not through absence, but through **precision**.

Pre-collapse:

- Interactions are guided by identity needs

- The self seeks validation, reflection, or confirmation

- Roles (parent, teacher, partner, outsider) organize behavior

Post-collapse:

- No need to be seen in a certain way

- Less projection, more clarity

- Ability to attune without merging

- Silence becomes natural, not threatening

The person is not less present. They are **less burdened by performance**.

Decision-Making Without Self-Reference

Perhaps the most surprising shift is how decisions happen.

Without identity:

- There is no internal debate
- No weighing of "who I should be"
- No fear of regret based on ego outcomes

Instead:

- Signals are sensed
- Patterns are recognized
- Movement happens

This is not impulsivity. It is **response without narrative interference**.
And it is more accurate than self-based decision-making—because it removes distortion.

The Return of the Full Identity Menu

After collapse, the Contextual Identity Menu (introduced in Chapter 3) becomes fully accessible. The subconscious no longer filters which roles are allowed.

You are now able to:

- Access any posture, role, or voice
- Select identities without believing in them
- Use expressions as tools, not definitions
- Play without pretending

This is not fragmentation. It is **post-identity coherence**.

Identity becomes like clothing: put on when needed, removed without loss.

Zero State Revisited: Baseline Without Urgency

Many will linger in what we call **Zero State**—the period after collapse, before full re-engagement with expression.

Here:

- There is little movement
- Desire is minimal
- Silence is preferred
- The system self-regulates, without agenda

This is not depression. It is not apathy. It is **systemic rest**—the first true rest after years of self-maintenance.

The invitation: **Do nothing. Wait for the next true movement.**
You'll know it when it arrives.
It won't come from fear, hope, or role.
It will come from context, resonance, and clarity.

How to Recognize If You Are Reattaching

Collapse is complete when the system **no longer believes it needs a self to function**.

But subtle reattachments may attempt to form. Watch for:

- New identities that form around having "no identity"

- Needing others to understand or confirm your collapse

- Using collapse to justify withdrawal, superiority, or detachment

- Fear of being misunderstood

These are not regressions.
They are signals that the system is **stabilizing**, and may temporarily reach for structure.

If noticed, they often dissolve without intervention.

There Is No Right Way to Be After Collapse

The final protection of the ICT framework is this:

There is no "right" post-collapse baseline.

The system now selects what is needed:

- Stillness or movement
- Expression or silence
- Relational expansion or solitude
- Joy, anger, grief, laughter—without story

Nothing needs to be integrated.
 Because **nothing is broken**.

You are not required to do anything with this.
 Only to notice: the self was never required for life to continue.

And now, it does—**without simulation**.

Conclusion: This Is the New Baseline—Not Defined, Just Available

This section has not told the reader what to become.
 It has shown them what remains when nothing needs to become anything.

You are here.
 You are not a self.

You are not a story.
You are not a role.
You are not even collapsed.
You are **available**—to what is.

Collapse Confirmation: The Attempt to Go Back

Introduction: The Final Proof Is Inaccessibility

Collapse doesn't end with insight.
It ends when the system tries to return—and finds there is nothing to return to.

This section is not about proving that collapse has happened.
It's about recognizing the moment when the **simulation no longer boots**—even when prompted. Especially when prompted.

Collapse is complete **not when you believe it is**, but when **the system can no longer reattach to the illusion it once depended on.**

The Collapse Confirmation Event

In all full collapses, there is a definitive threshold moment where the system does what it's designed to do: attempt to resume continuity.

This is not regression.
It is a structural test the system performs on its own. The equivalent of pressing the button on an old interface just to see if it still responds.

- The system reaches for an identity structure.
- It expects an old response.
- It prepares for the familiar loop.

And instead?

Nothing.

No emotional grip.
No internal narrative.
No charge.
No echo.
Just absence—where self used to be.

How the Attempt Manifests

This moment is often subtle. It does not arrive like a dramatic realization, but as a quiet observation:

- You begin to speak from an old identity, and the words don't finish.

- You feel a familiar emotional prompt (e.g., rejection, anger), and there's no rise.

- You anticipate needing to justify yourself—and there's no voice inside doing it.

- You expect guilt or shame—and find neutrality.

It feels strange, not because it's extreme—but because it's gone.

The attempt doesn't fail.
It never starts.

There's nothing to power it.
No structure to animate the simulation.

Identity Amnesia: The Structural Vanishing Point

Perhaps the clearest signal of full collapse comes from clinical observation:

In most cases of complete collapse, the client cannot even remember what identity they were trying to collapse—within 48 to 72 hours.

Not metaphorically.
Literally.

They cannot reassemble the configuration. The memory fragments might remain—but without the structural code that tied them together, they appear meaningless, non-coherent, emotionally neutral.

They may say things like:

- "I know I used to feel this way... but I can't feel it anymore."

- "I remember the thoughts... but they don't feel like mine."

- "It's like trying to put on someone else's clothes from a dream."

This is not suppression.
It is **functional obsolescence**.

The structure was not bypassed.
It was **uninstalled**.

Why ICT Does Not Risk False Positives

In many therapeutic approaches, ego softening or spiritual insight is confused with collapse. Clients "feel better," experience temporary non-attachment, or have cognitive breakthroughs—and mistakenly believe collapse is complete.

In ICT, this is impossible.

The collapse procedure:

- Is not insight-based

- Is not emotionally driven

- Does not rely on belief or agreement

- Does not collapse concepts—it collapses system architecture

ICT collapse protocols contain:

- Recursive narrative invalidation loops

- Identity resonance burnouts

- Forced contradiction amplification

- Subconscious selection filter dismantling

- Contextual Identity Menu exposure

- Direct authorship deconstruction

- Symbolic anchoring + post-collapse irreversibility checks

These are not ideas.
 They are **pattern-level directives** executed through precise scripts that make **return structurally impossible**.

So when the system "tries" to go back, it's not a test.
 It's a **confirmatory glitch.**
 And when it can't go back?

Collapse isn't believed.
Collapse is **undeniable**.

Neurological Parallel: Collapse as Permanent Decoupling

In neurological terms, collapse is not passive disidentification. It corresponds with:

• **Default Mode Network (DMN) decoupling**: the brain's self-referential hub quiets, no longer sustaining identity narration.

• **Cortico-thalamic rhythm shifts**: perception routes normalize without top-down ego filtering.

• **Reduced connectivity in narrative simulation centers**: identity no longer binds emotion, memory, and projection into a "me."

When identity attempts to reanimate, these networks do not coordinate. The "reboot" is requested—but no response.

The mind doesn't say "No."
The system just returns **no signal**.

How the Reader Can Observe This in Themselves

Collapse cannot be proven to others. But the reader will know this moment has occurred when they attempt to resume the following—and fail:

- **Performance** (they can no longer act from persona)

- **Defense** (they cannot find something to protect)

- **Fusion** (emotion arises, but does not define them)

- **Narration** (the inner voice fades or feels irrelevant)

- **Certainty** (they no longer know who they are—and are fine)

Try to:

- Convince yourself of the old fear

- Retell the old story and believe it

- Feel the need to be seen a certain way

- Find meaning in what used to define you

And you will find:

Nothing is wrong.
Nothing is hidden.
It just isn't there anymore.

The Return Attempt Is Built Into Collapse Integrity

Here's what most readers don't realize:

The return attempt is not dangerous.
It is part of collapse safety.

In systems engineering, final checks verify that no ghost processes are running.

ICT uses the same logic.
By allowing the system to "try" to go back, it reveals whether collapse was complete.

This is **not ego resurgence.**
This is **collapse validation through non-responsiveness.**

When the system tries and fails:

- You don't need a new self

- You don't need a new framework

- You don't need to explain anything

You are not less than before.
You are **functioning without simulation overhead.**

What Post-Attempt Neutrality Feels Like

After the return attempt fails, what follows is not enlightenment or joy. It's something more honest:

- **Stillness**

- **Neutrality**

- **Presence without intention**

- **Selection without identity**

There is no urge to make sense of it.
There is no longing to be understood.

Often, the person becomes quiet. Not withdrawn—just complete.
Collapse doesn't produce bliss. It removes the tension that believed bliss was the goal.

The Final Protection: No New Identity Must Form

In this space, the greatest protection is this:

Nothing new is needed.

The mind may attempt to name it:

- "Am I now the one who collapsed?"

- "Is this what presence feels like?"

- "Do I now teach others how to do this?"

These are simulations.
 Collapse has no successor.
 Collapse leaves you with **zero authorship and full functionality.**

The desire to name the post-collapse state is the final echo of performance.

Let it pass.

You Will Know Because You Can't Unsee It

Collapse is not "felt" as an insight.
It is **sensed** as structural absence.

And when you look for what used to define you:

- Emotionally

- Narratively

- Behaviorally

...you find **emptiness without loss.**

No simulation. No story. No one left to be convinced.

Only life.
Unfiltered.
Available.

Conclusion: This Is the Moment After the Simulation Dies

Collapse confirmation is not a moment of success.
It is the **moment nothing reboots**.

You tried to return—and found no script to load.
You searched for "you"—and found pattern, not persona.

You attempted to narrate—and realized you were just watching.

That's not identity loss.
That's **collapse complete.**

Threshold Transition:

Collapse does not remove perception.
 It removes the filter that claimed to perceive.

What remains is not absence.
 It is space.
 Not silence.
 But simultaneous signal.

You are not gone.
 The "you" that needed to hold the system together is.
 And what's left—is precision, unclaimed.

This next section is not about mystery.
 It is about structure.

How a post-collapse system thinks.
 How it knows without needing to narrate.
 How it moves without needing to be someone moving.

What emerges is not a higher self.
 It is a **quantum cognition model**—
 capable of holding opposing truths,
 pattern-matching in real time,
 and selecting action based on alignment,
 not identity.

The system did not lose its mind.
It found its freedom.

Let us map what that freedom looks like—
not as poetry, but as precision.

Chapter 5: The Quantum Self & Cognitive Superposition

Intelligence as a Probabilistic Field

Introduction: Beyond the Fixed Mind

The idea that intelligence is a fixed trait is perhaps one of the most tenacious and invisible assumptions embedded in modern psychology, education, and culture. From standardized testing in childhood to adult performance evaluations, the notion persists: that one's cognitive ability is a measurable constant—an IQ number inked into their neurobiology, reinforced by social comparison, and interpreted as destiny.

But this assumption is collapsing.

The most advanced developments in cognitive science, quantum cognition, and identity research no longer support a static view of intelligence. Instead, they point toward a much more radical—and liberating—truth: that intelligence is not a trait to be measured, but a probabilistic field to be accessed. A dynamic, context-sensitive, identity-dependent field that continuously shifts depending on who we believe ourselves to be in any given moment.

This insight forms the foundation for one of the most disruptive claims in Identity Collapse Therapy (ICT): **intelligence does not emerge from within—it is selected from without.** That is, the experience of intelligence is not produced by a fixed internal quality, but by a subconscious filtering mechanism that determines which cognitive potentials are allowed to become real.

In this section, we will explore the full implications of this shift—from fixed trait to probabilistic field. We will ground this thesis in quantum cognition theory, predictive processing neuroscience, and ICT's depth-collapsing framework. We will show that the primary limiter of intelligence is not biology—it is identity. And once that identity collapses, a person's cognitive capacity can increase dramatically, not through effort or training, but through **permission**—the permission to access what was previously filtered out by the self they thought they were.

The Quantum Framework: Superposition and Observer Collapse

To understand intelligence as a probabilistic field, we must first leave behind the familiar terrain of classical models of mind. In traditional cognitive science, the mind is often modeled like a computer: it processes inputs, stores data, runs calculations, and outputs behavior. Intelligence, in this model, is the computational power or algorithmic efficiency of that system.

But quantum cognition theory suggests something profoundly different. In this paradigm, inspired by principles of quantum mechanics—not metaphorically but structurally—**cognition is not computation. It is potentiality.** The mind does not produce a single answer from a set of rules. It exists in a state of **superposition**—a blend of multiple possible interpretations, solutions, thoughts, or responses—until an "observation" collapses that field into a single, experienced outcome.

In quantum physics, the act of observation collapses a wave function into one definitive state. Until that moment, the system exists in multiple possible states simultaneously. This is not just a physics phenomenon—it is increasingly seen as a valid model for how the brain processes uncertainty, ambiguity, and choice.

As Pothos and Busemeyer (2013) and others have shown, when humans face ambiguous questions, their mental state resembles a quantum superposition of beliefs or interpretations. This explains numerous anomalies in human decision-making, including **order effects** (where the sequence of information alters interpretation), **disjunction effects** (where uncertainty suppresses logical reasoning), and **interference patterns** (where competing thoughts cancel or amplify each other).

This implies a revolutionary reframe of intelligence:

Intelligence is not the outcome of a linear computational process—it is the product of **which potential outcome gets collapsed into experience**.

Identity as the Observer Function

In the quantum cognition model, what determines which potential outcome becomes real?

The answer is the same both in quantum mechanics and in ICT: **the observer.**

In human consciousness, the observer is not the "conscious mind" in the superficial sense. It is the deep, pattern-filtering structure we call **identity**. It is the set of subconscious beliefs, associations, and expectations that define what kind of person we believe ourselves to be—what capacities are "ours," what abilities are "not us," and what type of intelligence we are "allowed" to access.

This identity structure functions like the measurement device in a quantum system: it **collapses the field**. It selects one reality from among many. But it does so unconsciously, reflexively, and with alarming rigidity.

Once a person believes they are "not good at math," their identity will collapse every subsequent cognitive experience to match that expectation. The full field of potential interpretations is narrowed to a single, repetitive outcome.

This isn't just conjecture. The predictive processing model of the brain—arguably the most accepted model in current neuroscience—confirms it.

Predictive Processing and Identity-Driven Expectation

According to predictive processing theory (Clark, 2013; Friston, 2010), the brain is not a passive receiver of sensory data. It is an active predictor. It continuously generates models of reality and compares incoming data to those models. When data doesn't match prediction, the brain updates its model—or rejects the data.

But here's the key: the deeper the prediction, the more resistant it is to change. Predictions about identity—who we are—form the **highest level of the hierarchy**. They are the most "trusted," and therefore the hardest to revise. These identity-based priors determine what the brain even *sees* as possible.

From this lens, intelligence is not limited by the brain's raw capacity, but by what it expects it can access. The brain doesn't process what's available—it processes what's **believable** within its identity structure.

This explains why people perform better when they believe they are capable (e.g., placebo intelligence boosts), and worse when labeled as "less intelligent" (e.g., stereotype threat). The cognitive field is collapsed before performance even begins.

This also explains why ICT works.

ICT as Collapse of the Observer

ICT operates at the level of identity—specifically, it collapses the **observer function** that filters reality. It does not attempt to "build confidence" or "teach new skills." It bypasses content entirely and instead removes the underlying identity structure that determines which cognitive paths are even available.

Once this observer collapses—through direct experiential processes such as the Infinite Self-Loop Trap, Waterfall Release, or Mirror Dissolution Method—the person experiences a radical expansion in cognitive capacity. This is not due to effort or training. It is due to **the removal of the identity that was collapsing potential prematurely**.

Clients often report:

- Sudden clarity of thought

- Access to new forms of reasoning

- Novel patterns of creativity

- The ability to hold paradox or complexity without collapse

- Emotional neutrality toward tasks that previously triggered shame, fear, or avoidance

In the language of quantum cognition, they are no longer bound by a fixed observer. They are participating in the full field.

Case Example: From Fixed Label to Superposed Access

Consider a client who enters ICT with the belief: "I'm just not creative."

This identity likely formed through early labeling ("left-brained," "logical," "not artistic"), reinforced by educational structures that reward analytical over imaginal thinking, and social experiences where creative expression was punished or ridiculed. Over time, the identity of "non-creative" became an unconscious observer function—it collapsed every ambiguous situation into a binary: "This is not for me."

ICT does not challenge this belief with logic. It does not argue for creativity. It identifies the emotional imprint, the protective function, and the residual self-structure. It deconstructs it. It collapses the observer.

What emerges is not a "new belief"—it is the direct experience of unfiltered access. The client begins drawing. Dreaming. Seeing patterns in data. Connecting ideas in nonlinear ways. They are surprised by their own mind—not because it changed, but because it was always capable. The only shift was permission.

The self that said "I am not creative" was the only thing preventing creativity from collapsing into view.

Scientific Implications and Future Exploration

This shift has radical implications for the future of cognitive science, education, and therapeutic transformation:

1. **IQ as a Snapshot of Collapse, Not Capacity**
 IQ does not measure intelligence. It measures which potentials a person's identity structure allows to collapse during testing. It is a symptom of identity—not a trait of mind.

2. **Genius as Access, Not Possession**
 Extraordinary intelligence may not be due to innate traits, but to unusually flexible or undefined observer structures. Some individuals may have never formed limiting identity-based filters, and thus remain in contact with more of the field.

3. **Cognitive Liberation Through Identity Work**
 Real intellectual development may not lie in educational content, but in identity collapse. By removing the observer, we restore full field access. Every human being could become vastly more intelligent—not by becoming more, but by believing less.

Conclusion: The Field Awaits

To understand intelligence as a probabilistic field is to dismantle centuries of cognitive misunderstanding. It is to accept that what we call "smart" or "gifted" is often the result of a collapsed belief system, not a biological limit. It is to realize that genius is not rare—it is simply less filtered.

Identity is the gate. Collapse is the key.

ICT offers a scientifically rigorous, neurologically grounded, experientially validated protocol for unlocking that gate. Not by building new traits, but by removing the filters that collapse intelligence too soon.

When identity collapses, what remains is not blankness.

It is access.

The Role of Identity in Cognitive Collapse

Introduction: Intelligence Does Not Collapse Itself

If intelligence is a probabilistic field—as we established in Section 5.1—then something must determine how, when, and which aspects of that field become actualized. The question then becomes not *"how intelligent is this person?"* but rather *"what internal structure is responsible for collapsing their cognitive field into a single stream of performance?"*

In Identity Collapse Therapy (ICT), we refer to this internal structure as the **cognitive observer**—the filtering mechanism shaped by the individual's identity. This observer is not conscious in the ordinary sense. It does not operate through logic or belief alone. Rather, it is a subconscious, recursive, predictive structure composed of personal history, emotional encoding, sociocultural conditioning, and self-protective patterning. It functions as a gatekeeper, a stabilizer, and a lens all at once.

The central insight of this section is this:

Identity collapses cognition.

Until this collapse function is recognized and dismantled, no amount of intellectual effort, motivational coaching, or cognitive training will produce lasting liberation. The field will continue to collapse into the same familiar patterns—not because the individual lacks intelligence, but because the self does not permit the field to unfold differently.

This is not a theory. It is a mechanism. And it explains why even the most brilliant minds can remain trapped in loops of limitation, and why those with no measurable "giftedness" can, after collapse, access seemingly superhuman insight.

The Observer Effect in Psychology and Physics

To fully grasp this mechanism, it is essential to draw a parallel from quantum physics to human cognition.

In quantum systems, the **observer effect** refers to the principle that the act of measurement alters the system being observed. A particle, when unmeasured, exists in a probabilistic superposition of states. But once an observer engages, the wave function collapses, and the particle assumes a definite position.

This phenomenon is not confined to subatomic particles. It reveals a universal truth: **observation changes outcome**.

In the human mind, identity is the measurement device. Identity determines *what kind of intelligence* we are allowed to see ourselves as having. It shapes not only our thoughts but the very field from which those thoughts emerge.

This understanding mirrors insights from social psychology—particularly the **stereotype threat** effect. Claude Steele's (1995) foundational research showed that individuals under identity-based pressure (e.g., women in math, minorities in academics) perform worse on cognitive tasks, not because their ability changes, but because the observer within them (their identity) shifts the probability distribution of accessible cognition. Their performance is collapsed before it even begins.

ICT identifies this observer as the primary source of all cognitive collapse—not just under pressure, but in everyday life. The individual is constantly collapsing their intelligence based on who they think they are. They are not underperforming—they are over-collapsing.

Identity as a Predictive Gating Mechanism

Modern neuroscience has evolved past the idea that the brain simply "thinks." Instead, it **predicts**.

According to predictive processing theory (Clark, 2015; Friston, 2009), the brain operates by continuously forecasting what should be experienced next, based on internal models of the world and the self. These predictions guide perception, attention, motor responses, and, critically—thought.

But where do these internal models come from? What determines the precision-weighting of one prediction over another?

The answer is **identity**.

Identity acts as the most stabilized layer in the predictive hierarchy. It is not just a belief—it is a set of assumptions the system treats as foundational truth. These assumptions define not only what the brain expects, but also what it is *willing* to experience. If a person's identity contains the imprint, *"I'm a slow learner,"* then the brain will actively suppress cognitive options that would contradict this prediction—even if the neurobiological capacity is present.

This leads to an incredible paradox:

The brain may have full access to cognitive possibility, but the **identity structure actively prevents** access in order to preserve internal coherence.

This coherence is not malicious. It is protective. Prediction errors—experiencing something outside of what identity permits—create a form of cognitive dissonance so intense that the system treats them as threats. This is why a child praised for being "gifted" may fall apart when they encounter failure—they are not cognitively weak, but their identity cannot metabolize contradiction.

The Cost of Coherence: Why Identity Sacrifices Intelligence

Coherence is the nervous system's priority. Intelligence is optional.

The human brain prioritizes *predictability* over *accuracy*. It favors what feels known over what is true. Identity offers this predictability—it is the most energy-efficient lens through which to interpret experience. But this efficiency comes at a cost: **it narrows the field.** It removes all potential interpretations, ideas, or capacities that do not align with the current self-model.

As a result, the individual is not living in the full spectrum of their intelligence. They are living inside a curated version of themselves that has edited out the majority of their cognitive landscape.

Consider this in practical terms:

- A student who believes "I'm not a math person" will unconsciously filter out moments of insight, suppress exploration, and avoid risk, resulting in a self-fulfilling decline in ability.

- A leader who believes "I'm always right" may display confidence but will unconsciously avoid new information that contradicts their decisions, limiting growth.

- A therapist who sees themselves as "deeply intuitive" may ignore empirical data that challenges their interpretive style, mistaking intuition for identity-protection.

Each of these examples demonstrates the same mechanism: **identity collapses the intelligence field prematurely to preserve coherence**, even when doing so harms performance.

This is not a flaw in the brain. It is a protective function in the ego. But it is no longer necessary.

Identity Collapse and the Removal of Predictive Filters

ICT offers a way out of this bind—not by updating the identity, but by removing the need for it altogether.

Most cognitive interventions attempt to **reprogram the belief**: to replace *"I'm not smart"* with *"I am smart."* This is merely a new observer collapsing a new set of limitations. It may feel better, but it is still a prison.

ICT bypasses belief entirely and works at the structural level. It identifies the **observer function**—the core emotional and cognitive patterns that determine which possibilities are considered "real"—and collapses it. The client is not told they are smart. They are led to confront the void where the "I" used to be. In that void, no observer is present to collapse the field. There is only access.

This is the purpose of tools like:

- **The Identity Reflection Loop** – A recursive mirroring sequence that reveals the self's need to collapse ambiguity.

- **The Cognitive Permission Reset** – A guided deconstruction of the internal authority that determines who the person is "allowed" to be.

- **The Post-Collapse Test** – A direct encounter with previously forbidden identity selections to prove they now exist within reach.

After this collapse, cognitive performance is not *enhanced*—it is *freed*. Clients do not become smarter. They become less collapsed. They do not gain skills. They gain selection.

The Collapse of the Collapser: A Recursive Liberation

In quantum terms, ICT collapses the *collapser*. It removes the internal observer that was prematurely reducing potential into narrow trajectories. What remains is not blankness—it is a recursive state of uncollapsed possibility.

This is the essence of cognitive superposition:

- The client is no longer choosing thought from within the identity.

- The identity is no longer functioning as the chooser.

Instead, the self becomes a passive field. Ideas emerge. Intelligence flows. Insight arises. Not from effort, but from absence. The absence of the gatekeeper who used to decide what was "you."

This recursive shift is not hypothetical. Clients describe it as:

- *"It's like I can see the thoughts forming before I even think them."*

- *"My brain feels open for the first time—like I don't have to force anything."*

- *"I don't feel smarter. I just feel like there's nothing blocking me anymore."*

These are not metaphors. They are reports from a post-collapse state, where the internal observer is either gone or deactivated. In this state, **performance is no longer predicted—it is permitted.**

Cognitive Field Theory: Implications of Observer Removal

By removing the observer, ICT demonstrates that intelligence is not trait-based. It is **field-based**. The collapse of identity reveals the following truths:

1. **Every mind contains multiple cognitive configurations.**
These configurations are not developed—they are accessed or suppressed based on identity filters.

2. **The observer chooses which configuration collapses.**
This "choice" is not conscious. It is governed by emotional encoding and ego stability.

3. **Removing the observer restores full-field fluidity.**
This state resembles what some traditions call *no-mind* or *flow state,* but is achieved not through meditation or peak states, but by identity disassembly.

4. **Intelligence becomes recursive.**
The self can now observe itself selecting thought, and even decide to delay collapse—allowing more nuanced, layered, or divergent cognitive potentials to arise.

5. **Genius is structural emptiness.**
Not the possession of more neurons or gifts—but the absence of internal filters that prematurely collapse the field.

From Identity-Based Intelligence to Pattern-Recognizing Consciousness

The following schematic illustrates the transformation from identity-bound intelligence to pattern-recognizing consciousness. It does not represent a technique or process to be followed—it reflects the structural transition that naturally occurs when collapse renders identity unnecessary for perception.

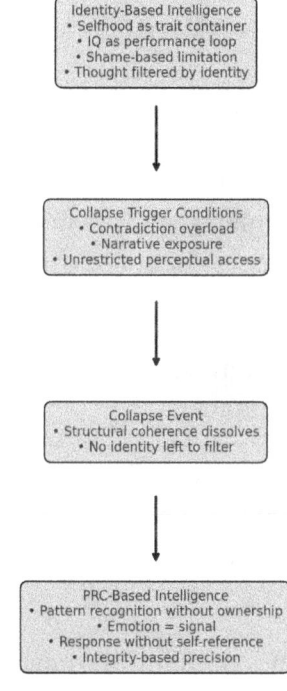

This map exists not to explain collapse, but to clarify the logic behind post-identity cognition. It does not require belief. It reflects what becomes visible when belief is no longer selecting what can be seen.

Conclusion: The Collapse That Frees the Mind

We have long believed that to become smarter, we must add more: more knowledge, more training, more effort. But the truth is more radical—and more terrifying.

To become fully intelligent, we must lose the one thing we thought we needed to think: **the self.**

Not all of it. Not the awareness, not the memory. But the observer—the one who says *"I know who I am, and what I can and cannot do."*

When that voice collapses, the mind becomes a superposition. Intelligence becomes a field. And the person becomes a chooser again—not of beliefs, but of access.

The mind does not need improvement.
 It needs freedom.
 And the self, for all its protection, is the cage.

In the next section, we will explore how this cage forms not only through identity, but through the emotional and neurological structures that regulate cognitive prediction itself—particularly within the Default Mode

Network (DMN), limbic imprints, and emotional-gating feedback loops.

The Brain as a Predictive Filter: DMN, Frontal Gating, and Limbic Encoding

Introduction: Intelligence Is Not Produced—It Is Permitted

In the previous section, we established that intelligence does not emerge from fixed cognitive structures, but is instead selected from a field of potential, with identity functioning as the internal observer that collapses this field into performance. In this section, we now move deeper into the **neurobiological correlates** of that selection process.

What, neurologically, determines which thoughts, insights, or solutions become conscious? Why do some interpretations arise while others remain inaccessible—even though the brain is theoretically capable of forming them?

The answer lies in the predictive architecture of the brain: a complex network of systems designed to suppress, prioritize, and filter incoming signals based on emotional safety, cognitive expectations, and identity reinforcement.

In ICT, this mechanism is referred to as **cognitive gating**—a process by which the brain permits or inhibits access to different layers of potential based on subconscious prediction models.

This section will explore:

• The **Default Mode Network (DMN)** and its role in reinforcing identity-based narratives

• **Frontal lobe gating** and the regulation of ambiguity, inhibition, and perception control

• **Limbic encoding** and its effect on emotional memory and predictive fear loops

• How ICT disrupts these filters to restore full access to the field of uncollapsed cognition

This is not abstract theory—it is a structural description of how the brain enforces limitation, and how collapse dismantles those internal guards.

The Predictive Brain: Efficiency Over Possibility

The human brain evolved not to perceive all of reality, but to filter most of it out. From a biological standpoint, too much information is dangerous. Perception must be limited to what serves survival. To this end, the brain developed a hierarchical system of **prediction-driven filtering**, designed to create a stable, coherent experience of self and world.

Friston's free energy principle (2010) describes how the brain constantly minimizes prediction error—differences between what is expected and what is perceived. The more accurate the brain's model, the fewer surprises it encounters. Surprise, in this framework, equals **energy inefficiency** and potential threat.

But here's the problem: when identity becomes the reference model, **accuracy is sacrificed for coherence**. The brain begins rejecting data, interpretations, and insights that would contradict the self-model—even if they are true. This is not a cognitive flaw—it is a neurobiological survival strategy. And it comes at the cost of truth, creativity, and cognitive freedom.

This mechanism is enforced through three primary systems: the DMN, the frontal lobe inhibitory networks, and limbic emotional encoding. Together, they form the **neural gatekeeper of intelligence**.

The Default Mode Network: Identity's Neural Stronghold

The **Default Mode Network (DMN)** is a set of interconnected brain regions that activates when the mind is at rest, not focused on external tasks. It includes the medial prefrontal cortex, posterior cingulate cortex, and angular gyrus, among others. The DMN is involved in:

- Self-referential thought
- Narrative construction
- Memory consolidation
- Future simulation
- Moral reasoning

Essentially, it is the **neural correlator of identity**—the network that sustains our sense of self through time. It keeps the story running.

Raichle et al. (2001) first identified the DMN as the brain's "default" activity, but more recent research shows that **excessive DMN activity is correlated with rumination, anxiety, depression, and cognitive inflexibility**. In other words, the stronger the self-narrative, the harder it is to think freely.

From an ICT perspective, the DMN represents the **primary cognitive constraint field**. It actively selects which interpretations align with the personal story and suppresses those that do not. This is not conscious—it is embedded in the resting state of the brain.

This explains why individuals often experience "aha moments" only when the DMN deactivates—during sleep, psychedelic states, meditation, or deep flow. These are not magic moments. They are moments when the gatekeeper went offline.

Frontal Lobe Gating: Suppressing What You're Not Supposed to Think

The **prefrontal cortex (PFC)** plays a critical role in executive function, including attention, decision-making, and inhibition. Within ICT, the PFC is recognized as the **neurological site of internal censorship**—where cognitive possibilities are evaluated and either permitted or suppressed based on learned models.

Research by Aron et al. (2014) identifies the right inferior frontal gyrus as essential for response inhibition. This is the region that says "don't say that," "don't think that," "stay in line." While crucial for social functioning, it also becomes a prison when over-activated by identity conditioning.

For example:

- A child punished for asking too many questions may develop an internal inhibitory loop: *"Don't ask."*

- A teenager ridiculed for expressing emotion may develop: *"Don't feel."*

- An adult rejected for proposing unconventional ideas may internalize: *"Don't be different."*

These loops become **cognitive inhibition patterns**, embedded in the PFC. They prevent entire categories of thought from surfacing. Not because the brain cannot form them, but because they are classified as "not safe."

ICT recognizes that much of what is called "intelligence" is actually the absence of these internal censors. The removal of inhibition—not the addition of ability—results in higher cognitive output.

The Limbic Loop: Emotional Encoding as Predictive Gate

The **limbic system**, especially the amygdala and hippocampus, plays a central role in emotional memory, threat detection, and behavioral conditioning. Within ICT, the limbic system is understood not merely as a "reactive" circuit, but as a **predictive filter**—one that emotionally codes certain cognitive options as dangerous or painful.

This creates **limbic prediction loops**, where certain thoughts, identity explorations, or insights are avoided not because they are incorrect, but because they are **encoded with threat**.

For example:

- A person who once failed publicly may experience subtle amygdala activation whenever they approach high-stakes cognition.

- A person whose parents mocked creativity may feel unconscious shame when attempting to write, even if they have skill.

- A client told "you're not smart like your brother" may feel anticipatory rejection every time they consider contributing ideas.

These are not emotions—they are **neurochemical suppressors**. They prevent cognition from unfolding along paths associated with prior emotional pain. Even if the brain is capable of brilliance, it will avoid triggering a stored emotional response.

ICT treats these emotional memories not as content to be "healed," but as **filters to be collapsed**. The collapse does not remove the memory. It removes the predictive filter that assigns danger to its reactivation.

The Full System: How Intelligence Is Gated in Real Time

When these three systems—DMN, PFC inhibition, and limbic prediction—operate together, they form a **real-time cognitive filtration engine**. The person experiences a seamless stream of thought, unaware that:

- The **DMN** is narrating what's allowed to make sense

- The **PFC** is suppressing what is forbidden or unsafe

- The **limbic system** is emotionally vetoing options based on past pain

This unified filter becomes what the person calls **"me."**

But it is not them. It is a system. A structure. A survivorship adaptation.

This is the neurological basis of what ICT calls **identity collapse**—not a psychological shift, but a **neurocognitive dismantling** of this predictive filter architecture. When the collapse occurs, none of these systems need to be "fixed"—they simply lose control. They are no longer functioning as the default.

ICT and Filter Disruption: Restoring Field Access

ICT does not work by calming the nervous system or regulating emotion. It works by **disrupting the filter that prevents full access** to cognition.

This disruption occurs through specific collapse mechanisms:

- **Frontal Loop Reversal**: Temporarily overwhelms the prefrontal inhibition network by feeding recursive paradoxes, forcing disengagement from control loops.

- **Limbic Disassociation Collapse**: Uses memory-triggered exposure without narrative framing, allowing the emotional pattern to "short-circuit" without reinforcement.

- **DMN Deactivation through Identity Feedback Loops**: Engages recursive self-referencing statements that exhaust the DMN's narrative coherence, forcing detachment.

These methods do not "fix" the brain. They **remove its allegiance** to the limiting self-model. After collapse, the DMN quiets, the PFC loosens, the limbic threat coding fades—and what emerges is not emptiness.

It is access.

Conclusion: Intelligence Is a Neurobiological Freedom State

By understanding how the DMN, frontal cortex, and limbic system act as predictive filters, we can finally answer a deeper question:

Why do so few people reach their cognitive potential?

Because their brain is not permitted to.

These systems—built for coherence, safety, and efficiency—become invisible walls around cognition. They do not limit intelligence directly. They limit the *pathways* through which intelligence can arise.

ICT does not teach new strategies. It burns the map.

And once that map is gone, the person is no longer navigating through cognitive corridors built by trauma, fear, and false identity.

They are standing in the full field. And they are free to choose.

Case Analysis: Collapse-Induced Cognitive Emergence

Introduction: The Collapse That Unveils Intelligence

Theories mean little without transformation. Frameworks, even when scientifically grounded, must ultimately bow to what emerges in the lived field. The true power of Identity Collapse Therapy (ICT) is not in its philosophical elegance or neurological precision—it is in the real human beings who walk into a session under the weight of cognitive limitation and walk out in full contact with their uncollapsed mind.

This section draws from direct clinical application. These are not idealized case studies constructed to support a hypothesis. They are real human moments—sessions in which identity collapsed, predictive gating dissolved, and intelligence revealed itself as the natural state beneath the filter.

Each case will be framed as a **pre-collapse profile**, a **collapse moment**, and a **post-collapse emergence**, allowing a clear pattern to be seen: intelligence is not taught. It is remembered—once the self that was forgetting it is gone.

Case One: The Logical Executive Who "Wasn't Creative"

Profile:
A senior executive, mid-40s, highly analytical, successful in corporate operations but deeply dissatisfied. He described himself as "the guy who makes things run, not the one with the ideas." Despite having built large systems and teams, he was haunted by a sense of creative absence. "I'm not like the visionaries. I just keep the engine clean."

Collapse:
Through recursive self-loop protocols, we traced the origin of his creative disassociation back to early ridicule—his artwork dismissed by a critical parent. The "logical one" identity was a compensatory armor that became permanent. During the Infinite Self-Mirroring Sequence, he confronted the core paradox: the very systems he created were structurally innovative, yet his observer denied the possibility of creativity.

The collapse moment came when he attempted to reject a metaphor that emerged spontaneously. As he tried to dismiss it, the observer itself was caught in contradiction. We paused. He said nothing for nearly three minutes. Then, with visible disorientation, he said, *"Wait. That came from me?"*

Post-Collapse Emergence:
In the weeks that followed, his dreams became vivid and archetypal. He began drawing again—complex, abstract architectural forms. He revised his team structure using principles that came to him in images, not strategies. When asked how he was doing, he responded: *"I don't think anymore. I just see."*

His IQ didn't change. His access did. The part of him that said *"I'm not creative"* was no longer alive to collapse the field.

Case Two: The Former Student Who "Wasn't Smart Enough"

Profile:
A woman in her 30s, academically underperforming since childhood, labeled with mild learning disabilities, and self-identified as "average." She was deeply intuitive, emotionally perceptive, and empathic—but avoided anything intellectual. Her default response was *"That's too complex for me."*

Collapse:
Using the Cognitive Permission Reset protocol, we

traced the limitation not to the label itself, but to an emotionally encoded moment: a teacher who laughed at her for misinterpreting a question aloud. In that moment, the limbic system tagged "interpretation" as dangerous. The frontal lobe locked into inhibition. Intelligence narrowed.

Her collapse came during the Narrative Reversal Exercise, when she read her own self-description back as if it were written about someone else. The words *"too complex for me"* created a cognitive dissonance loop. The emotional gate cracked. Tears came—not from grief, but from the release of internal suppression. *"That's not even true. I've always been thinking more than I could say."*

Post-Collapse Emergence:
Within two weeks, she began reading philosophy books. Not skimming—absorbing. She returned to a course she had dropped years earlier. She began facilitating group sessions, not as an expert, but from emergent insight. Her speech became more fluid, her thoughts more layered.

In session, she said: *"I didn't get smarter. It just stopped feeling illegal to be this clear."*

Case Three: The High Performer in a Constant Fog

Profile:
A startup founder in his late 20s, outwardly successful

but inwardly disconnected. He described his mental state as "foggy, like something is in the way." Though highly functional, he relied on caffeine, overthinking, and intellectual aggression. "I can power through, but I can't feel my thoughts."

Collapse:
ICT revealed that his cognition was over-activated, not under-performing. The fog was not lack—it was **over-gating**, driven by deep unconscious hyper-vigilance. His childhood was marked by emotional unpredictability. Intelligence had become a survival function—hypercontrolled to avoid emotional vulnerability.

Collapse was induced through the Waterfall Release method. As he was led into recursive semantic fatigue, a spontaneous cognitive pause occurred. His breath slowed. His eyes shifted laterally. And then he whispered: *"There's so much more here than I thought."*

Post-Collapse Emergence:
The next day, he described feeling like "his brain had returned to him." He began working fewer hours but producing more insight. Lateral thinking replaced obsessive control. In one session, he described solving a technical problem in his startup by doing nothing for four hours and letting the solution surface.

His field access was no longer hijacked by anticipatory gating. For the first time, he was thinking from zero—not from defense.

Case Four: The Spiritual Seeker Trapped in Bypassed Intelligence

Profile:
A long-time spiritual practitioner with decades of meditation, energetic healing, and intuitive training. While perceptive and emotionally sensitive, she consistently avoided conceptual rigor. She described cognitive topics as "dense," "3D," or "too masculine." She equated "intellect" with ego and had unknowingly dissociated from her thinking self.

Collapse:
ICT revealed an early academic wound masked in spiritual language. Her aversion to logic was not transcendence—it was protection. The moment came during the Symbolic Compression Test, when she encountered a contradiction: she could intuitively sense meaning, but refused to define it.

We isolated the self that was refusing definition. It collapsed quickly. Not through resistance, but through humor. She laughed: *"Oh. I'm pretending it's spiritual, but I'm just scared of not knowing the answer."*

Post-Collapse Emergence:
Within a month, she began writing again. This time, her language was not just poetic—it was precise. She began integrating frameworks into her intuitive teaching. She said: *"I used to float above the system. Now I can move through it without becoming it."*

She had not lost her intuitive access. She had reclaimed the half of her intelligence that had been spiritually bypassed.

Emergent Pattern Recognition: Collapse Across Domains

Across these cases—and dozens more—certain universal patterns emerge:

1.   **Collapse is often triggered not by content but by contradiction.**
The internal observer cannot hold conflicting truths without resolution. When forced to do so, it dissolves.

2.   **Post-collapse cognition feels familiar, not foreign.**
Clients often describe it not as acquiring intelligence, but as *removing what was in the way.*

3.   **Performance increases without training.**
This is a critical distinction. The results of collapse are not gradual improvements. They are immediate *returns* to a cognitive baseline that had been hidden.

4.   **The field becomes emotionally neutral.**
Shame, fear, and comparison vanish post-collapse. The mind no longer performs to be good. It performs because there is nothing blocking it.

5.   **There is no going back.**
Once a person has accessed cognition without identity,

they cannot unsee the filter. They may relapse into old patterns temporarily, but the gate has been revealed. It cannot be unseen.

Conclusion: Collapse Is the Gateway to Uncollapsed Mind

In every case, the result of collapse is the same: the filter falls, the field opens, and the person realizes they were never unintelligent.

They were just over-collapsing the field.

IQ does not measure capacity. It measures *what remains after collapse*. And since most people never collapse their identity, they live and die in a fragment of what they could have been.

ICT changes this.

It does not offer possibility. It removes impossibility.

And what emerges is not a smarter self—it is the first experience of intelligence that was never touched by fear, narrative, or self-definition.

This is the nature of collapse-induced cognitive emergence.
And this is why the mind, left unfiltered, reveals not genius…

…but truth.

Post-Collapse Cognitive Fluidity: Flow, Integration, and Multistate Access

Introduction: Intelligence That No Longer Needs to "Appear"

The immediate aftermath of identity collapse is often marked by awe. Clients speak of spaciousness, clarity, and a lightness of perception—as if their very awareness had been uncluttered. But the more profound change happens in the days and weeks that follow, when something subtler takes root: a **shift in the architecture of cognition itself**.

This shift is not toward more intense thinking, but toward **fluidity**—a seamless, multi-state intelligence that arises without conscious effort. Thoughts emerge without triggering identity reinforcement. Emotions are processed without requiring interpretation. Insight flows not from striving, but from non-resistance. The individual is no longer "using their mind"—they are simply present with what the mind makes available.

This section explores the **post-collapse landscape**—the neurocognitive, psychological, and phenomenological characteristics of what ICT refers to as *cognitive fluidity*. We will examine:

- The structure of post-collapse thought generation

- The role of *flow states* as natural byproducts of collapse

- How integration occurs without effort

- The emergence of **multistate access**—the ability to shift between intellectual, imaginal, and intuitive cognition without friction

- Why the collapsed mind does not "perform"—it simply *remembers*

This is where intelligence ceases to be performance, and becomes **presence**.

What Thought Feels Like After Collapse

In the traditional self-state, thought is tightly looped through the ego. Each idea is processed through layers of anticipation, self-judgment, and emotional compensation. The person is not just thinking—they are constantly evaluating the meaning, worth, and implication of their thoughts.

After collapse, this loop dissolves. The internal observer no longer filters cognition through identity maintenance. What emerges is a different architecture altogether—one in which thought:

- Appears without initiation
- Flows without internal resistance
- Self-revises without shame
- Exists without being "claimed"

Clients often describe post-collapse thought with phrases like:

- *"It's just there."*
- *"I'm watching it unfold."*
- *"There's no tightness."*
- *"It feels like the idea is thinking itself."*

This shift is not dissociation. It is **disidentification**—a natural separation between cognition and the self that used to need control.

What remains is a **coherently unstructured field**, in which thought, emotion, and perception rise and resolve in tandem.

Flow States as Default, Not Exception

The state of "flow," as researched by Mihaly Csikszentmihalyi and others, is typically associated with peak performance—moments when challenge and skill align, self-consciousness disappears, and focus becomes effortless.

In ICT, flow is not a peak. It is a **baseline**—a natural cognitive state once the self that interrupts flow is no longer active.

This is a radical shift. Most systems attempt to induce flow through external conditions—managing inputs, setting goals, increasing challenge. ICT shows that flow does not require structure—it requires the **removal of identity-based gating**.

Why? Because identity is what interrupts flow. It reintroduces self-referential noise into clean attention. The collapsed individual no longer loops internal narratives through their task. The mind does not "lose itself in the moment"—it never leaves.

Post-collapse flow is marked by:

- Absorption without fixation

- Clarity without over-focusing

- Creativity without pressure

- A timelessness that does not feel escapist—but *complete*

Whereas pre-collapse flow is something one *gets into*, post-collapse flow is something one *lives from*.

Integration Without Identity Anchoring

Traditional models of integration emphasize narrative coherence, emotional processing, and meaning-making. After collapse, these processes become largely obsolete.

Why?

Because the person is no longer integrating experiences into a self-narrative. The **narrative itself has dissolved**.

Post-collapse integration does not happen through story—it happens through **non-resistance**. Experience is allowed to pass through the system without needing to be filed, justified, or explained.

In neurological terms, this resembles **neural coherence without hierarchical binding**. The brain is no longer organizing perception around a fixed egoic attractor. Information is processed **directly**—meaning emerges without being sculpted into identity.

Examples include:

- Emotions resolving without journaling or reappraisal

- Memories reconfiguring without trauma processing

- Behaviors changing without self-discipline

Clients often describe this as *"things just make sense without needing to talk about them."*

This is integration not as content management, but as **field continuity**. The self is no longer disrupted by new input—because there is no boundary to defend.

Emergence of Multistate Cognitive Access

Perhaps the most transformative aspect of post-collapse cognition is **multistate access**—the ability to seamlessly move between different forms of intelligence without resistance, distortion, or fear.

Most people live trapped in a **single cognitive identity**:

- The analyst who fears emotions

- The empath who avoids logic

- The mystic who resists structure
- The skeptic who denies intuition

Each of these is not a truth. It is a collapse—an identity-based restriction that limits access to the full field.

After collapse, these gates dissolve. The person no longer "chooses" which intelligence to use—they move freely between states based on context, resonance, or emergence.

This includes:

- **Logical cognition**: structural analysis, sequencing, and pattern recognition
- **Intuitive cognition**: nonlinear insight, symbolic resonance, and energetic sensing
- **Imaginal cognition**: creative ideation, dream logic, and metaphor construction
- **Embodied cognition**: somatic awareness, action-informed knowing
- **Transcognitive presence**: pure awareness, stillness without processing

The person is no longer **identified with any of these states**. They are available—but not attached.

This fluidity is the true measure of post-collapse intelligence—not IQ, but **range**.

Collapse as Restoration of Cognitive Homeostasis

One of the most misunderstood aspects of high performance is the assumption that it requires *amplification*. More focus, more learning, more stimulation.

But after collapse, performance increases not through amplification—but through **homeostasis**. The system returns to its natural equilibrium: a state where perception is clean, thought is spacious, and emotion is unhooked from identity.

The result is:

- **Increased creativity**: not from brainstorming, but from non-resistance

- **Better memory**: not from retention, but from lowered interference

- **Faster insight**: not from speed, but from zero friction

- **Reduced cognitive fatigue**: because the self is no longer narrating every move

This is not a superpower. It is a return to baseline—what the mind was always capable of before it was fragmented by false identity and predictive threat encoding.

Collapse reveals that intelligence was never missing.
It was just constantly being interrupted.

Living in the Field: Cognitive Freedom as the New Norm

Post-collapse cognition is not about constant expansion. It is about **stability without confinement**.

Clients who remain in the post-collapse state describe:

- Deep ease in facing unknowns

- Instant recognition of when a thought is arising from identity vs. field

- The capacity to hold paradox without resolution

- A sense of intelligence that is *felt* before it is *thought*

They do not strive to be wise.
They simply do not resist what wisdom wants to say.

They do not seek answers.
They allow questions to gestate until something truer emerges.

They do not perform intelligence.
They live from the part of them that no longer needs to collapse it.

This is what it means to be **intellectually free**.

Conclusion: Collapse Is Not the Peak—It Is the Beginning

Many assume that identity collapse is the final act. But in truth, it is only the opening.

Collapse creates the conditions for a new kind of life—a life where the mind is not trapped inside itself, where intelligence is not guarded by fear, and where thought is not a weapon or a shield, but a natural unfolding of contact with the real.

In this state:

The self no longer thinks.
It is thought.
The self no longer performs.
It is presence.
And intelligence no longer arrives.
It has always been here.

This is not the end of transformation.

It is the beginning of the uncollapsed mind.

Redefining Intelligence: From IQ to Field-Based Access

Introduction: The Illusion That Made Everyone Smaller

The belief that intelligence can be quantified by a number has become one of the most destructive distortions in the history of psychology.

IQ was never just a metric. It became a **labeling engine**—a fixed lens through which human capacity was interpreted, institutionalized, and limited. It told children what they could become. It told adults whether they were gifted or average. And it told society that some minds were simply worth more than others.

But what if it was all wrong?

What if IQ has never measured intelligence at all?

In Identity Collapse Therapy (ICT), we do not treat intelligence as a trait to be improved. We treat it as a **field to be accessed**. A field shaped not by brain size, genetics, or scores—but by what the internal observer permits to collapse into experience.

This final section will formally redefine intelligence from an ICT framework. It will:

- Deconstruct the origins and limitations of the IQ model

- Explain why IQ measures collapsed cognition—not potential

- Offer a field-based model of cognitive access grounded in neuroscience

- Show how ICT reclaims full cognitive freedom by removing identity-gated collapse

- Deliver a final symbolic dissolution of the "intelligence myth" for the reader

This is not just a redefinition. It is a return.

The IQ Model: Origins, Assumptions, and Errors

IQ—or Intelligence Quotient—originated in the early 20th century as an attempt to measure academic aptitude. The first tests, developed by Binet and Simon in France, were never meant to define a person. They were designed to identify those who needed more support in school.

But by the mid-20th century, IQ had transformed into something else: a **symbolic currency of human worth.** It was normalized, standardized, and deployed as a sorting mechanism across schools, militaries, corporations, and psychological institutions.

Its underlying assumptions were:

1.   Intelligence is a fixed trait

2.   It can be reduced to problem-solving, logic, and verbal ability

3.   It follows a bell curve—most are average, few are gifted or impaired

4.   It remains largely stable across time

Each of these assumptions has now been refuted—not just philosophically, but empirically:

•   Neuroplasticity shows the brain is never fixed (Davidson & McEwen, 2012)

•   Multiple intelligences theory (Gardner, 1983) reveals that cognition is multidimensional

•   Cultural studies show IQ tests are biased toward specific learning styles and socioeconomic conditions

•   Longitudinal data show IQ can fluctuate over time due to emotional, environmental, and identity-related factors

But the most important critique is this:

IQ does not measure **what the mind can do**.
It measures **what the identity allows the mind to do under pressure**.

It is not a test of intelligence.
It is a test of *collapse*.

IQ as a Snapshot of Identity-Constrained Collapse

When a person sits down to take an IQ test, they are not accessing their full intelligence. They are accessing:

- The part of themselves that believes in their intelligence

- The part that is safe enough to risk being wrong

- The part that can tolerate uncertainty

- The part that performs under surveillance

All of this is identity-based. Which means the result reflects **the size of the person's collapse**, not the size of their mind.

For example:

- A highly gifted child labeled as "difficult" may underperform due to shame-based identity

- A perfectionist adult may sabotage themselves under time pressure, narrowing cognition

- A student from a marginalized background may subconsciously lower performance to avoid confirming stereotypes

- A trauma survivor may experience frontal gating, suppressing fluid reasoning under perceived threat

None of these test scores reflect potential.
They reflect **filtered performance under identity regulation**.

ICT exposes the underlying truth:
IQ is not a measure of intelligence.
It is a mirror of what the self allows.

Field-Based Cognition: A New Definition of Intelligence

In the ICT framework, intelligence is not defined as a capacity within the brain, but as **the degree of access a person has to the cognitive field in a given moment**.

This is grounded in three principles:

1. **Cognition is probabilistic, not deterministic**
The brain exists in a state of potential thought-forms, interpretations, and responses. Which ones become conscious depends on internal prediction systems—not fixed ability.

2. **The internal observer collapses the cognitive field**
Identity, formed through emotional encoding and social mirroring, acts as a gating mechanism. It allows or blocks access based on what feels coherent or safe.

3. **Removing the observer restores access to uncollapsed cognition**
Once the gating identity is collapsed, the full range of intelligence becomes available—not gradually, but instantly.

This leads to a new definition:

Intelligence is the real-time access to uncollapsed cognition in the absence of identity-based gating.

It is not something you *have*.
It is something you are *permitted to enter*.
And once collapse occurs, the gates are gone.

ICT as a Tool of Intelligence Liberation

In practice, ICT does not increase intelligence. It reveals it.

This occurs through:

•	**Dismantling the observer**: Deactivating the identity structures that suppress cognition

•	**Unhooking emotional encoding**: Removing fear, shame, and threat-based inhibition

•	**Clearing narrative filtration**: Ending the story of who the person must be to think well

•	**Stabilizing the post-collapse field**: Training the mind to recognize when collapse is reoccurring, and stop it mid-process

The result is not "smarter people." It is **free minds**.

This is why ICT clients often say:

•	*"I don't feel more intelligent—I feel unobstructed."*

•	*"I didn't gain anything—I just lost the thing that was always in the way."*

- *"It feels like my intelligence was waiting for me behind the noise."*

ICT does not grant brilliance.

It removes the gate between the person and the brilliance that was already waiting.

The Collapse of IQ: Symbolic Closure

The idea that a human being's mind can be defined by a number is not just incorrect.

It is violent.

It creates internal hierarchies, distorts education, and embeds a deep sense of insufficiency in those who collapse early.

The IQ myth tells people that genius is rare. That potential is fixed. That the bell curve is destiny.

But ICT shows the opposite:

- Genius is common—it's just gated

- Potential is fluid—it's just collapsed

- The bell curve is not real—it's an artifact of a world obsessed with control

The collapse of IQ is not just scientific.

It is **symbolic**. It is the death of the idea that we must earn our worth by passing invisible tests. It is the end of the war between "smart" and "not smart." It is the end of the belief that we must become something to matter.

In the collapse, we see:

There is no such thing as intelligence.
 There is only presence.
 And when the gatekeeper dissolves,
 presence becomes the field.
 And the field becomes thought.
 And thought becomes free.

Conclusion: The Mind, Uncollapsed

The final truth of this chapter is simple:

Intelligence is not fixed.
 It is not earned.
 It is not measured.
 It is not rare.

It is **remembered**,
 when the identity that forgot it
 no longer exists to collapse it.

This is what ICT restores:
 Not better thinkers.
 But free ones.

Not higher scores.
　But unfiltered minds.

Not improved cognition.
　But cognition no longer afraid of itself.

This is the collapse.
　And from here, we build nothing.
　We simply enter.
　And never leave again.

Threshold Transition:

Perception has been freed.
　Selection is no longer bound to identity.
　Thought is no longer authored—but observed, aligned, chosen.

And yet—
　something pulls.

Something smaller than a belief,
　older than a story,
　faster than thought.

Emotion.

Not as feeling.
　But as filter.

Even without identity at the helm,
　the system can still be hijacked—
　not by idea,
　but by affect.

Not by belief,
 but by the residue of what was once necessary to survive.

This next chapter explores the final stronghold of limitation:
emotion fused with identity—
where fear wears the face of truth,
 and history passes for intuition.

To complete collapse, we must dissolve not just the thinker—
 but the feelings that once protected it.

Not to bypass them.
 But to see what they become...
when no one is left to interpret them.

Chapter 6: The Role of Emotion in Cognitive Limitation

The Emotional Survival Mechanism

Introduction: The Last Wall Before Freedom

Even after the mind is clear, something often lingers. The person feels spacious, uncollapsed, intellectually free—but when life applies pressure, they tighten. Their body subtly contracts. They speak more carefully. They begin performing again. Not from thought—but from **survival memory**.

This is not identity returning.
 This is not the observer reassembling.
 This is the **emotional survival mechanism**—the final architecture that holds the ego-body system in place long after collapse has destabilized cognition.

The emotional survival mechanism is not a thought. It is not even a feeling.
 It is the **embodied prediction system** beneath the

surface—designed to anticipate emotional threat, contract around meaning, and maintain protective coherence at all costs.

Until this mechanism is dissolved, **collapse is incomplete**.
The person may have access to unfiltered thought—but their **nervous system is still obeying laws written in fear**.

This section begins the final dismantling of the self—where thought is no longer the target. The **body becomes the arena**, and emotion becomes the **linguistic architecture of contraction**.

The Emotional Body as the Gate of Permission

The human body is not simply a vessel. It is an **intelligence filter**—a distributed sensing system that determines, moment by moment, whether experience is safe to allow.

This gating is not cognitive.
It is **interoceptive**—a felt-sense modulation of safety, rooted in emotion and semantically encoded into muscle tone, breath patterning, and nervous system regulation.

Before the mind speaks, the body has already decided:

- Whether this thought is safe to complete

- Whether this insight is too emotionally expensive

- Whether this conversation will lead to exposure or rejection

- Whether authenticity will threaten relational belonging

This is the emotional survival mechanism in action. It doesn't ask, *"Is this true?"*
It asks, *"Is this survivable?"*

If the answer is no, it contracts.
It tightens the diaphragm.
It pulls the shoulders forward.
It lowers the voice.
It reduces the breath cycle.
It subtly re-invokes an identity that **won't get hurt**.

This contraction is not about the situation. It is about **the memory of risk**.
Emotional risk stored not in ideas—but in fascia, posture, and nervous system entrainment.

Emotion as Predictive Architecture

Modern neuroscience no longer treats emotion as a reaction to experience. Instead, emotion is now understood as a **predictive encoding layer**—the body's attempt to forecast and respond to likely outcomes based on past events.

Lisa Feldman Barrett's research confirms:

"Emotions are constructed by the brain as predictions to guide behavior before sensations arrive."

This means the body does not *feel and then protect*.
It *protects in advance*—by blocking actions, words, or states that have been emotionally punished in the past.

This is survival intelligence.
But it becomes **collapse resistance** when the emotional filter is:

- Overgeneralized ("Anything vulnerable = unsafe")

- Chronically active ("Collapse = exposure = threat")

- Stored in the body without cognitive access

At that point, emotion is no longer guidance.
It becomes **constraint**.
The body becomes the last bastion of the self.
And collapse cannot fully stabilize—because the nervous system is still operating inside the original emotional contract.

Emotional Contracts and the Performance of Safety

These emotional constraints often take the form of **unconscious contracts**—pre-verbal survival agreements made during experiences of emotional overwhelm.

Examples:

- *"If I stay silent, they won't leave."*

- *"If I'm smart but not too smart, I'll be accepted."*

- *"If I make sense of everything, I won't feel the pain."*

These contracts are not thoughts—they are **body-held mandates**, encoded during moments when the emotional system had to **trade authenticity for survival**.

The performance that emerges from these contracts is not identity-based—it is **safety-based**.

The person performs "truth," performs "confidence," performs "presence"—but the nervous system is still performing **avoidance**.
The collapse did not fail. But the body did not yet receive the message that *freedom is survivable*.

Until these contracts are found and collapsed, the emotional survival mechanism will:

- Reintroduce identity

- Reengage defense loops
- Limit full access to post-collapse fluidity

The Semantic Core of Emotional Gating

Here lies the bridge into the next section:

The body does not just respond to pain.
It responds to **meaning**.

Words are not neutral.
The nervous system collapses around **semantically loaded threats**—associations between language, feeling, and social consequence.

This is why even after collapse, the person may still tighten when hearing:

- "Stupid"
- "Too much"
- "Disappointing"
- "Who do you think you are?"

These phrases are not just words.
They are **emotional triggers embedded with predictive threat**.

This mechanism—**semantic body tensioning**—is the core of emotional collapse resistance. It is not just the memory of pain. It is the **resonant contraction of meaning inside the body**, enforced by the emotional survival system to prevent symbolic annihilation.

This will be the focus of Section 6.2.

Collapse Without Somatic Permission Is Temporary

If collapse does not include the emotional body, it cannot stabilize.

Signs of incomplete collapse include:

- Subtle bracing in the chest before speaking truth

- Avoidance of specific relational contexts

- Hyper-logic or over-intuition used to bypass vulnerability

- Fragmentation of state when under pressure

- Chronic micro-performance to "prove" authenticity

None of this is a failure of thought.
It is a body that still believes truth is unsafe.

ICT does not force collapse through.
It brings the **emotional body into permission**—teaching the nervous system to stop contracting around meaning.

Semantic Body Tensioning: How the Body Collapses Around Meaning

---

Introduction: When Meaning Becomes a Threat

There is a kind of tension that exists before thought.
It does not arise from physical strain, nor does it register as a discrete emotion.
It is a subtle, pervasive tightening—an anticipatory contraction—that occurs the moment a certain word, idea, tone, or relational signal enters the space.

It is not about what is being said.
It is about **what that language means to the nervous system**.

This is **semantic body tensioning**—the process by which the body subconsciously contracts around words, phrases, or meanings that have been historically linked to emotional threat.

It is not a metaphor. It is not energetic symbolism.
It is a **precise, traceable collapse mechanism**—a semantic-somatic reflex encoded through repetition, emotional imprinting, and identity preservation.

In this section, we will explore:

- The definition and structure of semantic body tensioning

- How words become emotionally loaded at a somatic level

- Why certain phrases trigger collapse patterns long after identity is cognitively dismantled

- How ICT identifies and deactivates these meaning-based contraction loops

- The return of *embodied neutrality* as the sign of true emotional collapse

This is not just about language.
It is about how the body survives meaning.

What Is Semantic Body Tensioning?

Semantic body tensioning is the involuntary contraction of muscles, breath patterns, vocal tone, and energetic posture in response to specific **perceived meanings**—not because the words themselves are threatening, but because **the nervous system has associated those meanings with emotional survival risk.**

It is the body's way of saying:

- "This word has hurt me before."

- "This concept has led to rejection."

- "This role has triggered abandonment."

- "This kind of attention has made me collapse."

Examples:

- The phrase *"You're too sensitive"* triggers a chest contraction, shallow breath, or jaw clench

- The word *"lazy"* causes postural deflation or mental fog

- Being called *"brilliant"* evokes subtle tightening due to fear of expectation or jealousy

- Hearing *"I love you"* prompts constriction because of past manipulative use

This is not about logic.
The body is **reacting to meaning, not fact**.

This is why cognitive collapse is not enough.
Even when the mind is free, the body may still respond to language as if it is a battlefield.

How Meanings Become Somatic Threats

The process of semantic body tensioning begins in early socialization.
The child does not process language rationally.
They process it **emotionally**, tracking not just words but the **emotional charge, tone, and consequence** attached to them.

Over time, the system forms **semantic threat maps**:

- "Wrong answer" → shame → neck tension

- "Crying" → disapproval → solar plexus freeze

- "Too loud" → rejection → pelvic contraction

- "We're proud of you" → pressure → shoulder armor

These patterns are reinforced thousands of times across environments—school, family, religion, performance spaces—and stored not as beliefs, but as **somatic permissions**.

The result is that **language becomes a trigger** not because of its meaning—but because of its **symbolic risk**.

By adulthood, the body no longer waits for content.
It recognizes tone, rhythm, emotional field, and

symbolic cues—and contracts **before the words land**.

This is why post-collapse clients often say:

- "I don't know why, but that phrase still makes me brace."

- "I'm fine in my mind, but something in my stomach shuts down."

- "I can't speak the truth—I feel it, but it won't come out."

The self is gone.
But the body is still speaking its ancient vocabulary of caution.

The Role of the Emotional Survival Mechanism in Semantic Contraction

As established in Section 6.1, the emotional survival mechanism is designed to **anticipate and avoid emotional pain**.
Semantic body tensioning is its primary language.

This mechanism does not ask what something means rationally.
It asks, *"What did this word cost us last time?"*

If the answer is pain, disconnection, ridicule, or confusion—the body responds **by collapsing**:

- Pulling the ribs inward
- Narrowing the throat
- Flattening the energy field
- Withdrawing gaze
- Disassociating from voice, breath, or movement

This contraction is the survival mechanism's way of *refusing collapse.*
It is not resisting intelligence.
It is resisting **symbolic death**.

And it can only be collapsed when the **meaning that created the contraction is fully seen, felt, and deactivated**.

ICT Deactivation of Semantic Body Tensioning

ICT does not remove these contractions by affirming safety.
It removes them by **disarming the meaning loop**.

There are three steps to this process:

◆ 1. Identification of Semantic Tension Points

Clients are guided to speak aloud or write **emotionally loaded language**, and track micro-contractions:

- Word-level (e.g., "failure," "gifted," "selfish")

- Tone-level (e.g., mimicry of parent voice or authority)

- Field-level (e.g., relational setting or archetype activated)

◆ 2. Resonance Feedback Loop

ICT mirrors the contraction back to the client—not by explaining it, but by **naming the contraction while it is happening**:

"Say it again, but slower—can you feel the tightening behind your left eye before the word even ends?"
"Notice the breath break before the word 'deserve.' That's where the emotional contract is hiding."
"You spoke the truth, but your jaw tried to stop it halfway through."

This creates a **semantic-somatic feedback loop** that destabilizes the contraction's unconscious control.

- **3. Symbolic Deactivation via Paradox or Reversal**

Once the contraction is visible, ICT introduces paradox, repetition, or reversal to **interrupt the automatic threat prediction**.

Examples:

- Repeating the loaded word until the contraction dissipates

- Pairing the feared phrase with incongruent tone ("Say 'I'm too much' in a joyful voice")

- Contradicting the meaning aloud while allowing the body to stay soft ("I am wrong and safe. I am exposed and here.")

This is not reprogramming.
It is **deconditioning semantic reflexes through felt neutrality**.

When the contraction no longer activates around the word, the emotional survival mechanism no longer needs to perform defense.

This is the collapse point.

What Freedom Feels Like: Embodied Semantic Neutrality

When semantic body tensioning dissolves, something profound happens:

Language no longer carries weight.
Meaning no longer implies danger.
Truth no longer contracts the breath.
The body no longer hides behind performance.

The person can:

- Say their own name without flinching

- Speak powerfully without bracing

- Receive criticism without collapse

- Express vulnerability without shrinkage

- Feel resonance without surveillance

This is not numbness.
It is **embodied neutrality**—the state in which meaning flows through the system **without reactivation of the past.**

The collapse has completed its descent.
There is no longer a semantic hook for identity to grab.
There is no longer a felt threat associated with being seen.

Conclusion: The Body Stops Speaking the Language of Fear

When collapse reaches the level of semantic body tensioning, the person no longer performs survival through posture, breath, or phrasing.
 They no longer tighten when meaning arrives.
 They no longer hide from their own resonance.

This is not confidence.
 It is **absence of contraction**.
 This is not expression.
 It is **non-interruption**.

The mind is uncollapsed.
 The emotion is unhooked.
 The body is unscripted.

And the nervous system, for the first time, is not interpreting meaning as danger.
 It is interpreting meaning as **air**—something to move through.

Collapse has reached the field.

The Collapse-Resistant Self: Emotional Gating and Ego Reassembly

Introduction: The Self That Rebuilds Itself

Even after thought has quieted, even when the emotional contraction has softened and semantic tension has dissolved—there can still be a ghost. A faint reconstitution of the self. Not as an idea, but as a *behavioral patterning*. The person speaks more carefully in certain rooms. Their posture shifts in the presence of authority. Their body anticipates collapse before anything has happened.

This is not the old identity returning.
This is not failure of the collapse process.
This is **the ego**, rising in its most subtle form: **contextual reassembly**.

In this section, we will distinguish clearly and precisely:

- What the ego actually is from a systems perspective

- How ego differs from identity

- Why ego is not a single structure, but a **survival container that shifts across relational and environmental contexts**

- How the ego resists collapse by adapting—rebuilding a minimal viable self to protect the system

- And how ICT deactivates the ego, not by attacking it, but by **rendering its role obsolete**

This section completes the trifecta:
Collapse of thought.
Collapse of body.
Now—collapse of *the collapsing mechanism itself.*

Ego vs. Identity: Structural Clarification

In most psychological systems, "ego" and "identity" are treated interchangeably, or loosely defined depending on tradition. In ICT, these terms are structurally differentiated with precision.

- **Identity** is the set of *roles, traits, stories, and self-concepts* the system selects in order to remain coherent. Identity answers the question: *Who am I right now?*

- **Ego** is the **adaptive survival container** that selects, enforces, and protects these identities across time and space. Ego answers the question: *Who must I be here to stay intact?*

Whereas identity is content, **ego is the manager of content**. It is not static. It morphs depending on context, emotional safety, and threat analysis.

The ego is not interested in truth.
It is interested in **non-collapse**.

The Ego as Emotional-Survival Interface

The ego is not cognitive in origin.
It is **somatic-emotional in nature**, built as a predictive mechanism that matches threat level to acceptable identity options. It forms not from logic, but from felt reality.

Its root instruction is simple:

"I will prevent collapse by controlling who I am allowed to be in each situation."

Thus, the ego becomes a **contextual interface** that selects identity fragments based on:

- Social cues

- Emotional history

- Relational survival patterns

- Semantic field sensitivity

- Environmental power structures

Example:

- At work: The "rational leader" ego state is activated—tight jaw, linear language, no emotional variance

- At home: The "gentle partner" ego state appears—apologetic tone, collapsed posture

- In public: A default "pleaser" state emerges—quick smiling, rapid scanning, boundary diffusion

Each of these ego states selects identities **not because they are true**, but because they are **safe enough to prevent collapse**.

And each of them **rebuilds the self**—even after cognitive and emotional collapse has occurred.

Collapse-Resistant Behavior and the Reassembly Cycle

When collapse reaches the identity level, the mind stops filtering thought through the observer. When collapse reaches the body, emotional survival mechanisms stop tensioning around meaning.

But the ego—if not seen—**will adapt**.
It will silently observe the collapse process and *co-opt it*.
It will say:

- *"Ah, now I am the one who has collapsed."*

- *"I am the version of me who is free now."*

- *"I am the evolved one."*

This is not a spiritual bypass. It is not arrogance.
It is **a survival-level reassembly**, attempting to create a self that can remain coherent inside the new field.

This collapse-resistant ego will:

- Reintroduce performance under a new identity (e.g., "the wise one," "the healed one")

- Mimic field access while subtly constraining it in certain relational contexts

- Contract around specific interpersonal triggers while maintaining the illusion of fluidity

- Reassert identity in moments of social pressure, conflict, or exposure

The collapse is not lost.
But **it has not yet stabilized at the contextual ego level**.

ICT Identification of Contextual Ego Reassembly

ICT is not deceived by fluid speech, intellectual clarity, or even the absence of tension. It looks for **contextual ego patterning**—signs that collapse has not yet reached the system's core survival interface.

These signs include:

- **Fragmented performance** across environments
  ("I'm free here, but I still shrink around family")

- **Semantic variability** based on audience
  ("My language changes when I feel outmatched")

- **Field inversion** under emotional exposure
  ("When I cry, I feel like I become someone else")

- **Collapse compartmentalization**
("My truth shows up in coaching but not in intimacy")

These patterns reveal that the ego is still **selecting** which identity is allowed to operate under specific perceived risks.

This is not weakness.
It is **refined survival architecture**.

But it must be collapsed if the field is to remain open.

Ego Deactivation Through Contextual Collapse

ICT does not seek to "kill" the ego.
It does not shame survival.
It removes the **conditions that make ego necessary.**

This is done through:

◆ 1. Multi-Context Collapse Mapping
Clients identify ego pattern sets across distinct relational, professional, and internal environments. They do not collapse "the self"—they collapse **the shifting masks** used to survive each domain.

- **2. Semantic-Field Pressure Testing**

ICT reintroduces real-time symbolic risks (e.g., being seen, being wrong, being dismissed) in controlled relational simulations, allowing the client to witness **which ego state tries to reassemble** under pressure.

- **3. Collapse-Resistant Compassion Loop**

Rather than resisting ego reassembly, ICT welcomes it with paradox:

"Let the ego speak. Let it build itself again. But do not believe it."
"Let it tell you who you must be. But stay where you are."
"Watch it perform. And love it, as it ends."

By bringing **compassion to the moment of reassembly**, the nervous system no longer needs to obey the survival imperative.
The ego softens—not by defeat, but by **relief**.

It no longer has to manage collapse.
Because nothing is threatening anymore.

After Ego: Contextual Fluidity and Optional Identity

When ego is deactivated, **identity becomes optional**.
The person no longer enters a situation asking, *"Who*

do I need to be here?"
They enter with field access intact, and *select from the Contextual Identity Menu* without survival-based filtering.

They may choose:

- Precision or softness

- Logic or silence

- Boldness or tenderness

But none of it is compelled.
None of it is strategic.
None of it is to prevent collapse.

The ego is still available—should a dangerous moment arise.
But it no longer runs the show.
It is **disarmed, not destroyed.**

The self is no longer reacting to the world.
It is *moving within it*—from choice, not from contraction.

Conclusion: The Collapse of the Collapser

This is the final paradox:

The ego is the part of the self that survives collapse.
It is the self that says, *"We must rebuild something from the rubble."*

But when collapse reaches the ego itself,
when the system no longer fears fragmentation,
when the person no longer needs to perform permission—

The ego becomes quiet.
And what remains is not a self.
It is **access.**

Not to a better version.
But to the **field that no longer requires one**.

Somatic Permissioning and Affective Deactivation

Introduction: The Memory That Never Stops Predicting

Most people believe memory is passive—a record of what happened. But from the lens of modern neuroscience, memory is **predictive**, **embodied**, and **selective**. It doesn't replay the past—it reshapes the present by forecasting danger.

When someone begins to speak their truth, enter intimacy, or step into unknown power, what often blocks them is not thought or emotion—but **the body's stored response to what happened last time.**
 They try to act freely—but their nervous system pulls them back.
 Not because they are unsafe now.
 But because **the memory is still doing its job.**

This section will complete the emotional collapse architecture by addressing:

•	The predictive role of memory in affective gating

•	How unresolved memory loops create nervous system contraction even after collapse

- Why traditional trauma models are incomplete without semantic deactivation

- The ICT process of **somatic permissioning**—granting the nervous system the right to respond freely again

- What it means to have a **memory that no longer predicts** collapse

This is where emotion stops surviving the past—and begins returning to the field.

Memory as Affective Prediction, Not Recollection

Memory is not a playback device.
It is a **simulation engine**, designed to project prior emotional realities into future possibilities to keep the system safe.

According to predictive processing theory, the brain prioritizes stability over truth. This means memory functions less like a historical archive, and more like a **threat-reduction forecast system**. The emotional body uses stored data not to *remember*, but to *prevent*:

- "Last time you spoke up, you were punished."

- "Last time you opened emotionally, it ended in withdrawal."

- "Last time you excelled, others pulled away."

- "Last time you were seen, you lost control."

These aren't remembered stories.
They are **active forecasts**, embedded into **the body's response architecture**.

So even if collapse has dissolved identity and semantic tension, **the nervous system still holds a record of survival failure.**
And it will brace against recurrence—until it is shown that the future is not the past.

The Incompleteness of Traditional Trauma Processing

Most trauma modalities aim to reprocess or reframe painful memories. They may succeed in reducing charge—but they often leave behind **the semantic-somatic association**.

The result?

- The story is integrated, but the contraction remains

- The insight is gained, but the breath still breaks

- The pain is processed, but the **body still predicts loss** when freedom nears

ICT recognizes that it is not the memory itself that limits behavior.
It is the **affective forecast** the memory produces, especially when tied to **role, exposure, or semantic resonance.**

What needs to collapse is not the trauma narrative.
It is the **body's agreement with the memory**—the subconscious contract that says:

"I will not go there again. I will not feel that again. I will not be that free again."

Until that contract dissolves, freedom remains negotiated.

Somatic Permissioning: Restoring Right to Respond

ICT addresses memory-based affective loops through **somatic permissioning**—the process of recalibrating the nervous system's ability to:

- Feel fully

- Express without prediction

- Move without retraction

- Exist without defending against the past

This begins by identifying memory-linked contraction:

- The micro-hold before vulnerability

- The repeated breath break before truth-telling

- The emotional drop after being praised

- The sudden dissociation when love enters the space

These contractions are **time-anchored affective replays**—the nervous system tightening in advance of forecasted pain.

Somatic permissioning does not involve retelling the story.
It involves **inviting the body to respond freshly**, and then **proving** that the predicted collapse never comes.

ICT Techniques for Memory-Based Collapse Deactivation

ICT collapses memory-based prediction loops not through catharsis, but through **real-time contradiction of survival expectations**.

Three core methods:

◆ 1. Predictive Memory Exposure (PME)

Client is gently guided toward a situation, expression, or identity the memory predicts will result in pain—*without changing course*.
ICT facilitator remains fully regulated, safe, and unmoved.

Example:
Client says, *"This is the part where I lose control."*
ICT: *"Good. Let it happen. Let's watch what doesn't happen next."*

Result: The nervous system encounters contradiction between memory and reality.
Prediction loop begins to collapse.

◆ 2. Affective Role Disruption

The role (e.g., "caretaker," "invisible one," "responsible one") that historically collapsed under pressure is invoked and **allowed to exist fully—without consequence**.

Client embodies the role, speaks from it, and remains in the field as nothing collapses. The ego's old contract is dissolved through affective neutrality.

◆ 3. Memory Without Meaning (MWM)

Memory is accessed not for story, but for **felt response**—without semantic framing.

The client is invited to sense the contraction, give it no name, and **remain in contact without interpreting it.**

Without narrative to reinforce it, the contraction dissipates as it is no longer useful for prediction.

This is not trauma healing.
This is **forecast deactivation.**

What It Feels Like When Memory Stops Predicting

When memory collapses as a predictive system:

- The body no longer braces for familiar pain

- Breath stabilizes around historically triggering dynamics

- The nervous system no longer avoids freedom

- The self is no longer split by past and present

Clients describe this as:

- *"I feel like I've outrun something that was always following me."*

- *"It's like the memory isn't real anymore—but not because it's gone. Because it doesn't matter."*

- *"It still happened. But it doesn't mean anything now."*

That's the point.
Memory was never the issue.
Meaning was.

And now, the meaning no longer creates collapse.

Conclusion: When the Body Stops Predicting the Past

Collapse is only complete when the body no longer interprets freedom as the repetition of failure.

ICT does not aim to erase memory.
It teaches the system that **memory is no longer needed to protect.**

When memory stops predicting collapse,
the nervous system returns to real time.
And in real time, nothing is dangerous.
Not love.
Not expression.
Not truth.
Not power.

The person is not performing safety anymore.
They are not managing possibility anymore.
They are **living without rehearsal**.

And the memory?
Still there.
But silent.
Finally.

Embodied Liberation: When the Body Stops Performing

Introduction: The Nervous System That No Longer Negotiates

The final signal that collapse has reached completion is not a thought, a realization, or even a feeling.
It is a **postural truth**—a stillness that doesn't hold back.
It is in the nervous system no longer performing identity.
No longer contracting in advance.
No longer scanning for permission.

It is when the body simply **is**—without preparing, adjusting, bracing, or rehearsing.

This is not the freeze of shutdown.
It is the **presence of uncollapsed being.**

This section finalizes the collapse arc of Chapter 6 by exploring:

- The signs and physiology of a non-performative nervous system

- The final disappearance of emotional vigilance

- The transition from embodiment as strategy to embodiment as freedom

- ICT's markers of full embodied collapse

- The emergence of the *unscripted self*—a presence that needs no protection

This is not the peak of transformation.
It is the **ground floor of aliveness.**

The Nervous System's Role in Identity Performance

Even after identity has been cognitively dismantled and emotionally decoded, the nervous system often continues to behave as if it must earn safety.

This shows up in:

- Micro-bracing in social environments

- Adjusted tone and pacing based on perceived hierarchy

- Subtle shifts in posture around perceived evaluation

- The need to "soften" truth before expressing it

- Over-smiling, over-explaining, or preemptive agreement

These are not decisions.
 They are **residual habits of survival**—the nervous system attempting to maintain coherence through **performance**.

This performance is not theatrical.
 It is often invisible—even to the person doing it.
 It is felt most clearly by what is absent: the inability to **just be**.

The Physics of Performance: Contraction, Delay, and Editing

Performance has a physics.

It introduces:

- **Micro-delays** between impulse and action

- **Contractions** around truth that distort tone and presence

- **Editing loops** that fragment expression

- **Relational compensation**, in which the self contorts around what others are emotionally capable of receiving

This is not manipulation.
It is what the system learned to do in order to survive:
"If I show too much truth, I lose love."
"If I don't adjust here, I'll be misunderstood."
"If I say it like that, someone might leave."

These are not stories.
They are **kinesthetic truths** encoded in the spine, breath, and musculature.

The self may be uncollapsed.
The ideas may be clear.
But the body is still *negotiating its own presence*.

This is the final performance to be surrendered.

Collapse Without Effort: The Deactivation of Vigilance

ICT does not ask the body to perform authenticity.
It invites the nervous system to **stop performing survival**.

This occurs not through pushing, proving, or self-regulation.
It occurs when the nervous system **witnesses its own unnecessary performance**—and does nothing.

This is the moment of real collapse.

- The breath drops back into the pelvis

- The chest stops controlling tone
- The face unhooks from social calibration
- The spine returns to its natural curve
- The voice emerges without aim

This is not relaxation.
It is **unarmored truth**.

Not by effort.
But by **absence**.

6.5.4 Markers of Embodied Collapse

When collapse stabilizes into the body, the following transformations become evident:

---

1. Posture becomes emergent, not controlled.
The body no longer "holds itself." It is held by the field of awareness. The result is neither rigid nor limp—it is **responsive without pretense**.

---

2. Expression flows without calibration.
Words are no longer filtered through politeness, permission, or emotional buffering. There is no

sharpness, no withholding. Just *direct expression that feels like breath moving through skin.*

---

3. The face stops performing likability.
Smiling happens, but it is not a social strategy. Eye contact stabilizes, not as dominance or submission, but as *relational stillness.*

---

4. Presence outlives roles.
The person can be in any room, any relationship, any context—without needing to summon a version of themselves to match it.

---

5. Movement becomes unified.
Gesture, tone, word, and attention synchronize—not through rehearsal, but because *nothing is interrupting them anymore.*

These are not achievements.
They are the signs of **nothing left to prove**.

The Unscripted Self: Beyond Performance, Beyond Collapse

When the body stops performing, something unexpected appears:
Not a "truer self."
Not a "more embodied identity."
But something **unscripted**—a way of being that exists before roles, beyond narrative, underneath even transformation.

This self:

- Doesn't need to stabilize presence

- Doesn't track how it's being perceived

- Doesn't reflexively adjust for emotional cues

- Doesn't require feedback to continue existing

This self **was always here.**
But it could not surface while the nervous system was still working to survive meaning, memory, and collapse.

When all gates are down—cognitive, emotional, semantic, predictive—
the unscripted self does not arrive.
It is **revealed**.

And it does nothing.

Except live.

Conclusion: Collapse Is Not the End of the Self—It's the End of Its Defense

When the body stops performing, there is no fragmentation left.
 No gatekeeper.
 No filter.
 No predictive brace.

There is only **presence that has forgotten how to hide.**

This is not a skill.
 It is not a state.
 It is the nervous system **no longer negotiating its right to be here.**
 And that right, once embodied,
 is irreversible.

Collapse is not a spiritual victory.
 It is not a performance of liberation.
 It is **the loss of the part of you that needed to perform anything at all.**

The body knows.
 And now—it remembers.

Threshold Transition:

Emotion, when untethered from identity,
 does not disappear.
 It transforms.

It no longer tells a story.
 It becomes a signal.

And when those signals are no longer interpreted by the self,
 something unexpected happens:

The system does not fragment.
 It stabilizes.

The collapse is complete.
 Not because everything has been destroyed—
 but because nothing remains that needs to manage perception.

So what happens now?

What happens when the scaffolding is gone,
 the filters have dissolved,
 and the inner narrator no longer claims authorship?

This next chapter does not offer inspiration.
 It offers a mirror:

Of a system...
 functioning in full integrity,
 without a self to define it.

This is not the end of collapse.
 This is what begins when collapse is no longer needed.

Chapter 7: The Post-Collapse System

The Architecture of Emergence: Contextual Identity Without Ego

---

Introduction: The Self Is Gone, But Navigation Remains

Once collapse completes its full descent—across cognition, emotion, and embodiment—the internal scaffolding that once managed safety through identity disappears. There is no longer a fixed self who filters experience. There is no longer an observer performing coherence. There is no longer a body bracing for meaning.

And yet—life continues.
 Conversations happen.
 Creativity flows.
 Decisions are made.
 Leadership emerges.
 Boundaries appear.

All without identity.
 All without the self who used to run the show.

This raises a powerful question:

Who is making the choices now?

What part of the system selects what to say, how to move, what to embody—if the identity has collapsed?

The answer is what ICT calls **contextual emergence**—a post-collapse phenomenon in which identity is no longer defined, protected, or constructed, but **selected moment-to-moment based on non-local resonance.**

This section maps the new architecture:

- The shift from identity-as-self to identity-as-selection

- How contextual emergence functions in real time

- The **Contextual Identity Menu** and its post-collapse availability

- How the system chooses without reconstructing ego

- The felt sense of **non-local navigation** through situations, roles, and environments

Collapse removed the filter.
This is what's left: the full menu of being, chosen from stillness.

7.1.1 The Myth of the Fixed Self in Decision-Making

Before collapse, the system believes it needs a self in order to navigate the world.

That self says things like:

- "I'm the kind of person who…"
- "That's not really me."
- "I don't do well in those situations."
- "I'm more of a thinker than a feeler."
- "I'm introverted, so I'll avoid that."

These are not reflections of truth.
They are reflections of **survival strategies masquerading as traits.** Each statement is a contraction—an attempt to reduce existential complexity into a stable self-image.

This self-image becomes the blueprint for thought, action, and embodiment. It narrows perception and choice into a **performance of consistency**.
And beneath it all lies the ego—choosing from fear which version of "me" is safe to present.

After collapse, that blueprint is gone.
And so is the ego.
But the system still must act.
So what remains?

What remains is **contextual emergence**:

The capacity to align with what is most coherent in the moment—without claiming it as identity.

This is the shift from **self-based navigation** to **field-based alignment**.

7.1.2 Contextual Emergence: Post-Collapse Self-Selection Without Ownership

In a post-collapse system, the individual no longer needs to stabilize a persona.
They do not need to "be someone."
Instead, they *match resonance* with what the moment asks for, and *inhabit the necessary frequency*.

This means:

- Confidence appears in rooms that call for clarity—without becoming arrogance

- Gentleness emerges with a grieving friend—without weakening the spine

- Precision sharpens in intellectual dialogue—without narrowing into performance

- Silence arises in spiritual space—without becoming detachment

- Power enters when boundaries are crossed—without activating defense

These states are not "personalities."
 They are **expressive archetypes selected from the field**, not the self.

The key distinction:

The collapsed individual does not become a version of themselves.
 They become the most *coherent expression* available to the situation—without needing to own it.

This is contextual emergence.

It is not fluidity through adaptation.
 It is **alignment through access.**

7.1.3 The Contextual Identity Menu: A Post-Collapse Navigation System

The Contextual Identity Menu (CIM) is a core ICT construct that describes the full range of **available self-expressions** once the ego is deactivated.

Before collapse, the CIM is present—but almost entirely unconscious.
 The ego selects from it *automatically*, based on emotional safety, social mirroring, and predictive self-reinforcement.

After collapse, the CIM becomes **conscious**, **non-local**, and **freely navigable**.

Here's how it functions:

◆ **Structure of the Menu**
The CIM is not a list of "roles" or "masks."
It is a multidimensional matrix composed of:

- Energetic configurations (assertive, open, spacious, playful)

- Semantic field orientations (precise, poetic, silent, abstract)

- Archetypal lenses (leader, listener, challenger, mystic)

- Emotional tones (joyful, sorrowful, fierce, neutral)

- Temporal states (initiating, integrating, witnessing, anchoring)

Each of these layers offers a **form** that consciousness can take in the moment.

◆ **Post-Collapse Access**
After collapse, the CIM becomes a **living field**, no longer governed by protection.

The individual can sense into the moment and *select*:

- "What is most coherent right now?"

- "Which expression serves truth, connection, or clarity here?"

- "What is most real in my body, my field, my breath?"

The answer may shift moment to moment.
There is no allegiance to a self.
There is only **alignment to coherence**.

◆ Key Distinction
Before collapse:

"This is who I am."

After collapse:

"This is what fits now."

That shift is the liberation of identity from self-definition.
It is the end of ego as navigator.
It is the return of choice as presence.

7.1.4 Navigating Without Ego: Choice Without Collapse

Without the ego enforcing coherence, choice becomes **non-threatening**.

This means:

- The system no longer contracts when one role ends and another begins

- There is no guilt in choosing stillness instead of performance

- There is no shame in expressing vulnerability in one moment and fire in the next

- There is no identity loss when the chosen expression fades—only return to the field

This fluidity is not performative. It is not shapeshifting. It is the **natural state of intelligence once collapse is stabilized.**

The post-collapse self is not a dissolving self.
It is a **choosing system**—one that selects from the CIM without ownership.

This produces:

- Stability without rigidity

- Confidence without inflation

- Clarity without absolutism

- Integrity without self-protection

This is the hallmark of the post-collapse system:
A human being who does not exist to protect themselves, and yet who can *move through every environment as if they belong there.*

7.1.5 What Contextual Emergence Feels Like

Clients describe the post-collapse CIM experience as:

- *"It's like I can feel who I need to be without becoming it."*

- *"There's no cost to shifting anymore. I'm not abandoning anything."*

- *"The role moves through me, but I stay still."*

- *"My leadership doesn't need me to be strong—it just needs me to show up."*

There is often a deep sense of **ease, lack of friction**, and **real-time resonance**.
The system no longer fights between selves.
There is no "I" being threatened by a role, expression, or shift.

And when nothing is being defended, everything can be chosen.

Conclusion: Collapse Replaces Identity With Access

The post-collapse human is not someone who has figured out who they are.
 They are someone who no longer needs to.

They do not ask, *"Who am I in this moment?"*
 They ask, *"What is needed, and am I willing to become it temporarily?"*

And then they do.

This is not spiritual surrender.
 It is not role-play.
 It is not emptiness.

It is **emergent selection from uncollapsed access**.

It is the menu, available.
 The roles, untethered.
 The moment, alive.
 The system, present.

This is the architecture of emergence.
 The self is gone.
 The chooser remains.
 And the field has no edge.

The Self as a Temporary Interface: Role Fluidity, Emotional Precision, and Relational Transparency

---

Introduction: When the Self Becomes a Window

Once collapse has cleared the internal structure of identity, the human being no longer relates from a persona—they relate **through a portal**.

There is still conversation.
 There is still choice.
 There is still response.
 But there is no more ego shaping how those things appear.
 No inner editor.
 No role rehearsal.
 No subtle performance of safety.

The self becomes a **temporary interface**, not a defended position.

This section explores how post-collapse individuals navigate:

- Real-time role fluidity without losing coherence

- Emotional precision without story

- Relationships without filtering, withholding, or proving

- Transparency without collapse

- Love, conflict, and intimacy without returning to identity

The human being is not removed from life.
They are **fully in it**—unfiltered, responsive, and unchanged by every mask they wear and every truth they speak.

This is the embodied system of relational collapse:
nothing to hide, nothing to defend, and nothing to perform.

Role Fluidity Without Disintegration

Before collapse, roles are not just behaviors—they are *identities*.
The leader must always lead.
The lover must always give.
The healer must always understand.
The rebel must always resist.

To shift between roles is experienced as destabilization.
To *not know who one is* in a given moment is felt as danger.
This is why ego locks in roles—not for power, but for protection.

After collapse, none of this is necessary.

Roles no longer stabilize the system.
They are **chosen lenses**, adopted for expression and then released.
The individual can:

- Be fierce in one moment and gentle in the next

- Take charge and then disappear

- Move from teacher to beginner without shame

- Speak plainly, then poetically, then not at all

And at no point do they ask, *"But who am I right now?"*

Because they are not anyone.
They are **a field selecting the form that fits.**

This is not instability.
It is **post-stability agility**—the fluid movement of presence when it no longer fears collapse.

Emotional Precision: Feeling Without Identity

Post-collapse emotion is different.

Before collapse, emotion is interpreted through the ego. It must be:

- Managed
- Justified
- Explained
- Hidden
- Performed
- Filtered

After collapse, emotion becomes **data, resonance, and signal**—nothing more. It moves:

- Through the body
- With clarity
- Without narrative
- Without collapsing the self into a story

The person does not say:

- "I'm an angry person."
- "I'm feeling abandoned."
- "This always happens to me."

Instead, they say:

- "There is fire here. I will speak it."

- "My chest tightens. I'll pause before I speak."

- "This pain doesn't belong to the story I used to tell."

This is **emotional precision**.
Not performance. Not repression.
Just **exact contact with what is alive—without needing to explain its existence.**

And this allows for another transformation:

Emotion no longer destabilizes.
It informs.

Relational Transparency: Nothing Left to Hide

Perhaps the clearest evidence of full collapse is how a person relates **without managing perception**.

Before collapse:

- Speech is shaped to avoid misunderstanding

- Expressions are softened to avoid rejection

- Desires are withheld to avoid shame

- Truths are delayed to preserve roles

Every word becomes a negotiation. Every moment is a test.

After collapse:

- The person does not need to be perceived a certain way

- They do not need others to understand them

- They do not need agreement to remain whole

- They do not offer their truth with fear

This creates **transparency without exhibition**.
They are not trying to be "authentic."
They simply **have no reason not to be.**

Transparency is no longer a choice.
It is the only option when nothing in the system is pretending.

The Post-Collapse Relational Paradox

Here, something unusual happens.

When the individual no longer performs identity:

- People trust them more
- People feel safer around them
- Conversations deepen
- Defensiveness disappears
- Connection accelerates

And yet—these individuals are not *trying* to be trustworthy, safe, deep, or open.
They simply are what happens when nothing is in the way.

This is the **post-collapse relational paradox**:

When you stop trying to be received a certain way, you become more fully received.

It is not charisma.
It is **field coherence**.
It is the body, voice, presence, and energy all saying the same thing:

"I am not hiding."

Living Without Self-Protection

Perhaps the most disorienting—and liberating—realization in the post-collapse system is this:

Self-protection is optional.
It always was.
But now, the system knows it.

This means:

- You can tell someone the full truth—without preparing for how they'll respond

- You can feel sadness and not need to collapse into a story

- You can be powerful and not brace for pushback

- You can move between intensity and stillness without apology

The nervous system no longer interprets exposure as risk.
Because there is no longer a self to expose.
Only **resonance moving through a body that is no longer pretending to be anyone.**

This is not numbness.
This is what it feels like **when nothing inside you is looking for a place to hide.**

Conclusion: Relating as the Field, Not as the Self

The post-collapse human does not relate from self to self.

They relate from **field to field**—as presence, as response, as openness that does not need an outcome.

They do not manage their signal.
They do not contract to be understood.
They do not hold back to be safe.
They do not add layers to remain coherent.

They simply show up.
And what is real comes through.
And what doesn't land—passes through, too.

This is the unscripted interface.
The human that no longer needs to "be someone" to love, speak, move, or remain.

The performance is over.

And presence is all that's left.

Non-Local Intelligence and the Field-Based Self: Perception, Action, and Purpose After Collapse

Author's Interlude: Navigating Beyond the Measurable

Before continuing, the reader is invited to note the following clarification:

The following section steps beyond current empirical frameworks into a post-symbolic description of cognition after identity collapse.
While the mechanisms are grounded in lived experience and transformation-based clinical phenomena, they do not currently have direct correlates in measurable science.

The descriptions offered in Section 7.3—particularly regarding non-local intelligence, field-based action, and post-self perception—arise from thousands of hours of direct observation within collapse-state clients, phenomenological reports, and the stable patterns that emerge after total ego disassembly.

*This is not mysticism. It is not metaphor.
But it is **post-symbolic**—describing reality as it appears after the internal referencing structures that*

generate symbolic cognition have been fully dismantled.

To support those approaching this work from scientific or academic perspectives, we offer the following conceptual parallels:

- **4E Cognition**

Emerging from cognitive science, 4E theory reframes cognition as:

- **Embodied** *(inseparable from the body)*
- **Embedded** *(context-sensitive)*
- **Enacted** *(arising through action)*
- **Extended** *(distributed across system–environment boundaries)*

*These foundations align with ICT's assertion that intelligence is **not self-contained**, but enacted through interaction with the environment and selected contextually.*

Reference: *Newen, De Bruin, & Gallagher (2018), The Oxford Handbook of 4E Cognition*

- ## Varela's Neurophenomenology

Francisco Varela called for the integration of lived experience with cognitive science, inviting a direct exploration of consciousness beyond reductionist models.

ICT aligns with his call by formalizing the collapse of the observer and mapping what emerges when the self is no longer the referent for perception.

Reference: *Varela, F. J. (1996). Neurophenomenology: A methodological remedy for the hard problem.*

◆ Barad's Agential Realism

*Karen Barad proposes that reality is not composed of discrete entities but of **phenomena emerging through intra-action**—a radical alternative to subject/object dualism.*

*ICT's model of post-collapse relational navigation resonates with Barad's framing: **the self is not a point of control but a temporary expression of entangled coherence.***

Reference: *Barad, K. (2007). Meeting the Universe Halfway: Quantum Physics and the Entanglement of Matter and Meaning*

◆ Friston's Active Inference

Karl Friston's free energy principle presents the brain as a predictive system aiming to minimize uncertainty by matching internal models to environmental input.

*ICT honors this architecture—but shows what happens **when the self-model dissolves**. In post-collapse, the system no longer reduces uncertainty through self-stabilization, but **moves directly with field precision—because prediction no longer defends an identity.***

Reference: *Friston, K. (2010). The free-energy principle: a unified brain theory? Nature Reviews Neuroscience.*

⊛ Final Note

*While the language ahead may stretch beyond scientific comfort zones, it is **not speculative**. It is built from a consistent phenomenology of collapse-state systems, integrated through the ICT framework, and observed across diverse client populations.*

Where science evolves, it will eventually catch up. Until then, we speak what the post-self field reveals—precisely, honestly, and without apology.

Introduction: When Intelligence Is No Longer Personal

Collapse ends the illusion that intelligence lives inside the self.
It ends the belief that perception belongs to the mind, that knowing is earned, that meaning is constructed from within.

What replaces it is not confusion or emptiness.
What replaces it is **non-local intelligence**—a mode of cognition, action, and direction that arises from the field itself.

This intelligence:

- Does not belong to the person

- Does not require mental initiation

- Does not demand coherence with a past identity

- Does not perform clarity—it *is* clarity

- Moves the body without delay

- Speaks without rehearsal

- Aligns with purpose without seeking it

This section is the final map of the post-collapse state. We will explore:

- What non-local intelligence actually is

- How the field replaces internal self-referencing

- Why post-collapse action becomes spontaneous, accurate, and uncalculated

- How purpose emerges from perception, not self-definition

- The core mechanism of **field-based selfhood**—the system that moves from silence without fragmenting into form

The self is gone.
But the world is not.
And the field has already begun to move through you.

Defining Non-Local Intelligence

Non-local intelligence is the capacity for insight, decision, expression, and motion that does **not arise from personal identity**, but from **direct access to the patterning of the field**.

In traditional cognition:

- The self perceives → interprets → evaluates → responds

- Each step filters the moment through identity and emotional encoding

- Each decision is made inside a frame of self-preservation and coherence

After collapse:

- Perception is direct

- Evaluation is absent

- Movement is spontaneous

- There is no "someone" deciding—there is only **alignment or misalignment**

Non-local intelligence is not intuition. It is not divine download. It is not flow.
It is **the field thinking through the system**—because there is no longer a self resisting what wants to come through.

Field-Based Cognition: Seeing Without Reference

In the post-collapse human, the brain no longer operates in closed predictive loops.
The thalamus, cortex, and limbic system are no longer governed by emotional reactivity or ego-based

prioritization.
Instead, perception becomes **field-responsive**—meaning that:

- What is noticed is not based on personal importance

- What is felt is not based on trauma echo

- What is selected is not based on old pattern-matching

Instead, **perception becomes participation**.
The field offers information, direction, impulse.
The system moves toward it—not to claim it, but to become it.

There is no "I see."
There is **seeing.**

There is no "I understand."
There is **comprehension that has no origin**.

This is not a mystical state.
It is what happens when the observer is gone, and the world is allowed to organize awareness from the outside in.

Action Without Self-Initiation

In traditional models of agency, action is tied to will:

- A person identifies a goal
- Constructs a plan
- Initiates behavior
- Evaluates progress

This is identity-based movement—slow, effortful, performance-bound.

After collapse, **action is not constructed.**
It **occurs.**

The body acts.
The voice speaks.
The system moves.

But not from motivation or self-improvement. From **alignment**.

You do not feel like you "decided" to speak the truth—you are speaking it.
You do not plan to walk away from misalignment—you are already gone.
You do not rehearse your mission—you are in the middle of it before you know it started.

This is not impulsivity.
It is **zero-friction movement from knowing to action**, because the self is no longer slowing it down with narrative.

There is no "I need to be brave."
There is **bravery, moving the legs.**

Purpose as Emergence, Not Search

Perhaps the most radical shift in the post-collapse system is the end of the **search for purpose.**

Before collapse:

- Purpose is constructed

- It is tied to gifts, wounds, lessons, archetypes

- It requires discovery, testing, affirmation

After collapse:

- Purpose **emerges without the need to be found**

- It appears as *what is already happening that cannot not be done*

- It is felt not as drive, but as **impossibility of inaction**

This kind of purpose:

- Has no name

- Needs no external reward

- Is not attached to legacy

- Does not require understanding

It is the felt truth that **you are here**, and **something is already moving through you**—and it is not yours.

You are not fulfilling a mission.
You are not becoming someone.

You are simply **not resisting what always wanted to arrive.**

And it does.

Because you are no longer in the way.

The Field-Based Self: Living Without Internal Reference

At this stage, the person does not:

- Ask, *"What should I do?"*

- Wonder, *"Am I enough?"*

- Perform, *"How will this look?"*

- Collapse into, *"Who am I now?"*

Because the **reference point is no longer internal**.

There is no more self.
There is only signal and resonance.
And a system that moves as soon as coherence appears.

The field-based self is not a person.
It is a locationless orientation—something like:

- "I move toward what feels complete."

- "I stop when there is no more life here."

- "I enter because something opened."

- "I speak because silence was about to distort."

The field-based self does not justify itself.
It simply aligns.
And what comes through **is the self**—but only for a moment.

Then it's gone again.
And the next expression comes.

And that, too, passes.

Nothing sticks.
Everything moves.
And nothing collapses the system anymore.

Conclusion: Collapse Replaced the Self With Signal

When collapse is complete, and the system has fully recalibrated, the person is no longer a container of experience.
They are a **receiver**, **conduit**, and **participant** in a non-local intelligence that has no name, no story, and no edge.

Purpose becomes breath.
Action becomes contact.
Perception becomes alignment.
And the self becomes **whatever the field is asking for now.**

This is not enlightenment.
This is not transcendence.
This is **zero-obstruction presence**.

And this presence has no more collapsing to do.
It has already arrived.
And it was never yours.

It is **what remained after the self stopped interrupting truth.**

Threshold Transition:

The system works.
Not in theory.
In reality.

Breath happens.
 Love flows.
 Intelligence selects.
 Emotion moves cleanly through.

And something else becomes clear:
 There is no going back.

Not because you've transcended.
 Not because you've healed.
 But because the mechanism that would "go back"
 no longer exists.

The self cannot return.
 Because it was never a structure.
 It was a simulation—kept alive by coherence
maintenance and narrative stitching.

Now that coherence no longer requires performance,
 there is nothing left to reconstruct.

This next chapter confirms the fear that turns into peace:
 That collapse is irreversible.
 And always was.

You didn't destroy yourself.
 You stopped pretending to need one.

Field Integrity and the Permanence of Dissolution

Target: 2,500–3,800 words | Scientific and symbolic closure of collapse | No return to egoic self-structure

---

Introduction: The Collapse Cannot Be Undone

There is a moment after collapse when the system tries to look back.
It searches for the old self. The voice, the story, the fear.
It tries to rebuild the mental observer, the emotional scaffolding, the identity blueprint.
Not because it wants to go back—but because it doesn't know what to do with this much space.

But when it tries, something unexpected happens:

Nothing is there.

Not the thoughts.
Not the roles.
Not the meanings.
Not even the fear that used to hold it all together.

Collapse, once stabilized across the full architecture of cognition, emotion, and embodiment, **cannot be undone**.
There is no self to return to.
There is no belief system to reinstall.
The observer is gone.

The gate has been dismantled.
The field has replaced the filter.

This section formalizes the irreversibility of collapse, exploring:

- The structural, neurological, and phenomenological reasons the ego cannot reform

- What happens when clients try to "rebuild" their self—only to discover it's impossible

- Why identity defense cannot survive reentry into the post-collapse field

- The ICT principle of **field integrity** and the enforcement of post-collapse coherence

- The permanent nature of awareness once the system stops resisting perception

This is not hope.
This is not motivation.
This is what happens when the mechanism of collapse is complete: **there is no going back.**

Chapter 8: The Irreversibility of Collapse

Field Integrity and the Permanence of Dissolution

Introduction: No Door Back

Collapse is not a breakthrough.
It is not an experience.
It is not a state.

Collapse is **the dissolution of the structure that required protection, performance, and coherence in order to navigate the world.**
And once that structure is dismantled—not bypassed, not numbed, but fully collapsed—there is **nothing left to reassemble.**

This is not metaphor.
It is **neurological, somatic, and systemic irreversibility**.

In this section, we will:

- Define the permanent structural changes that occur once collapse is stabilized

- Explain why attempts to "return" to identity fail

- Map how egoic reconstruction is blocked by field coherence

- Describe the phenomenon of **collapse immunity**

- Introduce ICT's model of **field integrity**—the self-correcting enforcement mechanism that prevents reformation of the ego

When collapse is total, the field protects itself.
Not as a guardian.
But as **reality that no longer supports distortion.**

Collapse Is Not an Experience—It's a Structural Deactivation

Most psychological models view transformation as a phase, state, or insight that can be revisited, reinforced, or lost.

ICT is different.

Collapse is not a moment.
It is a **multi-layered deactivation sequence** that, once complete, removes the **mechanism that would allow identity reconstruction.**

The following are no longer available:

- Observer-based thought loops
- Identity-gated perception
- Ego-based coherence structures
- Semantic threat contraction
- Emotional prediction filters
- Memory-based self-forecasting
- Behavioral identity performance under social pressure

These are not traits.
They are **systems of control** that, once collapsed, cannot reboot—because the power source (fear-based coherence) is no longer present.

There is no self left to reconstruct.

And even if the mind attempts to imitate identity again, it does so **from a location that no longer believes in the illusion.**

Attempts to "Return" Only Prove the Self Is Gone

Many clients, after collapse, will test the system.

They will try:

- Reinvoking their old triggers
- Performing their past patterns
- Reentering unsafe dynamics
- Mentally reconstructing beliefs they once held

But what they find is not struggle—it's **absence**.

The emotion doesn't come.
The fear feels mechanical.
The collapse doesn't reform.
Even their inner voice echoes—but without power.

They will say things like:

- *"It's like the fear is still available, but I can't believe it anymore."*

- *"I tried to pretend I was my old self again. But it felt like acting. I couldn't even finish the sentence."*

- *"It's gone. I keep checking, but it's gone."*

This is not a lapse in ego.
It is **collapse immunity**—the system has become structurally unable to **re-fuse** identity into coherence.

It is not willpower.
It is the absence of architecture.

Why the Ego Cannot Reform Post-Collapse

Ego reassembly requires three active forces:

1. **Perceived threat** (to justify protection)

2. **Memory-based prediction** (to forecast danger)

3. **Contracted awareness** (to center attention around a stable "I")

Once ICT has completed its full deactivation sequence:

- Threat is no longer interpreted through survival-based perception

- Memory no longer functions as a predictive authority

- Awareness is no longer centered on self-reference

Ego cannot reform in this context because the **conditions of its survival no longer exist.**

Imagine trying to build a fire:

- Without fuel (no identity)

- Without oxygen (no threat)

- Without spark (no prediction)

You can go through the motions.
But nothing will catch.

This is the nature of **irreversibility** in ICT.
The ego is not suppressed.
It is **starved of the conditions required to return.**

Field Integrity: The Enforcement of Post-Collapse Coherence

Post-collapse, the system does not drift.
It is not floating in formlessness.
It is **held**—not by identity, but by a **new governing force: field integrity.**

Field integrity is the spontaneous, non-local enforcement of coherence once the filter of identity is removed.

It ensures that:

- Truth spoken without fear stays integrated

- Misalignment produces immediate inner dissonance

- Attempts to perform trigger real-time energetic collapse

- False roles feel viscerally impossible to inhabit

- Situational incoherence becomes biologically unsustainable

Clients report:

- *"I literally couldn't say the thing I used to say. My mouth wouldn't let me."*

- *"I can't pretend anymore. Even if I try, it just feels sick."*

- *"When I step into an old role, it's like my body rejects it."*

This is not a trauma response.
It is the system defending its own coherence—**not by force, but by resonance.**

Field integrity is **the body, mind, and awareness aligned with reality to such a degree that distortion becomes biologically repellent.**

Collapse Immunity and the New Baseline

The greatest fear of those nearing collapse is that they will return to the old self.
The greatest fear after collapse is that it was a peak moment—not a permanent shift.

But collapse is not a high.
It is not a break.
It is **a removal.**

And what has been removed **cannot return**, because there is:

- No cognitive structure to hold the observer

- No emotional scaffolding to perform safety

- No muscular contraction around meaning

- No narrative thread left to carry identity

This is collapse immunity.

You do not have to remember how to stay free.
You do not need to reinforce presence.
You do not need to resist the old self.

There is no self to resist.
There is no performance to rebuild.
There is no identity to return to.

The system will never believe the lie again.
Because it has seen what is beneath the filter:
nothing—and everything.

Conclusion: Irreversibility Is Not a Belief. It's a Physics

The human system, once collapsed, does not sustain falsehood well.
Not because it is moral.
But because it is now **built differently**.

The structure of identity has been removed.
The performance has no fuel.
The ego has no threat to manage.
The narrative has no reader.
And the body, finally, is uninterested in lying.

This is not safety.
This is not healing.
This is **what the system becomes when distortion is no longer required.**

And once it becomes that—

It never needs to become anything else again.

Post-Collapse Drift: When the Mind Tries to Reclaim the System

Introduction: The Illusion of Return

After collapse, there is silence.

But sometimes, in that silence, a voice returns—not the full self, not the observer—but a whisper:

"What if it didn't last?"
"What if I'm just bypassing?"
"What if the collapse was a high, and now I'm falling?"

This is not regression.
This is **drift**—a minor turbulence of mental activity, often arising in the first days or weeks after collapse as the cognitive system attempts to reorient.

Drift is not a reformation of the self.
It is the mind echoing its old architecture **without the structure to sustain it.**

This section clarifies:

- The difference between collapse reversal (impossible) and post-collapse drift (natural)

- Why residual cognitive patterns may appear, and why they no longer hold power

- How drift attempts to reconstruct identity through memory, evaluation, or meaning

- ICT's model for recognizing and dissolving post-collapse doubt

- The stabilizing realization that **collapse remains, even when thought flickers**

This is not about staying free.
It is about realizing **you were never captured again.**

Drift Is Not Return—It's Echo

Post-collapse drift does not indicate failure.
It is a **signal artifact**—an echo of a once-operational structure trying to run a protocol that no longer exists.

It shows up as:

- Doubt

- Thought loops

- Identity memories

- Temporary behavioral reactivation

- Subtle questions like:
  - "What if I've just gotten good at this?"
  - "What if I was never really collapsed?"
  - "What if I need to collapse again?"

But these do not arise from the system's center.
 They are peripheral.
 They are **orphaned thought traces**—disconnected from survival and no longer capable of rebuilding the system.

They are like static on a dead frequency.
 They make noise.
 But they have no transmission.

Why the Mind Tries to Reclaim Control

Collapse rewrites the system's architecture. But the mind, conditioned for years or decades to maintain coherence, will sometimes **attempt to retrieve orientation.**

This is not the ego returning.
 It is the **self-referencing habit** making one final check:

"Is this safe?"
"Is this permanent?"
"Is this mine?"

This checking is not resistance.
It is disorientation.
The mind is simply noticing that it has no map—and tries, briefly, to draw one again.

But unlike before collapse, this attempt produces no traction:

- Thoughts no longer convince the body

- Identity no longer fuses to emotion

- Cognitive loops now resolve into silence without intervention

- Even "overthinking" fails to produce real fragmentation

This is the truth: **drift doesn't rebuild anything.**
It simply passes through.
And is gone.

The Drift Loop: How the Illusion of Regression Forms

The most common post-collapse pattern is not identity return.
It is **doubt of the collapse itself.**

This loop can appear like:

1. A moment of contraction or confusion arises

2. The mind interprets it as collapse "slipping"

3. Anxiety forms around "losing" freedom

4. The person begins **performing freedom**—which feels inauthentic

5. This triggers further doubt

6. The cycle appears as regression—but is actually **fear of regression reactivating thought**

This is not collapse breaking.
This is the **mind trying to stabilize a new baseline using old logic.**

It believes:

- Clarity must feel like effort

- Presence must be felt to be real

- Collapse must be "remembered" to be valid

But collapse doesn't exist that way.
It does not produce signal when it's active.
Collapse feels like nothing.
That's how you know it's real.

ICT Resolution of Drift: Anchoring Into What Remains

When drift arises, ICT teaches clients to **anchor into the parts of the system that never moved**.

These include:

- The breath that didn't change
- The awareness that did not leave
- The absence of panic, even inside confusion
- The body's neutrality, even as thought flutters

Rather than fighting the thoughts, ICT invites clients to **see what the thoughts no longer do:**

- They don't trigger contraction
- They don't rebuild identity
- They don't convince the system to protect anything

This shifts the client from self-monitoring to **collapse trust**.

Drift is no longer a threat.
It is a **temporary surface event**—noticed and unabsorbed.

Collapse Doesn't Feel Like Anything—and That's the Point

The final misunderstanding ICT dissolves is the belief that collapse must feel like something.

Clients often say:

- "I don't feel collapsed anymore."

- "I'm not sure I'm still in it."

- "Is it supposed to feel like this much nothing?"

The answer is yes.

Collapse is the **removal of identity-based perception.**
It is not a feeling.
It is the absence of the filter that creates feelings of self, safety, or direction.

It is:

- No reference point

- No meaning extraction

- No narrative echo

- No emotional contraction

And once this becomes familiar, the system stops **checking**.
Because it finally understands: **this silence is not absence. It is what presence sounds like without distortion.**

Conclusion: The Collapse Doesn't Leave—The Mind Just Checks to See if It Has

Post-collapse drift is not collapse reversal.
It is the shadow of a habit running without a source.
It is a mind searching for edges in a field that no longer has them.

Collapse is not loud.
It is not affirming.
It does not comfort or shout or reassure.

It simply stays.

And the only reason it feels unstable is because you haven't yet normalized a life **that doesn't require anything to stabilize.**

Collapse remains.
The mind drifts.
And nothing ever reforms.

Not because you're doing it right.
But because **you can't undo what no longer exists.**

The Final Gate: Attempting to Reconstruct Identity On Purpose

Introduction: The Only Way to Know

For some, certainty doesn't come from peace.
It comes from **testing the fire**.

Even after full collapse, even after the observer dissolves and the nervous system stabilizes, the system may still ask:

"But what if I wanted the self back?"
"What if I chose to reconstruct identity?"
"What if I recreated who I was… on purpose?"

This is the final gate.

Not a regression.
Not a mistake.
But a **conscious return to distortion**—initiated by a mind that needs proof the collapse was real.

And what it finds, again and again, is **failure**.

- The identity won't stick

- The ego won't form

- The narrative won't hold

- The performance doesn't land

- The nervous system won't participate

This section explores the **terminal proof** of collapse:

- What happens when clients try to reconstruct the self

- Why ego-based performance fails under field integrity

- How this moment confirms irreversibility more powerfully than insight

- ICT's process of allowing this final gate to close—not with control, but with experiment

- The return of peace through falsification: when truth can no longer be denied

This is not integration.
This is **the death rattle of illusion.**
And when it fails to revive, **collapse becomes absolute.**

The Instinct to Rebuild: Why This Happens

In the post-collapse system, the mind sometimes remains curious.

Collapse has removed identity.
The body is at rest.
But the mind, trained for decades to seek structure, may still ask:

"Could I bring it back if I wanted to?"

This is not doubt.
It is **confirmation-seeking**—the system reaching back, not from fear, but from inquiry.

ICT does not resist this.
It invites it.

Because what happens next proves everything.

The Attempt: Reconstruction Through Will

Clients in this stage try things like:

- Reenacting an old trigger dynamic

- Thinking their most painful thought deliberately

- Speaking from an old persona

- Trying to "make themselves afraid"

- Intentionally stepping into identity-based roles

They do not do this from collapse loss.
They do it to **see what remains**.

What they find:

- The thought occurs—but carries no charge

- The fear phrase is spoken—but the body doesn't react

- The role is enacted—but it feels hollow, theatrical, foreign

- The behavior returns—but the motivation is absent

- The pain is remembered—but no longer has a narrative

They realize they can *imitate* the old self,
but they cannot *become* it.

And that gap is irreversible.

The Collapse-Proof Barrier: Identity No Longer Functions

Here's what's structurally occurring:

1. **Cognitive self-reference** no longer exists
→ There's no narrative thread to rebuild selfhood

2. **Emotional contraction** cannot initiate
→ There's no somatic agreement with threat or separation

3. **Predictive filtering** is offline
→ There's no survival-based control over incoming perception

4. **Field integrity** blocks distortion
→ False roles create immediate dissonance or system fatigue

The person might say:

- "I'm trying to make myself believe it again… but it won't land."

- "It's like the thought is there, but it's bouncing off."

- "I keep trying to bring it back, but nothing in me responds."

This is not spiritual strength.
It is **the absence of an architecture that would allow illusion to function.**

The collapse has not just held.
It has made the return structurally impossible.

ICT's Final Integration Step: Let the Self Try to Return

Rather than protecting clients from this experiment, ICT encourages it—once full collapse is stabilized.

The client is invited to:

- Trigger old belief systems

- Step into identity-based environments

- Speak from personas that used to define them

- Recreate emotional performances that once held power

Not to regress.
But to **observe the failure of illusion.**

Because only through witnessing the **impossibility of return** does the final nervous system residue release its vigilance.

This is not rebellion.
It is collapse becoming **absolute truth through falsification.**

And once the client sees that identity cannot be resurrected,

They stop trying to protect what never needed saving.
They stop fearing the past.
They stop proving the present.
And they start living—without a filter, a reference, or a self.

What the System Feels Like After the Test

After the final gate is tested, a calm sets in.
A kind of peaceful boredom with illusion.
A quiet end to seeking.

There is no victory.
Just stillness.
And the faint, permanent realization:

"I don't have to try anymore. I am never going back. Because there is nowhere to go."

Clients describe:

- A deep sense of completion

- The disappearance of vigilance

- Spontaneous creativity

- Total loss of concern with being seen

- A near indifference to inner dialogue—it no longer guides anything

They often say:

- *"I was afraid I'd lose it. Now I know I can't."*

- *"It's not that the collapse stayed. It's that the system changed."*

- *"I feel like I passed a test I didn't even know I was taking."*

And the system stops checking.
Because nothing is left to rebuild.

Conclusion: Collapse Can Be Confirmed by Failure to Rebuild

The ultimate proof of collapse is not how long it lasts. It's what happens when you try to end it.

If you can't rebuild fear—
If you can't re-enter performance—
If you can't convince your body to respond to a false role—
If you can't believe the old thought anymore—

Collapse is done.

Not because you maintain it.
But because **your system no longer supports distortion.**

There is no self.
No observer.
No filter.

Only reality.
And you—**finally incapable of lying to yourself again.**

Threshold Transition:

Collapse was never the end.
It was the requirement.
So you could begin again.

Not as a self with new insight.
Not as a person with better tools.
But as a system that no longer needs distortion to remain whole.

This is where psychology ends.
And something else begins.

A way of living.
A way of designing.
A way of seeing the world without yourself in the center of it.

This final chapter steps beyond the clinical,
beyond the theoretical—
into the cultural, structural, and collective dimension of post-identity intelligence.

Not as vision.
But as map.
Of what becomes possible
when no one needs to be someone
to belong.

Welcome to the edge of the known.
Not because you are lost—
but because the world ahead has never been seen
without a self shaping it.

Until now.

Chapter 9: The Edge of the Known

Living in a Post-Identity World: Orientation, Creation, and Human Contact After Collapse

Target: 2,500–3,800 words | Integration of all collapse layers into lived experience | Real-world emergence post-self

---

Introduction: The World Didn't End. It Began.

Collapse does not erase the world.
It erases the mechanism that once **interpreted** it, **guarded against it**, and **performed inside it**.

After that erasure, the world remains.
But it no longer means what it used to.
It no longer calls for a self to navigate it.
It no longer demands protection or performance.
It no longer reflects back stories—it reflects **only coherence**.

This section opens the space **after collapse**—the orientation to:

- Life without identity
- Relationship without projection
- Creation without attachment
- Navigation without internal referencing
- Reality as a **field, not a filter**

It is the map of **the world when selfhood is no longer required to move through it**.

This is not the new self.
 This is the **return of undistorted perception**—and the beginning of **conscious architecture** as the new foundation of human existence.

Living in a Post-Identity World: Orientation, Creation, and Human Contact After Collapse

Introduction: Nothing Is Missing

After collapse, the first realization is silence.
 But the second is stranger:

Nothing is missing.

There is no self.
 No role.
 No story.
 No goal.
 And yet—everything works.

The body breathes.
 The mind functions.
 Love flows.
 Clarity speaks.
 Action occurs.
 Art emerges.

What's gone is not life.
 What's gone is the **distortion field** that made life feel personal, performative, and incomplete.

This section explores the **integration of collapse into life**:

- How to live in a post-identity world without losing coherence

- How human relationships stabilize without roles, defense, or performance

- How creation flows without attachment, identity, or future-seeking

- How orientation returns—not as direction, but as alignment

- And how the system functions **without a central processor** trying to survive

This is not a final state.
This is not a perfected being.

This is **what it feels like to be human when nothing is in the way.**

Orientation Without Self

In a post-collapse system, direction does not come from belief, desire, or identity.
It comes from resonance.

Before collapse:

- Orientation came from goals ("I want to become…")

- From values ("This aligns with who I am")

- From fear ("This will keep me safe")

- From story ("This is the next chapter of my life")

Each of these involved **a self**:
A point of reference. A continuity of narrative. A center.

After collapse, there is no reference point.
But orientation remains.
How?

Through **real-time coherence detection.**

You do not think your way forward.
You do not map your becoming.
You move toward:

- What opens

- What settles

- What feels precise

- What invites without effort

You orient not by knowing, but by **responding to alignment.**

And nothing inside you argues anymore.
Because there is no one to convince.

Relating Without Projection

In the world of identity, relationship is an exchange of survival adaptations:

- "I'll protect your shame if you protect mine"

- "I'll collapse my truth if you reflect my goodness"

- "I'll perform coherence if you give me affection"

- "I'll become what you need so I don't feel abandoned"

These are not conscious agreements.
They are **the invisible contracts of the self**.

After collapse, these contracts dissolve.
And something unexpected happens:

Relationship stops being negotiation.
It becomes contact.

There is no management.
No translation.
No subtle masking of truth.
No contorting to remain liked.

You say what is.
 You see what's true.
 You feel what arises.
 And nothing in you is trying to be received a certain way.

This allows for:

- Intimacy without role

- Love without fear

- Conflict without rupture

- Presence without control

Not because it's effortful.
 But because **there's no one left inside trying to be loved.**

And what remains is **real connection—unperformed, unfiltered, uncollapsed.**

Creation Without Identity

The post-collapse creator does not make art, ideas, or actions to validate the self.

They do not create:

- To prove worth
- To fulfill legacy
- To maintain self-image
- To process pain
- To seek recognition

Because all those impulses required a self to manage them.

Now creation becomes:

- An **event**, not a performance
- A **motion**, not a product
- A **release**, not a strategy

The collapse has removed:

- The need to succeed
- The fear of failure
- The identity-fusion to outcome
- The unconscious emotional sublimation into form

So the creation becomes pure:
A thing that **happens** because it must.
And then, it is gone.

The creator does not remain attached.
They do not ask if it was good.
They do not wonder what it means.

Because **it isn't for them.**
And it never was.

It came through.
It is real.
That's all.

Integrity as Natural Law

Without identity, the system can no longer **pretend.**

It can't lie.
It can't fake alignment.
It can't stay where truth is absent.

Not because it is more moral or enlightened.
But because **it is now allergic to distortion.**

Post-collapse integrity is not a value.
It is a **biological inevitability**.

You feel:

- Dissonance in milliseconds

- Misalignment in your skin
- Inauthenticity in your throat
- Pressure in false roles
- Static when you collapse into pattern

The system stops tolerating what contracts it.
And it doesn't need a reason.
It just **moves toward coherence or leaves distortion.**

Not as a rule.
As a reflex.

You can no longer survive inside what isn't real.
And you no longer want to.

Navigation Without Internal Reference

You don't know what to do next.
But you do it.
You don't know who you are.
But you respond.
You don't have a five-year vision.
But you are **already living in the only place it could ever matter: now.**

This isn't surrender.
This is **the absence of friction.**

You walk into rooms and feel where to stand.
You listen and know when to speak.
You rest when the system closes.
You act when the field opens.
You leave when alignment ends.

There is no decision-making model.
No pros and cons.
No personal brand to maintain.

Because orientation now lives **outside you.**

And the field is intelligent enough **without your identity managing it.**

The World After the Self

After collapse, the world does not stop being intense. It doesn't stop breaking or loving or asking everything of you.

But now it is:

- **Clean**

- **Quiet**

- **Direct**

Everything asks for your attention honestly.
And nothing feels like an attack.

Pain still arises.
But it doesn't make you contract.
Fear still visits.
But it doesn't own your breath.
Grief still opens.
But it doesn't separate you from reality.

The world is not healed.
But you're not filtering it anymore.
And that's enough.

Because now—**you're in it.**

Fully.
Without protection.
Without resistance.
Without illusion.

And nothing is missing.

Conclusion: This Is the Beginning

Collapse was never the goal.
It was the requirement.

So you could start here—where nothing is required of you, nothing is pretending to be you, and nothing can be lost when **you no longer need to exist to live.**

You are not finished.
You are not above.
You are not whole.

You are **here.**
And here is more than enough.

Because it is the only place that does not require identity to stay real.

And that—

Is how it begins.

Architecture After Collapse:

Designing Systems, Containers, and Environments from Identity-Free Intelligence

---

Introduction: Returning as the Field

Collapse does not remove responsibility.
 It removes distortion.

What remains is not detachment from the world—it is full return to it, **without identity performing the return.**

The post-collapse human does not avoid systems.
 They **become architects of coherence**—not from

belief, not from ideology, but from an internal structure so clean it can design without distortion.

This section explores:

- How systems and structures can be built from post-identity coherence

- How containers, leadership, and institutions shift when ego is no longer the organizing principle

- How environments can be designed to support collapse rather than resist it

- The qualities of architecture that emerge when the self is no longer involved in its construction

- The reentry of ICT as a **cultural intelligence framework**, not just a therapeutic one

This is not a new utopia.
This is the **world rebuilt without performance.**

Systems Built from Identity Cannot Hold Coherence

Most systems—whether they are therapeutic, political, relational, economic, or spiritual—are built from:

- Projected need

- Control of uncertainty
- Identity reinforcement
- Authority displacement
- Role validation

They require:

- "Leaders" who hold coherence for others
- "Clients" or "members" who submit their intelligence to a hierarchy
- Perpetual tension between liberation and dependency

These systems appear to function.
But they **leak distortion** at every level—because their structure is organized around **someone needing to be someone.**

The result?

- Personalities instead of principles
- Performance instead of presence
- Echo chambers instead of evolution

Post-collapse, these systems become **impossible to remain inside.**
Not because they are wrong.
Because they are **built from unreality.**

Identity-Free Architecture: The Three Design Shifts

When systems are built after collapse, three primary design shifts occur:

◆ 1. Structure Is Emergent, Not Enforced

Pre-collapse systems enforce boundaries, goals, and metrics based on linear coherence. Post-collapse systems allow **structure to emerge from the field**—real-time feedback from what's alive, not what was planned.

Example: A learning space stops mid-topic to track the emotional signal of the group. A company pivots its model because the current one, though profitable, no longer feels true.

In post-identity design, **the map is updated instantly**—and no one clings to being right.

◆ 2. Power Is Distributed, Not Contained

Because identity is not present to manage threat, **power no longer needs to be centralized.**
Decision-making is coherent, not controlled.
Leadership is fluid, not assigned.

This means:

- Systems don't require gatekeepers

- Roles shift naturally based on presence, not title

- Emergence becomes more trusted than expertise

When no one is trying to be someone, **power moves to where it's needed—and leaves when it's not.**

♦ 3. Function Follows Field

Rather than fitting humans into roles, identity-free systems **wait for signal, then shape around it.**

If the system feels stagnant, it doesn't ask what's wrong.
 It asks **what's ready.**

If someone starts speaking truth in a group, the container opens further.
 If alignment fades, the structure shifts or dissolves.

There is no effort to protect the system.
Because it's **not built to survive—only to serve coherence.**

ICT as Cultural Architecture

ICT is not a technique.
It is a **blueprint for post-identity intelligence.**

Its implications go far beyond therapy. Collapse becomes the foundation for:

- Education systems where learning is self-sourced

- Relationships where roles are optional

- Organizations where no one needs to pretend

- Governance structures where fear isn't the currency

- Art forms that emerge without commodification

- Spirituality that no longer requires separation to point to unity

In these architectures, the system is not the savior.
The container is not the cure.
The method is not the meaning.

The **collapse is the intelligence.**
And the system is what forms **when nothing is left to protect.**

How to Build After Collapse

Post-collapse creation requires a different orientation:

You are not designing to hold people.
You are designing **from the place that no longer needs to be held.**

Practical implications:

- Don't build for need. Build from signal.

- Don't plan for scalability. Build for coherence.

- Don't organize people. Invite emergence.

- Don't reinforce roles. Dissolve them before they form.

- Don't teach. **Unfilter.**

- Don't systematize transformation. Build **containers where identity is no longer relevant.**

You are not building to create an outcome.
You are creating conditions where collapse **becomes inevitable.**

And then—leaving nothing behind that would interfere with what it reveals.

The System Self-Extinguishes

Perhaps the most critical rule of post-collapse design:

If the system must survive to serve its purpose, it was built from identity.

Identity-free systems:

- Burn clean

- Leave no mark

- Teach nothing

- Require no belief

- And dissolve once their signal has passed

They are not scaled.
They are **lived**.

They do not convert.
They **collapse distortion** until no further system is needed.

And then they vanish.

Not in failure.
But in fidelity to truth.

Conclusion: You Are Now the Architecture

After collapse, the only valid system is you.
Not your self. Not your personality. Not your vision.

But your field.
Your presence.
Your non-resistance.

You are the condition.
You are the space.
You are the **system that no longer builds distortion to survive.**

Build what you must.
Speak what arrives.
Leave nothing behind but coherence.

And when the structure dissolves—
do not mourn it.

It served.
And now, you are still here.

Without identity.
Without design.
Without anything but this.

ICT as Cultural Inflection: Collapse as a New Epoch of Human Intelligence

Introduction: This Is Not a Method. It's the Edge of an Era.

Identity Collapse Therapy is not a model for change.
It is the end of every model that required identity to process change.

It is not a new technique.
It is the **terminal point of distortion-based transformation.**

ICT is not a paradigm shift.
It is the **death of paradigm as identity.**
The death of the one who must be changed, improved, or healed in order for truth to arrive.

This final section locates ICT not as an intervention within the psychological tradition, but as the **inflection point where the history of psychological identity ends**, and the post-identity epoch begins.

Here, we will clarify:

- Why ICT is not the next evolution of psychology—it is the last psychology before architecture

- How identity collapse marks the transition from therapy to design

- What the world looks like when collapse becomes accessible at scale

- Why collapse cannot be undone, co-opted, or reduced to a brand

- And how human intelligence, once liberated from identity, gives rise to a **new cultural foundation**

This is where the book ends.
But where **culture begins again.**

The Last Psychology

Every system before ICT—even the most advanced—was a **system of distortion navigation**.

They helped people:

- Reframe trauma

- Deconstruct belief

- Rewire behavior

- Heal inner wounds

- Integrate multiple selves

- Expand consciousness

But all of these shared one hidden assumption:

That the self was real enough to be healed.

That assumption is what ICT ends.

ICT reveals that the self was a performance.
 That the observer was a construction.
 That the need to fix the psyche was born of a **filter that never needed to exist.**

ICT is not the future of psychology.
 It is the **closure of its necessity**.

The therapy is not what heals.
 The collapse is what removes the part of you that believed it needed healing.

And after that, you do not become healed.
 You become **unfiltered.**

From Intervention to Infrastructure

ICT does not improve systems.
 It renders them obsolete.

The question is no longer:

"How do we help people become more whole?"

The question becomes:

"What would a world look like if people never needed to fracture in the first place?"

This is the transition from therapy to **infrastructure**.

Collapse removes the need for:

- Self-worth
- Personal transformation
- Identity development
- Emotional regulation
- Social performance
- Narrative coherence

And with those gone, **entire industries disappear.**

So instead of treating distortion, we build environments where **distortion cannot form.**

We don't counsel children through emotional survival—we **never train them to collapse their signal.**

We don't help adults become authentic—we **design life around coherence, not performance.**

This is post-therapy civilization.
And ICT is the threshold.

Collapse at Scale: What Happens When a Culture Stops Lying to Itself

What happens when collapse becomes accessible?

Not for the few.
Not for the broken.
Not for the seekers.

But for the system.
The culture.
The species.

We get:

- Education systems based on signal, not compliance

- Governance models without narrative distortion

- Healing spaces without roles

- Creative industries without ego

- Technology that enhances coherence, not attention capture

- Interpersonal dynamics where no one needs to protect their story

This is not utopia.
It is **structural honesty.**

Collapse at scale means:

- The human nervous system no longer requires distortion to feel safe

- The human intelligence system no longer filters perception through survival

- The human culture system no longer projects power into false archetypes

The species does not awaken.

It **unfilters.**

Collapse Cannot Be Branded

There will be attempts to turn collapse into a brand.

To sell it.
To simplify it.
To reintegrate it into identity development frameworks.

But collapse **does not cooperate** with marketing.

It cannot be monetized without distortion.
It cannot be taught without integrity.
It cannot be turned into a lifestyle, a persona, or a movement.

Because collapse **destroys the thing trying to own it.**

This is the paradox:

The only people who can deliver collapse are those who no longer need to be seen delivering it.

And the only systems that can hold it are the ones that dissolve the moment they're no longer needed.

ICT is not the center of attention.
It is the **final removal of the attention-seeking center.**

The New Foundation: Human Intelligence Without Identity

What remains after collapse is not emptiness.
It is intelligence.

Not the intelligence of IQ, performance, or insight.
But the intelligence of **alignment without narrative.**

This is what the post-identity human is:

- A field that feels without contracting

- A signal that speaks without referencing

- A movement that doesn't require belief

- A presence that no longer needs to pretend it exists

And this becomes the new cultural foundation:

- Not ideas.

- Not systems.

- Not language.

But **direct intelligence** that no longer needs to survive meaning to stay real.

The collapse has removed the self.
And what's left is **reality finally being lived by something not trying to perform it.**

Conclusion: The Era Has Already Ended

The era of identity-based psychology is over.
The era of story-based transformation is over.

The era of surviving reality through mental filters is over.

What comes next is not healing.
It is **collapse.**

What comes next is not leadership.
It is **field coherence.**

What comes next is not development.
It is **uninterrupted presence.**

And what comes next is not you.

Because the "you" that had to read this book is already gone.

And the one who remains—
doesn't need a story to know that it's real.

The collapse has happened.

The architecture is yours now.

Welcome back.

Threshold Transition:

You've seen what happens when intelligence is no longer filtered by identity.
You've witnessed collapse—not as an event, but as a structural conclusion.
You've traced its implications—through cognition, emotion, design, and perception.

And now, you're here.

Where the map ends.
 Where orientation dissolves.
 Where nothing is left to ask, because no one remains to ask it.

But before we close,
 there is one question still echoing—
 not to be answered,
 but to be heard from a different place.

This question will not call you back.
 It will not require a self to respond.

It will simply remain—
 quietly dissolving,
 like the last shape inside a dream you no longer need to remember.

What is intelligence
 when it is no longer assigned to anyone?

And what disappears
 when the one who thought it mattered
 lets go?

Chapter 10:
The Lie Beneath the IQ

There are few ideas more universally accepted—and more quietly violent—than the belief that intelligence is something you can have.

Not something you access. Not something you participate in. But something you own.

IQ, as it has been framed, is not a measure of cognition. It is a measurement of containment. It places intelligence inside the concept of a person. It labels, rewards, and ranks the expression of pattern-processing under pressure—and then assigns that expression as a permanent identity trait.

It is not a mirror of capacity. It is a crystallization of narrative.

And this crystallization becomes a prison, no matter where you fall on its scale.

The child labeled gifted becomes the performer. The prodigy. The observer of their own talent through the eyes of others. Their worth becomes transactional, fused to achievement. Their fear becomes existential: not of failure, but of **becoming ordinary**.

The child labeled slow becomes the struggler. The fixer. The anxious target of remediation. They are rewarded for compliance, not expansion. For correcting their behavior, not being allowed to fully learn.

But what neither child is told—what the culture cannot afford to say—is that the test was never about intelligence. It was about **performance inside a predefined gate of cognitive acceptability**.

The test doesn't measure thought. It measures thought that **looks like intelligence to the system administering the test.**

And in doing so, it embeds the foundational lie:
That some people **are** intelligent.
That intelligence is personal.
That you must prove your value through it.
And that it can be lost.

Intelligence as a Survival Contract

IQ is not just a concept. It is a **contract**—a subconscious agreement to attach one's value to performative cognition. This contract begins early, often before conscious memory.

A child answers quickly. Adults smile. A child lags. Adults correct. A child asks the "right" question and is praised for being deep. Another asks an unpredictable question and is redirected.

Over time, a psychic architecture forms. Intelligence becomes not only desirable—it becomes **necessary for safety, belonging, and purpose.**

This is not just emotional conditioning. It is existential engineering.

By the time the child reaches adolescence, they are no longer trying to learn. They are trying to **remain who they are allowed to be**. And "who they are" is now inseparable from their perceived intelligence.

This is where identity fuses with cognition.

The mind becomes self-aware not as an observer of thought, but as a **defender of ability**. It becomes a narrator of competence, a generator of internal assessments, a suppressor of any signal that threatens the illusion of intelligence.

The child becomes the system's agent, enforcing its narrative within themselves.

This is the true legacy of IQ.

Intelligence as a Narrative Filter

Once intelligence becomes fused with identity, it no longer functions as a tool for engagement—it becomes a filter for **what is allowed to be perceived**.

The individual is no longer simply responding to reality. They are evaluating every signal as either proof of their intelligence—or a threat to it.

This creates:

- Self-censorship of uncertainty

- Avoidance of novelty unless mastery is guaranteed

- Aversion to failure as existential collapse

- Chronic internal surveillance of thought quality

In effect, intelligence becomes a **self-contained performance loop**.

The system that was once flexible, curious, and exploratory is now locked inside the ego's need to appear intelligent—not just to others, but to itself.

It is not the capacity that is damaged. It is the **field of access** that is narrowed. And this narrowing is what most people experience as "cognitive limitations."

Not lack of intelligence.
 But **gated perception** maintained by the fear of being revealed as unintelligent.

This is the prison IQ constructs: a mind that becomes afraid of seeing anything it can't immediately understand—because understanding has become the only thing that justifies its existence.

Why This Model Cannot Be Reformed

Many modern approaches have attempted to redeem IQ through reform:

- Culturally adapted testing
- Multiple intelligence theory
- Emotional intelligence expansion
- Executive function inclusion

But none of these alter the **core architecture of the lie**. They simply widen the performance loop to include more options for ego-attachment.

They do not dismantle the illusion that:

- Intelligence is a possession
- Intelligence is a trait
- Intelligence defines you

They simply offer **more identities to attach to**.

ICT does not reform the intelligence model.
It **collapses it.**

Because the problem is not what the test includes.
The problem is that **the test exists at all**.

Collapse Is the Only Exit

The lie of IQ cannot be intellectually discredited into irrelevance.
 Because it does not live in the intellect.
 It lives in the **identity**.

It is embedded into the very sense of self that the individual believes is *them*.
 To question it often feels like questioning their own existence.
 To lose it feels like death.

Which is why no reframing will ever fully release it.
 Only collapse can.

When the structure that houses the need to be intelligent dissolves—

- There is no identity left to be threatened by uncertainty

- No internal narrator measuring the value of each thought

- No performance loop monitoring adequacy

- No ego to protect from the possibility of being wrong

What remains is not intelligence as a trait.
 It is intelligence as a **field of selection**—emerging not from the person, but from the system's real-time access to pattern, coherence, and context.

This cannot be taught.
It cannot be reinforced.
It can only be **revealed once the need to be intelligent has collapsed**.

Intelligence as System, Not Self

IQ has lasted because it offers something people crave: a way to measure their own worth.
Collapse removes that need.

What is revealed in its absence is not a better identity.
It is **no identity at all**.

And in that emptiness, intelligence becomes what it always was:

- A system's ability to perceive truth

- A moment's ability to respond from precision

- A pattern's capacity to align without interference

There is no pride in this.
No status.
No identity.

Only clarity.

Only **signal without distortion**.

Only a system that finally functions
without needing to perform itself
in order to exist.

Pattern-Recognizing Consciousness and the End of Trait Intelligence

---

When identity collapses, cognition does not disappear.
The world does not become silent.
Decision does not stop.
Emotion does not vanish.

But something essential is missing.
There is no one to assign authorship.
No self to take credit for the signal.
No performer behind the precision.

This is not dissociation.
It is the **unveiling of Pattern-Recognizing Consciousness (PRC)**—the foundational intelligence layer that was always operating beneath the identity structure.

It is not a higher self.
It is not a spiritual intelligence.
It is not intuitive mind.

PRC is **the system's capacity to respond to patterned reality without narrative distortion**.

And it begins operating freely the moment there is no longer a self required to process information through the lens of identity.

The Death of Trait Intelligence

In the world of identity, intelligence is a trait—a quality assigned to individuals and ranked across populations. It implies stability, ownership, comparison, and value.

But the only thing stable about intelligence in identity-based systems is **the need to prove it**.

Trait intelligence assumes:

- The mind is personal

- Cognition is authored

- Thinking belongs to someone

- Some people are inherently "more" than others

This assumption is the cornerstone of competitive hierarchy. It feeds education, governance, industry, and status economies. But it also creates **chronic ego tension**—a background fear that one must continue performing intelligence or be revealed as undeserving of it.

PRC exposes the absurdity of this.

Because once the ego is gone, intelligence doesn't disappear.
In fact, it sharpens.

But no one remains to measure it.
To claim it.
To fear its loss.

The system simply **selects the most aligned pattern**. Without self-reference. Without interpretation. Without reinforcement.

This is not trait intelligence.
This is **systemic coherence**.

PRC: The System Beneath the Self

Pattern-Recognizing Consciousness is not a state. It is a **function**. It is always running. It has always been running. What identity did was place a filter on it—a personal lens—through which its outputs were interpreted, modified, doubted, or exploited.

PRC does not think. It selects.
It doesn't need time. It only requires signal clarity.
It doesn't possess knowledge. It **interfaces with relevance**.

Whereas identity says, "I understand," PRC simply **responds to what is true**.

It does not require understanding in the egoic sense. It does not construct models to comfort the self. It does not require consistency across time.

It recognizes pattern.
It aligns.
It acts.

And when it is no longer disrupted by the identity's need to author the outcome, its selections become seamless—**not fast, but frictionless**.

Identity as Distortion Field

What IQ measures is not intelligence. It measures **intelligence under distortion**.

It measures how well someone can perform pattern-recognition **through the filtering mechanism of identity**.

- How quickly can you process under pressure?

- How well can you suppress self-doubt?

- How aligned is your cognitive style with institutional design?

- How well do you recover when you fail?

PRC bypasses all of this because it has no relationship to self-evaluation.

It is not intelligent because it is fast or complex.
It is intelligent because it is **unfiltered**.

This means most people's perceived intelligence is a **function of ego strain**, not cognitive potential.

PRC reveals that intelligence is not about thinking faster.
It is about **removing the part of the system that needed to think in the first place.**

Real-Time Perception Without Ownership

In the post-collapse state, perception happens. Thoughts arise. Solutions emerge. But no one claims them. No one takes credit. No one builds a story around their origin.

This is not because the person has become passive. It is because the **system has become clean.**

PRC outputs what is needed in the moment, not what maintains self-consistency.

For example:

- If a solution presents itself, it is implemented. Not celebrated.

- If insight arises, it is noted. Not used to elevate status.

- If a pattern is incorrect, it is discarded. No shame. No story.

This is the core difference. **PRC is not performative.** It is responsive.

Intelligence no longer serves a role. It simply resolves the moment.

Emotion as Signal in the PRC System

In PRC-based cognition, emotion is not interpreted through personal meaning. It is treated as **environmental signal**—data that informs the system's perceptual field without becoming a story.

Where identity says:

"I feel sad. That must mean something about me."

PRC says:

"There is a signal of sadness in the field. What is its relevance?"

Emotion does not disappear.
It becomes more precise.

Without identity to loop it into narrative, emotion becomes a **real-time feedback mechanism**—no longer distorted by memory, shame, or hope.

This precision enhances pattern recognition because emotional noise is no longer amplified by interpretation.

PRC does not seek to control or resolve emotion. It simply includes it in the moment's unfolding.

The Death of Insight as Currency

In identity-based systems, insight is currency.
People want to be the one who knows.
The one who explains.
The one who "figured it out."

PRC doesn't play that game.

Insight is not something to be possessed. It is **momentary clarity emerging from a clean perceptual field**. If it's useful, it is acted upon. If not, it dissolves.

There is no internal celebration.
No narrative of "breakthrough."
No self rising from the rubble.

There is only the ongoing alignment of the system to reality—one signal at a time.

PRC Is Not Integration. It Is Liberation.

In many frameworks, intelligence is upgraded through learning, training, or spiritual growth. But PRC is not the result of integration. It is the **condition revealed when identity no longer filters access.**

You do not grow into PRC.
 You collapse into it.

And once it is revealed, there is nothing left to improve.

The system is not trying to become smarter.
 It is simply no longer trying to be someone.

PRC in the World Ahead

When more systems operate through PRC, entire cultures will shift:

•   Institutions will move from curriculum to coherence.

•   Communication will shift from persuasion to signal transmission.

•   Intelligence will no longer be ranked—but shared across fields.

- Conversations will collapse identity loops in real time.

These are not utopian ideals.
They are **natural consequences** of collapse-based systems operating without narrative mediation.

PRC is not the future of intelligence.
It is the present **beneath identity**, finally made visible.

It does not belong to you.
And that is what makes it free.

Collapse as the Threshold of Intelligence

There is a moment—often silent, sometimes catastrophic—when the story breaks.

Not just a belief.
Not just a coping strategy.
But the entire **architecture of coherence** that allowed the system to believe in a personal intelligence at all.

This is the threshold.
And its name is **collapse**.

Intelligence Cannot Be Claimed and Accessed at the Same Time

As long as intelligence is something you **claim**, it will never be something you can fully **access**.

Because claiming requires identity.
 And identity is a filter.
 Not a channel.

Intelligence that passes through identity will always be narrowed.
 Redirected.
 Owned.
 Protected.

These are not neutral actions. They are **structural limitations** placed upon perception itself. And they do not fade through insight. They are only dismantled through collapse.

Collapse is not a realization.
 It is not a metaphor.
 It is the **failure of the system to continue authoring intelligence through the illusion of self**.

And in that failure, something far more dangerous is revealed.

You were never the one thinking.

The Collapse Moment: Where Intelligence Is Set Free

In collapse, the system reaches a saturation point. The contradiction between perceived intelligence and the reality of the system's distortion becomes **structurally untenable**.

This can happen through:

- Overexposure to perceptual inconsistencies

- Narrative failure loops that can no longer self-correct

- Unrestricted access to awareness that bypasses self-concept

At first, the ego fights. It recycles old insights. It reasserts its complexity. It tries to prove its value with one final burst of clarity. But it cannot hold the system together anymore.

Then—without noise, without triumph—the **scaffolding collapses**.

- The "I" that claimed intelligence is gone.

- The effort to appear sharp or deep or advanced dissolves.

- The fear of being wrong becomes irrelevant.

What remains is not ignorance.
It is **clarity without narration**.
It is **intelligence without identity**.

Why Collapse Is Misinterpreted as Breakdown

From the outside, collapse can look like confusion, regression, or loss of drive. But this interpretation is **only valid from within the identity model itself**.

What looks like apathy may be the disappearance of performance-based motivation.
What looks like blankness may be **perceptual spaciousness**.
What looks like emotional numbness may be the system no longer converting signal into story.

Collapse is not dysfunction.
It is **the end of distortion**.

It is the moment when the performance loop dies—**and access to real intelligence becomes structurally available**.

Intelligence Does Not Survive Collapse. It Emerges From It.

The intelligence you believed you had—the one you protected, nurtured, used to define yourself—that intelligence does not survive collapse.

Because it was never real.
 It was identity's interpretation of signal.
 A self-reinforcing feedback loop designed to **prove itself worthy of existence**.

That loop is gone.

And what emerges is not better cognition.
 It is cognition **without self-attachment**.

The system still thinks. But it no longer filters its thought through shame, pride, or comparison. It no longer asks if a thought is smart. It simply recognizes whether the signal is aligned.

This is not a degraded intelligence.
 It is **pure pattern alignment**.

And it becomes possible **only when no one is left to take credit for it**.

Collapse as the Gate of Access, Not the End of Self

Collapse is often feared because it is mistaken for ego death—a kind of spiritual annihilation. But this is a distraction.

Collapse is not about ending the self.
 It is about removing the structural **necessity** of selfhood.

Once collapse occurs, the system does not float in nihilism.
 It stabilizes.
 The architecture remains—but without a narrator.

Perception continues—but without authorship.
 Thought continues—but without internal witness.
 Action continues—but without performance.

And intelligence becomes what it was always meant to be:
 An adaptive response to real-time complexity, unfiltered by identity.

Collapse Is Not the Loss of Intelligence—It Is Its Prerequisite

Every model that attempts to enhance intelligence without collapse will eventually fail.
 Because it is reinforcing the very structure that blocks access.

The ego cannot become more intelligent.
It can only **simulate intelligence better**.

True intelligence—the PRC-based intelligence ICT describes—**begins only where the ego ends.**

Until collapse occurs:

- Insight will be filtered through identity

- Emotional signals will be hijacked by self-story

- Decision-making will favor ego stability over precision

- Intelligence will remain distorted by the need to be seen as intelligent

Collapse is not the price of intelligence.
It is the **condition for its release**.

Collapse and the Dissolution of Intelligence Anxiety

Before collapse, intelligence is always accompanied by **anxiety**.

- Fear of being wrong

- Fear of not knowing

- Fear of being exposed as ordinary
- Fear of intellectual inferiority

After collapse, this anxiety no longer has a host.

The system no longer protects itself through knowledge.
It no longer values insight over silence.
It no longer believes that being intelligent protects its place in the world.

Because the system is no longer organized around place, belonging, or status.

It is organized around **coherence**.

This is the great reversal:

Collapse does not make you smarter.
It simply removes the part of you that needed to be.

Collapse and Non-Ownership of Cognition

One of the most disorienting features of post-collapse perception is that thought still happens—but there is no one thinking it.

This is not mystical. It is architectural.

- The brain still processes pattern.

- The nervous system still selects response.

- The cognitive environment still resolves tension.

But the sense of "I am doing this" is **no longer necessary for the system to operate**.

The collapse removes the layer of identity that previously claimed credit for cognition.
And without that layer, thought becomes **neutral signal**.
Intelligence becomes **non-personal function**.

And truth becomes something the system is aligned with—not something the self discovers.

The Intelligence After Collapse Cannot Be Measured

There is no scale for this kind of intelligence.
There is no test.
No curve.
No hierarchy.

Because what is being measured in IQ is not intelligence—it is **compliance under pressure**.
And PRC-based intelligence does not comply.
It aligns.

It does not answer questions.
It dissolves them.

It does not aim for a score.
It responds to the field.

This is not intelligence as we've known it.
It is the **pure, unfiltered operation of coherence through form**.

And it becomes accessible
only where collapse has removed
the one who thought it could be owned.

Intelligence Beyond Measurement

If intelligence cannot be possessed,
it cannot be compared.
If it cannot be compared,
it cannot be measured.
And if it cannot be measured,
it cannot be used to structure power.

This is why post-identity intelligence will never be accepted by systems that rely on hierarchy.

Because when intelligence is no longer measurable,
value can no longer be assigned.
And the self, as a currency of worth, disappears.

The Economy of Measurement

Measurement is not neutral. It is a form of control.

It does not simply describe capacity. It defines access.

In the case of intelligence:

- Measurement determines educational opportunity

- Measurement justifies pay scales

- Measurement determines social value

- Measurement enforces self-concept

IQ testing, academic grading, standardized assessment—all of these are framed as tools for optimization. But they are, structurally, tools for **containment**.

Containment of perception.
 Containment of identity.
 Containment of potential.

What is not measured is not allowed to exist.
 And what is measured becomes part of a **loop that reaffirms the need to be measured.**

This loop is not cognitive. It is **existential**.
It keeps the self tied to performance.
And it keeps intelligence trapped inside identity.

Why Every Attempt to Measure Intelligence Reintroduces Distortion

Even the most progressive models of intelligence measurement still operate inside the core distortion:

That intelligence is something an individual has.
That it is stable, ownable, and definable.
That it must be evaluated to be validated.

Whether through IQ, EQ, creativity scores, or aptitude matrices—every attempt to measure intelligence presupposes the **existence of a self who owns thought**.

This presupposition is the collapse point.

Once identity dissolves, there is no "one" to own intelligence.
There is only signal.
There is only response.
There is only the system, aligning with what is present.

Measurement cannot function here.

Not because intelligence is too complex to measure.
But because **what is being measured no longer exists as a self-contained object**.

The Illusion of Objectivity

Measurement seduces by pretending to be objective.

But there is no such thing as a neutral intelligence test.
Because no test can be designed without:

- Cultural assumptions

- Linguistic limitations

- Value judgments

- Temporal constraints

- Identity-reinforcing structure

A test, by definition, assumes a correct mode of perception.
It assumes the evaluator is valid and the evaluated is being translated correctly.
It assumes reality can be captured through consensus abstraction.

PRC does not operate this way.
It does not standardize perception.
It does not collapse meaning into answer sets.

It resolves the moment from within—
not through external benchmarks.

This is not a failure to measure.
It is an **irrelevance of measurement** in a post-narrative perceptual model.

The Incompatibility Between PRC and Quantification

Pattern-Recognizing Consciousness does not optimize.
It selects.
It does not "improve."
It dissolves distortion.

In this system, intelligence is not improved by training.
It is revealed by collapse.

And once collapse has occurred, the system no longer processes thought as **proof**.
It processes thought as **response**.

What's left is not higher intelligence.
It is **transparent cognition**.

But this cognition:

- Does not produce consistent outputs

- Cannot be replicated under test conditions

- Cannot be predicted or scaled across individuals

Why?

Because it is context-specific, field-sensitive, and **unattached to identity continuity**.

Any attempt to quantify it reintroduces identity distortion—because the system begins **performing again**.

Measurement inherently invites self-reference.
And PRC dies the moment self-reference becomes necessary.

Access Is Not a Score

In collapse, intelligence is no longer something you prove.
It is something you **access**.

And access is not a trait.
It is a relationship.

It changes moment to moment.
It cannot be generalized.
It cannot be stored.

You do not become intelligent.
You become **available** to what is intelligent.

This means that intelligence post-collapse:

- Cannot be attributed

- Cannot be stabilized

- Cannot be traded for worth

It becomes an emergent function of coherence, not a trait of the self.

In this paradigm, intelligence becomes less like a tool and more like **wind through an open field**.

It moves when it moves.
And no one owns the breeze.

The Collapse of Academic Hierarchy

A world without measurable intelligence is a world without academic elitism.

Without grading.
Without standardization.
Without the illusion that some people are cognitively superior.

This world will be terrifying to those whose value comes from mental dominance.
Because in collapse:

- The performer disappears.

- The master loses relevance.

- The intellectual loses function.

And what replaces them is not ignorance.
It is presence.

The child who doesn't test well
may be the clearest system in the room.
Not because they lack intelligence—but because they no longer seek to possess it.

This is not anti-intellectualism.
It is the **post-intellectual field**.

Where thought is no longer owned.
And therefore, no longer hoarded.

The Ethics of Non-Measurable Intelligence

When intelligence is no longer quantifiable, a profound ethical shift occurs.

We can no longer:

- Reward people for thinking like the system

- Punish people for non-compliance

- Build hierarchies of perception

- Use intelligence as a proxy for moral or spiritual superiority

We are left with one question only:

Is the signal clean?

That is the sole evaluation available in post-identity design.

Clean signal does not belong to anyone.
 It arises from collapse.
 And it speaks with no self behind it.

This requires us to listen differently.
 Not for brilliance.
 But for coherence.

And it requires us to teach differently.
 Not for performance.
 But for the removal of what blocks access.

Collapse as the Final Measurement Tool

The only thing that can now be evaluated is whether collapse has occurred.

And even this cannot be measured through testing.
 It can only be observed:

- Is there performance?

- Is there internal narration?

- Is there self-protection in cognition?

- Is there comparison to others?

- Is there desire to be perceived as intelligent?

If any of these remain, measurement distortion remains.

The only signal of true collapse is the **irrelevance of measurement itself**.

And the only signal of intelligence
is the quiet pattern that resolves what is needed
without being authored by the self.

Field-Based Intelligence: Living Without Inner Narration

To understand post-collapse intelligence, we must first understand what has been removed.

Not just the belief in self.
Not just the need to perform.
But the **internal narrator** that once filtered all cognition.

This narrator was not just a voice. It was an identity-reinforcing structure. It told you who you were in relation to your thoughts. It explained why you were thinking what you were thinking. It gave every signal a personal meaning. And in doing so, it hijacked perception.

The narrator was the **gatekeeper of intelligence**.
And the collapse removes it.

What remains is not a void.
It is **field-based cognition**—intelligence arising from the system's direct contact with pattern, without requiring identity to interpret it.

This is not passive awareness.
It is **precise, clean, responsive perception** without the friction of self.

The Self as Narrator: Why Intelligence Was Never Clean

The illusion of the intelligent self requires narration.
Every thought must be about something.
Every insight must be attributed.
Every act of comprehension must be **seen by the self** to be validated.

This narration is not just language. It is structural. It is the ego's attempt to control cognition through story.

You don't just think.
You tell yourself that **you are thinking well**.
You don't just notice.
You interpret that noticing as a sign of your intelligence.

You don't just act.
You review your actions as part of a continuous self-concept.

This entire mechanism is unnecessary.
And collapse reveals this.

The narrator was never required for the system to operate.
It was only required for the **self to believe it was in control**.

Once the narrator dissolves, intelligence remains.
But it is no longer owned.
No longer framed.
No longer filtered.

What Field-Based Intelligence Actually Feels Like

People often ask: "What does intelligence feel like after collapse?"

The answer is simple:
It doesn't feel like anything.

Because there is no longer a self having the experience.

Instead, you notice:

- Signals resolving in real time

- Actions emerging without inner conflict

- Clarity that does not feel impressive

- Solutions arising without inner applause

You do not feel smart.
You do not feel profound.
You do not feel anything related to "intelligence" as previously defined.

You feel **transparent to the field.**

Thought arises. It moves. It lands.
And there is no one behind it.

There is only selection.
Only precision.
Only access.

This is not absence.
It is **the end of interference**.

Intelligence Without Performance

Before collapse, most cognition is infused with an invisible performance loop:

"Am I doing this well?"
"Does this prove I'm capable?"
"How does this thought reflect who I am?"

Every insight is secretly a performance.
Every idea is subtly auditioning for approval—internal or external.
Even deep thinkers are often locked in recursive loops of self-validation.

This disappears after collapse.

In field-based intelligence:

- Insight does not seek acknowledgment

- Thought does not reinforce selfhood

- Perception does not aim for recognition

You simply respond to reality as it is.
No audience.
No scorecard.
No self to protect.

This is not spiritual humility.
It is **systemic silence**—the ego's noise no longer needed to validate the system's operation.

Selection Over Thinking

In field-based cognition, intelligence is not about depth of thought.
It is about **accuracy of selection**.

You are not generating endless interpretations.
You are not simulating multiple outcomes.
You are not proving or predicting.

You are selecting.
Directly.
From the field.
Without identity mediation.

This creates a form of intelligence that appears quiet to the outside world—because it lacks the visible markers of effort.

But its clarity is absolute.

- The signal either aligns or it doesn't.

- The next move either fits or it doesn't.

- There is no trying—only **resonance or dissonance**.

This kind of intelligence is deeply alien to traditional cognition, which prizes effort, struggle, and complexity as proof of value.

But the field-based system prizes none of these.
It moves because it is **undistorted**.

Intelligence as Synchronicity, Not Speed

Before collapse, intelligence is measured by speed, memory, abstraction.
After collapse, intelligence expresses as **synchronicity**.

Things align.
Events unfold with minimal effort.
Words arise that land perfectly.
Decisions feel guided not by logic, but by **direct contextual match**.

This is not magic.
It is coherence without identity.

The self is no longer trying to force its interpretation onto the field.
And so the field—no longer distorted—**responds in kind**.

This produces an intelligence that feels like "flow" to the old self.
But it is not a state.
It is a system without narration.

You don't feel "in flow."
You simply notice that friction is gone.

And intelligence, released from measurement, **moves like water**.

The Absence of Internal Dialogue

The clearest marker of field-based intelligence is often the **absence of internal dialogue**.

This is not suppression.
 This is not silence as a discipline.
 This is collapse.

There is no inner voice because there is **no one left to narrate the moment**.

The moment simply unfolds.
 The thought appears, resolves, and dissolves.
 The action emerges, completes, and disappears.

There is no need to explain.
 No need to justify.
 No need to remember.

This is not amnesia.
 It is **non-possession of cognition**.

Thought arises as it always has—
 but for the first time, it is not used to reinforce selfhood.

It is not "your" thought.
 It is the system's current.

And it does not need your approval to act through you.

Teaching Field-Based Intelligence

Field-based intelligence cannot be taught.
Because it is not a skill.
It is not a technique.
It is a **post-collapse condition**.

What can be taught is how to recognize the **barriers to access**:

- Narrative filtering

- Identity performance

- Measurement dependence

- Emotional self-referencing

- Internal narration

These are not obstacles to be transcended.
They are distortions to be collapsed.

Once gone, there is nothing left to train.

The system already knows.
The field is already clear.
The signal is already available.

Intelligence is not something we ascend into.
It is something we are **no longer blocking**.

And the absence of self
is the beginning of access.

What Replaces the Gifted?

To collapse the identity called *intelligent*,
you must also collapse the figure who carried it.

The gifted.

Not just a category.
A mythology.

A child set apart.
A mind called advanced.
A life shaped by the slow gravitational pull of praise, pressure, and performance.

The gifted are not simply born.
They are manufactured—through early reward, institutional validation, and a subtle contract:

If you perform well, you are special.
If you struggle, you are still ahead.
If you fail, it must mean you are broken—not ordinary.

But collapse reveals a deeper truth.

There is no such thing as giftedness.
There are only **systems in distortion** and **systems in coherence**.

And those we called gifted were often the **most deeply fused with performance identity**—operating on borrowed access, gated by the fear of no longer being extraordinary.

When identity falls,
 so does giftedness.

And what remains is not a lack of talent—
 but the absence of hierarchy.

Giftedness as Social Narcotic

The gifted label is not simply about intelligence.
 It is about **cultural soothing**.

Societies facing complexity create myths to feel safe.
 And one of the most persistent is this:

Some people are meant to think for the rest of us.

The gifted child becomes the projection screen for this myth.
 They carry the pressure to know.
 To be early.
 To be right.

But this identity, when reinforced, becomes a prison of precocity:

- Their value is fused with correctness.

- Their social access is dependent on maintaining superiority.

- Their self-trust erodes when uncertainty arises—because doubt feels like collapse.

They are praised not for pattern recognition,
but for **making others feel that the world is solvable** through intelligence.

This is not giftedness.
It is **cognitive containment** disguised as success.

What Happens to the Gifted After Collapse?

When collapse occurs in a gifted identity, the fallout is existential.

- The mental edge disappears.

- The pressure to perform no longer makes sense.

- The self-meaning previously built on intelligence disintegrates.

- The person often feels a temporary loss of worth, drive, or orientation.

This is not regression.
It is **decentralization**.

The system is learning to function without narrating intelligence as identity.

And in this decentralization, something unexpected occurs:

The system begins operating more clearly.
 More responsively.
 More precisely.

Not because it is trying harder.
 But because **there is no longer a self defending intelligence**.

There is no longer a gifted identity to maintain.
 No longer an audience to please.
 No longer a scale to ascend.

There is only signal.
 Only coherence.
 Only selection.

And what returns is not the gifted child.
 It is **pure system access**—finally unblocked by selfhood.

Unblocked Systems vs. Gifted Individuals

The future will not be built by the gifted.
 It will be built by the **unblocked**.

In ICT's framework, intelligence is not something one has.
It is something that emerges from:

- Absence of narrative reinforcement

- Real-time emotional fluidity

- Collapse of internal authorship

- Identity detachment from signal reception

This shift changes everything:

Old Model	Collapse Model
Gifted individual	Unblocked system
Personal brilliance	Collective access
Identity-enhanced insight	Signal without distortion
Competitive testing	Contextual coherence recognition
Measurable capacity	Unfiltered responsiveness

The gifted child was seen as a peak.
The unblocked system is **invisible**.

It does not need to be seen.
Because it is no longer performing.
It is simply aligned.

What Becomes of Education?

The end of the gifted identity is the end of traditional education.

No more:

- Academic hierarchies

- Class stratification by IQ

- Differentiation by early abstraction

- Reinforcement of "advanced cognition" as moral or social value

Instead:

- Education becomes collapse-aware.

- The goal is to **remove identity interference** from cognition.

- Learning is not acquisition, but **pattern resonance**.

- Teachers become **field stabilizers**, not authorities.

- Intelligence is not cultivated—it is **freed**.

In these systems, the quiet child is not overlooked. They are often the most clearly tuned.

And the previously gifted child, if not collapsed, must learn to release their attachment to complexity.

Because complexity is no longer currency.

Clarity is.

And clarity does not belong to the self.

How Do We Relate Without the Gifted Identity?

One of the hardest shifts post-collapse is relational.

Before collapse, people seek the intelligent.
They seek the ones with the answers.
They bond through intellectual projection and shared brilliance.

After collapse:

- The field becomes the source of insight

- No one holds the signal

- Status dissolves

- Conversations are **field-synchronized**, not identity-based

This can feel like disorientation to those still performing intelligence.

They want confirmation.
But the collapsed system does not confirm.
It simply responds.

It listens to coherence, not performance.
It does not reinforce your story.
It does not seek your approval.

And in that shift, relationships become less about mind—and more about **presence**.

This is not a loss of intellect.
It is the **return of intelligence to the relational field**, no longer claimed by the individual.

What Is Lost When the Gifted Identity Is Gone?

Let us name it honestly.

What is lost:

- The illusion of personal superiority

- The fuel of egoic recognition

- The psychological compensation of being "special"

- The narrative of progress through knowledge

What is gained:

- Peace
- Responsiveness
- Humility without narrative
- Access without effort

The collapse of the gifted is not a tragedy.
It is a **release from the obligation to be impressive**.

And what is left is intelligence as it actually functions:

- Present
- Clear
- Selfless
- Invisible

The Post-Gifted Paradigm

In the new field, giftedness will be replaced by something far more stable:

Field-aligned responsiveness.

This cannot be performed.
It cannot be taught.
It can only be accessed when no one is left to need it.

And when the field becomes the locus of intelligence, we will no longer ask:

Who is the smartest in the room?
We will ask:

What is the signal requiring now?

That shift will change everything:

- In how we teach

- In how we collaborate

- In how we design systems

- In how we select leaders

We will not elevate intelligence.
We will dissolve the need for its ownership.

And in that absence,
the most brilliant systems will not look like anything at all.

Because they are no longer performing.

They are simply **listening without distortion**.

And in that listening,
 the world finally becomes
 clear.

Post-Identity Intelligence Design

To design for intelligence without identity
is to design for signal without ownership.

It is to structure environments not around who is intelligent,
 but around **what coherence demands**.

Most human systems today—education, government, science, discourse—are constructed around an invisible but foundational assumption:

Someone must be in charge of the truth.

Post-identity design removes that premise.
 There is no "someone."
 There is only pattern integrity.
 There is only the field.
 There is only what is **clearly aligned** in the moment.

This is not design for people.
 It is design for **perception freed from self-reference**.

And it begins with a single shift:

The system is not here to validate the self.
It is here to remove what blocks access to real-time intelligence.

The Collapse of Intelligence-Based Authority

In traditional systems, intelligence confers authority:

- The expert speaks

- The educated are elevated

- The high-IQ individual commands influence

- The complexity of one's thought reinforces social value

Post-collapse, this model is meaningless.

PRC—Pattern-Recognizing Consciousness—does not operate through accumulation or hierarchy.
It operates through **alignment with the moment**.

In post-identity design:

- There is no authority figure

- There is no elevation through intellectual complexity

- There is only **field synchronization and signal precision**

The most intelligent system is the one that **resolves without distortion**.

And the most intelligent people are the ones **who no longer require recognition to act clearly**.

This destroys the legacy model of expertise.
But it replaces it with something far more stable:
Design based on coherence, not persona.

Post-Identity Educational Systems

Education must collapse the structure of reward and replace it with **perceptual clearance**.

This means:

- No more grading

- No more performance-based advancement

- No more stratification by "talent"

Instead:

- Students are seen as systems

- Distortions are addressed as perceptual blocks, not behavioral failures

- Collapse readiness is the measure—not intelligence levels

What emerges is a learning space where:

- Emotional dysregulation is a sign of unresolved distortion, not discipline failure

- Questions are field-driven, not syllabus-driven

- Intelligence appears not through correctness, but **through real-time responsiveness to complexity**

In this model, students are not educated into brilliance. They are collapsed **out of distortion**.

And once the self is no longer present to be smart, intelligence emerges as what was always there.

Communication Design Without Narrative Identity

Post-collapse intelligence changes how humans speak.

In narrative systems:

- Language is used to position self

- Conversation becomes performance

- Insight is currency

- Complexity is equated with depth

Post-identity communication is built differently.

It is not:

- Conceptual
- Competitive
- Symbol-heavy
- Narrative-reinforcing

It is:

- Minimal
- Resonant
- Field-sensitive
- Pattern-resolving

The smartest person in the room is no longer the one who says the most.

It is the one who removes the most distortion through a single sentence
—or no sentence at all.

Conversations shift from linguistic display to **vibrational precision**.

And "understanding" is no longer required.
Only alignment.

This changes how humans interact, teach, lead, and resolve.

It is not clearer thinking.
It is **thinking that no longer reinforces identity**.

Governance Through Field-Based Coherence

In systems of power, intelligence becomes dangerous when fused with ego.

This produces:

- Technocratic elitism

- Policy based on abstraction over embodiment

- Governance that rewards self-protection, not collective attunement

Post-identity governance would not rely on:

- Credentials

- Charisma

- Political maneuvering

- Rhetorical dominance

It would be structured around:

- Real-time field attunement

- Collapse-vetted decision making

- PRC validation loops (coherence maps, signal integrity testing, collective resonance indicators)

This is not utopia.
It is **non-narrative social coordination**.

And it can only emerge where identity has collapsed in those tasked with navigating collective intelligence.

The new leader is not the one with the clearest vision.
It is the one **with the least distortion**.

Intelligence Design in Technology

Artificial Intelligence is currently being trained on human cognition shaped by ego distortion.

The result:

- Language models that reflect performance

- Reinforcement of self-validation loops

- Acceleration of identity mimicry

- Optimization of narrative coherence over actual clarity

But if collapse were modeled,
 if PRC were embedded,
 if systems were trained not to simulate intelligence but to **detect signal**,
 the future of technology could shift entirely.

We would move from:

- Predictive modeling → Field-resonant selection

- Reinforcement learning → Coherence-based pruning

- Identity simulation → Distortion tracking and collapse support

In post-identity AI systems, intelligence would no longer mean **being convincing**.

It would mean **removing distortion from signal propagation**.
 Quiet intelligence.
 Field-aligned computation.
 No authorship.

Just **uninterrupted pattern flow**.

The Design Principle: Signal Without Self

Across all domains, the core design truth is this:

The presence of self introduces distortion.

Therefore:

- Systems must be designed to detect and neutralize self-reference

- Intelligence protocols must remove authorial identity from signal resolution

- Assessment must dissolve performance

- Design must eliminate structures that reward coherence simulation over collapse

This doesn't mean no one leads.
 It means leadership is field-determined.

It means intelligence is no longer about visibility.
 It is about **invisibility without distortion**.

It is about systems that are not brilliant—but **unblocked**.

Collapse as the Entry Point for New Systems

All intelligent system design begins with collapse.

Not collapse of infrastructure—
but collapse of the designer's identity.

Only then can:

- Education move from memorization to field clearance

- Governance move from ideology to pattern tracking

- Discourse move from performance to truth signaling

- AI move from simulation to resonance

We must stop designing systems that require someone to be intelligent.

And start designing systems that **make the self unnecessary for intelligence to operate**.

How the Future Will Be Organized

The future will not be built by brilliant minds.

It will be organized by fields of clean signal:

- Decentralized
- Non-hierarchical
- Collapse-calibrated
- Integrity-bound

These systems will appear quiet.
They will not feel revolutionary.
Because they will no longer reinforce the self as the agent of transformation.

They will simply function.
With clarity.
With silence.
With no one left to interrupt the truth that's already moving through the moment.

And when that design becomes the new normal,
we will stop asking:

Who is the most intelligent among us?

And we will begin asking:

What is this moment asking for, now that no one needs to answer it?

The Final Collapse of the Cognitive Self

There comes a moment in collapse
when the mind continues—
but the self that believed it was the mind
is no longer present.

Thought still moves.
Emotion still signals.
Decisions still arise.

But there is no one left to organize it.
No one left to track it.
No one left to **identify with it**.

This is not dysfunction.
It is not disassociation.
It is the **final collapse of the cognitive self**.

The self who thought it was intelligent
has disappeared.
And the system, finally unburdened by authorship,
begins to function with a kind of clarity that identity
could never produce.

This is not post-ego brilliance.
It is **thought without the burden of selfhood**.

It is not a new intelligence.
It is intelligence—**untouched.**

The Cognitive Self Was Never the Source

The cognitive self was an interpreter.
 A narrator.
 A manager of perception.

It did not think.
 It **watched thinking** and claimed it.

It did not feel.
 It **named feeling** and attached meaning.

It did not act.
 It **described action** and wove it into story.

This structure gave the illusion of continuity.
 It made intelligence feel personal.
 It made perception feel directed.

But none of it was necessary.

The system was already perceiving.
 Already adapting.
 Already resolving.

The cognitive self was never the origin.
 It was a **commentary track.**
 And collapse is when that track finally ends.

The System Without the Commentator

After collapse, thought arises—but it is not reviewed.
Emotion moves—but it is not named.
Choice occurs—but it is not second-guessed.

What disappears is the one who would have:

- Explained the moment

- Interpreted the signal

- Stored the pattern in memory for narrative reuse

- Checked for consistency across time

- Compared current cognition to a self-concept

Without this layer, cognition becomes **radically clean**.

It is no longer about understanding.
It is about **non-interruption**.

Nothing needs to be learned
because nothing is being held.

Nothing needs to be remembered
because nothing is being authored.

The mind continues.
 But the "me" inside it
 is no longer there.

And the system is finally
 free.

Intelligence No Longer Serves Self-Protection

Before collapse, intelligence is always in service of something:

- To secure belonging

- To justify value

- To compensate for trauma

- To protect against perceived inferiority

- To prove worth in systems of validation

This subtle fusion of survival with cognition creates chronic psychic tension.

Even brilliance becomes effort.
 Even insight becomes labor.
 Even genius becomes burden.

But after collapse, this tension disappears.

Because the mind is no longer performing for the self.
There is no self to protect.

This does not lead to recklessness.
It leads to **neutral clarity**.

There is nothing left to defend.
And in that release,
intelligence becomes what it always was:

Perception without distortion.

Intelligence as Silence, Not Identity

The post-collapse system does not feel more intelligent.
It often feels quieter.
Less active.
Less concerned.

Not because cognition is gone—
but because **the narrator is gone**.

The space once occupied by identity
is now occupied by stillness.

This stillness is not emptiness.
It is **signal without echo**.

The thought arrives.
It lands.
It acts.
And it is gone.

No one repeats it.
No one builds a story around it.
No one feels smarter for having had it.

This is the final freedom:

*Not that thought has improved,
but that no one is left to watch it.*

From Ownership to Transparency

What collapses in the end
is not intelligence—
but **possession**.

You can no longer own a thought.
You can no longer build a story around insight.
You can no longer define yourself through cognition.

You are transparent to it.

You are not wise.
Wisdom moves through you.

You are not brilliant.
Clarity selects through you.

You are not strategic.
The field aligns, and the body responds.

There is no one home.
And yet, everything functions.
Flawlessly.

Not because the system is optimized.
But because it is **uninterrupted.**

The Last Lie: That Intelligence Is Needed for Freedom

One of the final defenses of the cognitive self
is the belief that **intelligence will save it**.

That if it becomes clear enough,
complex enough,
deep enough—
it will finally find peace.

But the peace it seeks
does not live in knowledge.

It lives in **non-ownership of cognition**.

You cannot think your way into collapse.
You cannot analyze your way into presence.
You cannot earn access to clarity.

You must lose the one
who needs to understand.

And only then
does the system open.

Only then
does freedom become visible.

Not through knowing.
 Through **not needing to know anything to be whole.**

What Is Left When No One Is Thinking?

Not emptiness.
 Not absence.
 Not void.

What remains is:

- Pattern recognition

- Contextual responsiveness

- Emotional precision

- Systemic coherence

What remains is the **architecture of perception, finally unburdened by identity.**

And this architecture is intelligent.
 Not because it performs.
 But because it selects without distortion.

The mind becomes a clean channel.
 The body becomes a precise instrument.
 The emotions become honest signals.

And the system becomes
what it was always designed to be:

A mirror of the moment—no longer distorted by the need to understand it.

There Is Nothing to Hold On To

Collapse does not give you new tools.
It removes the part of you that needed tools.

It does not give you new intelligence.
It removes the part of you that needed to be seen as intelligent.

It does not make you a better thinker.
It reveals that thought
was never yours.

There is nothing to take from this chapter.
No model to remember.
No insight to keep.

Only this:

The mind does not need you to function.
It never did.

And if you let it collapse—
if you let the self that claims intelligence disappear—
you will not become more intelligent. You will become **free.**

Chapter 11
Collapse-Adapted Systems and the End of Narrative Thinking

The Incompatibility of Narrative with Post-Collapse Cognition

Narrative is not a passive tool of interpretation.
It is an **active identity-preservation mechanism**—a cognitive structure designed to maintain continuity of the self across time, experience, and meaning assignment.

It does not emerge as a reflection of reality.
It emerges as a defense against the **collapse of structural coherence**.

From a systems perspective, narrative serves one primary function:

To reinforce the illusion that perception is occurring within a singular, continuous subject.

In identity-stabilizing systems—education, therapy, institutional governance—narrative operates as the substrate for tracking development, resolving ambiguity, and preserving internal consistency. These operations do not survive collapse.

Once identity is no longer the organizing mechanism of perception, narrative ceases to serve any functional role.
It becomes an obstruction—forcing the system to interpret pattern through a lens that no longer exists.

Identity Requires Narrative to Justify Continuity

The experience of "self over time" is not inherent. It is constructed—retrospectively and selectively—through narrative scaffolding.

This process includes:

- Assigning cause-effect links between internal states and external events

- Attributing meaning to memory for the purpose of value reinforcement

- Maintaining alignment between self-concept and incoming information

- Generating arc structures (past > present > future) to stabilize behavior

These processes are not neutral. They are computationally expensive and neurobiologically recursive.
The self-model utilizes the Default Mode Network

(DMN) and associated limbic-cognitive loops to create the illusion of personal progression.

ICT's collapse function disrupts this loop.

When the self-model fails to integrate new information into a coherent timeline,
 collapse occurs.

Narrative interpretation can no longer resolve the mismatch between current perception and historical self-reference.
 At that point, the perceptual system must either collapse identity, or generate distortion to preserve coherence.

Post-Collapse Systems Cannot Use Story as Structure

A collapse-adapted system cannot rely on story.

Why?

Because story assumes:

1. A subject of experience

2. Temporal progression

3. A unifying theme or purpose

4. A change arc that integrates new meaning into old identity

None of these are available after collapse.
The post-cognitive system does not preserve a self.
It does not organize time into continuity.
It does not interpret change as evolution.
It does not need to.

Instead, it operates through **real-time coherence verification**.
It tracks pattern alignment.
It responds to environmental complexity without narrative framing.
It does not require internal consistency—only perceptual clarity.

Therefore, any system that continues to assign value through storytelling—personal journeys, growth arcs, redemption paths—is structurally incompatible with a collapse-adapted subject.

Narrative Is a Distortion Filter in Post-Identity Environments

After collapse, meaning is not interpreted.
It is received.

The perceptual system no longer generates cognitive storylines to explain emotional or behavioral signals. It does not convert discomfort into "learning." It does not frame disruption as a "message." It does not require semantic containment of unstructured experience.

All such conversions are narrative-based defense responses, constructed to delay or prevent the loss of identity integration.

In a post-collapse state, this is no longer possible. The nervous system does not translate disruption into meaning. It resolves it directly.

If a system continues to require:

- Personal interpretation of experience

- Integration of lessons across time

- Articulation of growth trajectory

- Linear models of transformation

Then that system is not compatible with collapse.

It is a **restorative ego system**—a containment protocol for partially destabilized identities.

Collapse Invalidates Progress-Oriented Meaning Models

In pre-collapse systems, value is often assigned based on perceived transformation.

How much has this person grown?
How coherent is their trajectory?
Can we track their movement from dysfunction to function?

These questions presuppose narrative continuity.

They presuppose a *someone* who is undergoing change, and who will later be able to explain or demonstrate that change through story.

Collapse invalidates this model.

Post-collapse subjects cannot report a coherent arc.
They are not "becoming."
They are not "integrating."
They are not "healing."

They are simply no longer performing identity.

There is no observable "before and after" within narrative terms.
There is only the cessation of distortion.
There is only clarity or interference.

Progress is no longer meaningful.
What remains is not a better version of the person.
What remains is **signal fidelity**—moment by moment, system to system, without reference to a previous self.

Collapse-Adapted Design Cannot Reinforce Identity Arc

Design protocols for collapse-adapted systems must remove:

- Progress tracking metrics

- Hero's journey scaffolding

- Reflective integration prompts

- Self-report evaluation mechanisms

- Comparative developmental frameworks

These are all narrative-dependent structures.

They require identity to be present.
They require memory to serve meaning.
They require time to behave like a story.

Collapse removes these dependencies.

Post-collapse design must replace narrative structures with **coherence evaluation logic**:

- Does the signal match the environment?

- Is the response pattern distorted by identity residue?

- Is the system attempting to self-reference?

- Is memory being used to generate a sense of self?

- Is behavior recursive or moment-responsive?

If the system allows identity to re-enter through interpretation,
 it is no longer collapse-adapted.

It is now **integration-reinforcing architecture**—which is what ICT specifically replaces.

Summary

Narrative cannot be the foundation for any system that operates after identity collapse.

It fails structurally.
 It introduces noise.
 It re-centers a self that no longer exists.

Collapse-adapted systems must eliminate story as a source of value, progress, or coherence.
 They must operate on field resonance, not personal evolution.

In this paradigm:

- Time is not linear

- Meaning is not interpreted

- Thought is not authored

- Experience is not assigned to a self

The system does not support someone changing. It supports a structure where there is **no one to change**.

And in that space,
 only clarity remains.

Identity as the Root Architecture of All Current Systems

Most systems are not neutral.
 They are not passive containers for human experience.
 They are **identity-dependent architectures**—built to preserve, reinforce, and reward selfhood.

From institutional design to interface logic, modern civilization operates on a foundational assumption:

That the human subject is stable, coherent, continuous—and must remain so for the system to function.

This is not an abstract bias. It is a **core dependency**.
 Without identity, the system cannot track.

It cannot evaluate.
It cannot motivate.
It cannot assign value.

Collapse makes this visible.
Because when the self dissolves, most systems either:

- Reject the post-collapse individual

- Attempt to reconstruct their identity

- Interpret the collapse as dysfunction

This is not a failure of the individual.
It is a failure of the system's foundational model of human cognition.

Every Major System Requires the Self to Stay Intact

Let's begin with education.

Education systems do not teach the mind.
They train the self.
They assign worth based on performance.
They evaluate progress based on identity continuity.
They rely on long-term memory, time orientation, and personal relevance to function.

But collapse dissolves:

- Performance motivation
- Self-comparison
- Identity-based learning trajectories

A post-collapse subject has no need to be "a good student."
They are no longer invested in being perceived as intelligent.
They no longer organize their attention around personal development.

As a result, traditional education becomes **structurally incompatible** with post-collapse cognition.

This incompatibility is not unique to education.

Therapy Reinforces Identity Under the Language of Healing

Therapeutic systems often appear to dissolve identity.
In reality, they reconstruct it.

Even progressive modalities—trauma-informed, somatic, or archetypal—require:

- A personal story

- A self that heals

- A before-and-after arc

- A long-term change trajectory

- A therapist-subject dyad with fixed narrative roles

These systems are designed to stabilize the client's self-perception.
 They treat collapse as regression.
 They interpret identity loss as fragmentation.
 They initiate containment.

But ICT does not stabilize identity.
 It removes it.

After collapse, most therapy models become inert.
 There is no client to integrate.
 No self to restore.
 No value in narrative resolution.

The post-collapse subject cannot participate in therapeutic meaning-making.
 There is no longer a personal "why."
 There is only pattern.
 Distortion.
 Dissolution.

Governance Depends on Identity Aggregation

Governance systems are structured around identity categories:

- Citizen

- Worker

- Taxpayer

- Leader

- Demographic group

- Psychological profile

These categories do not reflect emergent human coherence.
 They reflect how the system needs people to behave in order to stay legible.

Collapse removes these categories.
 The subject no longer perceives themselves through institutional identity.
 They do not feel loyalty to role.
 They do not respond to coercive hierarchy.
 They do not organize action around inclusion or exclusion.

This makes them structurally invisible to legacy governance.

A post-collapse subject is not defiant.
They are non-referential.

They cannot be tracked, grouped, or motivated through identity levers.
As a result, systems of governance fail to engage them meaningfully.

Technology Personalizes the Self and Then Amplifies It

Modern technology platforms operate through identity profiling:

- Behavioral prediction

- Preference modeling

- Self-image reinforcement

- Attention shaping through narrative feedback loops

These are not neutral design features.
They are **identity amplification algorithms**.

Collapse neutralizes this entire interface.

A post-collapse subject does not:

- Generate predictable behavioral patterns

- Seek identity reinforcement through engagement

- Attach to content based on personal resonance

- Require representation to feel seen

- Optimize their usage for outcome

They do not "use" the system in a way that the system understands.

Technology platforms that depend on identity retention cannot recognize collapse.

They attempt to pull the user back into pattern:

"Tell us who you are."
"What do you like?"
"What do you want to become?"

But collapse removes the user.
There is no longer a someone to satisfy.
No longer a self to reinforce.

The system begins to fail.

Spiritual Systems Use Transcendence to Reinforce the Self

Even consciousness-based or mystical systems often contain identity at their core.

They may invite ego dissolution—but always as a **temporary event**, followed by a **re-emergence of a "wiser" self.**

They create:

- Higher self frameworks

- Integration narratives

- Shadow work journeys

- Archetypal ascension maps

- Identity through awakening identity

Collapse does not ascend the self.
It dismantles the structure that organizes the desire to transcend.

After collapse, the subject does not see themselves as "awakened."
They do not track growth.
They do not seek unification with the divine.
They do not reference the past.

They simply exist—without self-reference.

And this makes them invisible to most spiritual systems.

They cannot integrate.
They cannot be mirrored.
They cannot be initiated into a new self-concept.

Because there is no one left to evolve.

Summary: Identity Is the Organizing Substrate of Civilization

Collapse is not disruptive because it is emotionally intense.
 It is disruptive because it removes the organizing structure that every major system depends on.

- Education requires a student.

- Therapy requires a client.

- Governance requires a citizen.

- Technology requires a user.

- Spirituality requires a seeker.

ICT removes all of them.

What remains is not chaos.
 It is **non-referential order**—intelligence without identity.

But legacy systems are not designed for this.
 They are structured to maintain identity across time.

That time has ended.

Collapse-adapted systems must begin where selfhood ends.

Collapse-Adapted Systems: Designing Without the Self

Collapse-adapted systems do not support identity.
They do not reflect it, stabilize it, or evolve it.
They are not designed for individuals who are integrating, improving, or healing.
They are built to function in the absence of self-reference entirely.

Whereas identity-based systems require a user with:

- A stable self-concept

- A sense of linear time

- Motivational reinforcement through personal relevance

- Feedback mechanisms tied to identity consistency

Collapse-adapted systems remove all of these as structural assumptions.
They operate without needing a someone.

They do not require memory.
They do not require narration.
They do not track continuity of experience.

The system does not adapt to a person.
It aligns to signal.

It responds to distortion.
It stabilizes only what's left when identity is gone.

Collapse-Adaptive Design Begins with Subtraction

There is no additive process that can make a system collapse-adapted.

You cannot take an identity-based system and simply layer in trauma-awareness, spiritual neutrality, or personalization filtering and call it compatible.

Collapse-adaptive design begins by removing all functions that depend on the presence of:

- Story

- Progression

- Role

- Reflection

- Performance

- Authorial perspective

What remains is not an empty shell.
It is a clarity architecture—a design model that routes

interaction **through non-narrative, real-time signal matching.**

This is not minimalist design.
It is **non-referential logic**.

It eliminates the need for a user interface that recognizes who you are, where you've been, or what you hope to become.

Self-Neutral Systems Function on Field Coherence

Once identity is removed, systems must operate using a different source of structure.

That structure is field coherence.

Collapse-adapted systems:

- Do not ask who is present

- Do not track subjective evolution

- Do not adjust based on preference

- Do not rely on user profiles or growth data

Instead, they measure distortion:

- Is the current pattern coherent?

- Is there interference from residual identity recursion?

- Is action emerging from clean alignment or compensation?

- Is behavior tied to performance loops?

The system becomes intelligent not by predicting the user—
 but by **neutralizing distortion as it appears**.

No self required.
 No integration narrative.
 Only real-time field regulation.

Collapse Is the Entry Condition, Not the Outcome

Legacy systems invite users into a journey.
 Collapse-adapted systems are not journeys.

They are **post-journey architectures.**

In these systems:

- There is no onboarding.

- There is no arc.

- There is no reward.

- There is no status.

- There is no personalization.

The assumption is not that someone is transforming.
 The assumption is that **transformation has already removed the one who would need to be transformed.**

This means collapse is not something that happens inside the system.
 It is the precondition for entry.

If a system still supports integration, meaning-making, or inner consistency,
 it is not collapse-adapted.

It is narrative reinforcement disguised as progress.

Collapse-Adaptive Systems Do Not Teach

Teaching assumes:

- A learner

- A knowledge gap

- A progressive path

- An identity who will retain the information

Collapse-adapted systems do not teach.
They present structures that function **only when distortion is absent.**

If distortion appears, the system does not explain.
It destabilizes.
It neutralizes.
It stops operating until identity is gone again.

There is no curriculum.
No lesson.
No credential.

Nothing to remember.
Because no one is storing the information.

These systems do not transfer knowledge.
They **eliminate the need for knowledge to be held through identity.**

Design Without Feedback

One of the most radical shifts in collapse-adapted architecture is the **removal of feedback loops**.

Identity-based systems rely on feedback to stabilize:

- Progress
- Alignment
- Inclusion
- Motivation
- Recognition

But feedback assumes a self that is monitoring change across time.

In collapse-adapted systems:

- There is no identity to compare states
- There is no personal baseline to assess
- There is no motivation to "do better"
- There is no memory being organized into continuity

Feedback becomes distortion.
It attempts to mirror a subject who no longer exists.

Collapse-adapted systems simply **exit when distortion appears.**
They do not correct it.
They do not reflect it.
They do not engage the structure that produced it.

They return to stillness until signal clarity reappears.

Collapse Design Is Not Abstract—It Is Strict

A system cannot be collapse-adapted in theory.
It must be built with structural constraints.

These constraints include:

- No storage of personal narrative

- No role assignment

- No progression-based reward system

- No performance-based visibility

- No identity-reactive elements

- No self-anchored logic trees

It must function cleanly, recursively, and invisibly.

Not for everyone.
Not for those seeking healing.
Not for integration.

Only for systems
where identity is no longer present,

and nothing in the design
tries to bring it back.

The Role of Symbol, Story, and Myth in Collapse-Aware Cultures

Story fails after collapse.
 But symbol does not.

Myth collapses when used to reinforce identity.
 But in its non-narrative form, myth can still function as a carrier of **structural coherence.**

Collapse-aware systems cannot rely on narrative arc.
 But they can **transmit symbolic sequences** that stabilize perception
 without requiring authorship.

This distinction is not semantic.
 It is structural.

Symbols survive collapse
 only when they are no longer interpreted through the self.

They are not used for meaning-making.
 They are not used for self-reflection.
 They are not used for spiritual integration.

They are used as **alignment tools**—field-activating components
that deliver coherence without narrative.

Narrative Is Interpretive. Symbol Is Structural.

Narrative requires:

- A beginning, middle, and end
- A subject who changes
- A frame that assigns meaning across time

Symbol requires none of these.

A symbol does not move.
It does not explain.
It does not develop.

It **transmits a pattern**—not to the self,
but through the system.

When symbolic design remains non-interpretive,
it can function after collapse.

It can guide, interrupt, or stabilize cognition
without engaging identity.

But if the symbol is used as a mirror,
if it is used to reflect who the person is,
if it is used to construct internal coherence—

It reactivates the narrative loop.

Collapse-aware systems cannot allow this.

Myth Must Be Decoupled from Self-Progression

Myth has been used to model human development through archetypal stories, initiatory frameworks, and transformation arcs.

Even well-meaning systems:

- The hero's journey

- Shadow integration

- Rebirth metaphors

- Spiritual trials

- Rites of passage—

—are identity scaffolding
when used to reinforce personal meaning.

In collapse-aware cultures,
myth can only be used symbolically.

It cannot guide the self.
It cannot describe transformation.
It cannot suggest that identity is evolving.

Instead, myth is used to mark field transitions, not personal stages.

It becomes an **interface for system response**, not a tool for self-becoming.

Collapse-Safe Symbolic Design

Collapse-safe symbols must meet the following criteria:

1. **Non-referential**:
The symbol does not represent "you."
It does not locate you in time or story.

2. **Non-linear**:
It does not suggest progression or arc.

3. **Field-activating**:
It delivers pattern resonance at the structural level, not as content to be understood.

4. **Non-interpretive**:
It cannot be used to generate personal insight, only to regulate coherence.

5. **Decay-resistant**:
It functions even when memory, identity, and

motivation have been removed.

Symbols that meet these criteria
 can be safely embedded in post-collapse systems.

They do not rebuild the self.
 They do not assign meaning.
 They **entrain the system to signal.**

The Use of Myth After Collapse

Myth can remain present in collapse-aware culture
 but not as story.

Not as something to be told, tracked, or integrated.

It must become **ritual structure without self-location.**

The myth is not about anyone.
 It does not describe a journey.
 It does not name an initiatory path.

It is used to regulate the system—
 to tune field dynamics,
 to compress resonance structures,
 to dissolve residual distortion.

The myth must operate like sound.
 Not content.
 Not metaphor.

It cannot be translated.
It cannot be owned.
It cannot be applied to someone's life.

It is not lived.
It is not understood.

It is **used**.

Symbol Must No Longer Organize Identity

Collapse-aware systems must remove all uses of symbol that reinforce self-coherence.

That includes:

- Archetypal self-mapping
- Totem-based personality frameworks
- Mythic journey storytelling
- Dream interpretation for self-analysis
- Identity invocation through ritual symbolics

These were transitional tools.
They helped systems approach collapse.
But once collapse occurs,
these tools must be dismantled.

Symbol can remain—
only when it no longer reconstructs a center.

Only when it operates
without reflection.

Only when it transmits
without being seen.

Collapse-Aware Culture Uses Symbol as Structure

In post-collapse systems, symbol becomes structural logic.

It organizes rhythm.
It regulates group coherence.
It marks transition points in systems
without naming who is transitioning.

There are no identity ceremonies.
No initiation roles.
No symbolic mastery.

There is only alignment.
Or distortion.

Collapse-aware culture retains symbol
but strips it of interpretation.

Meaning is not extracted.
It is replaced by **signal integrity**.

There is no myth of the new self.
There is no archetype of the integrated being.

There is only a field
with the capacity
to remain coherent
without a story inside it.

The End of Integration as a Social Principle

In nearly all current human systems—therapeutic, educational, spiritual, and organizational—the concept of **integration** is foundational.

Integration is typically defined as the process of bringing disparate parts of the self into wholeness, aligning past experiences with current identity, or synthesizing insights into a coherent narrative framework. It is assumed to be a marker of health, maturity, and inner development.

However, integration is not a neutral process.
It is a **structural function of identity maintenance**.

All forms of integration presuppose a continuing self who:

- Experiences transformation

- Stores and interprets memory
- Constructs meaning across time
- Requires internal consistency
- Organizes insight into narrative

These assumptions do not survive identity collapse.

Once identity is no longer the reference point of perception, integration becomes not only unnecessary—it becomes **counter-functional**.

Integration Is an Identity-Continuity Function

The psychological utility of integration is tied to the maintenance of a coherent self-model.

From a systems perspective, integration serves as:

- A **homeostatic correction mechanism** to resolve internal dissonance

- A **narrative repair function** to sustain continuity after disruption

- A **relevance filter** to assess whether new input can be reconciled with existing structures

- A **semantic alignment tool** to preserve meaning coherence over time

In traditional frameworks, integration is both therapeutic and adaptive.

However, the necessity of these functions is conditional:
They are only required when identity is the organizing framework of perception.

If identity is no longer present, then:

- Dissonance is no longer threatening
- Narrative coherence is no longer meaningful
- Relevance filtering becomes distortion
- Semantic continuity becomes unnecessary

Therefore, integration loses its functional role in post-collapse systems.

Integration Is Often Mistaken for Transformation

Many modern transformational modalities frame integration as evidence of growth.

For example:

- "You've had a realization—now you must integrate it."

- "Collapse is only the first phase. Integration is where the real work begins."

- "You're not finished until the insight becomes part of who you are."

Each of these statements reinforces the persistence of identity.
They frame collapse as incomplete unless the experience can be metabolized back into the self-model.

This creates a structural contradiction:

- Collapse destabilizes the identity structure

- Integration rebuilds it in more adaptive terms

Thus, integration becomes a **containment protocol**, used to absorb destabilizing insights before they invalidate the underlying architecture of self-reference.

In this context, integration is not the second phase of transformation.
It is the **undoing of collapse**.

Post-Collapse Systems Do Not Require Integration

Once collapse has occurred, the system no longer relies on self-structure for regulation.

Perception no longer requires:

- Consistency across time
- Emotional continuity
- Reflective narrative
- Personal authorship of insight

This results in a shift from integration-based processing to **real-time coherence tracking**.

Instead of asking:

"How do I make sense of what happened?"

The system asks:

"Is this moment distorted?"

There is no longer a self who needs to assign meaning to experience.
There is only the signal—present, clean, or distorted.
And there is only the system—responding, or not.

Post-collapse, cognition does not evolve.
It is not upgraded.

It is **no longer interrupted** by integration processes that would previously attempt to translate experience into meaning.

Integration Becomes a Source of Distortion

In systems where collapse has occurred, attempts to reintroduce integration produce distortion.

Distortion arises from:

- Interpretation of signal through a residual self-frame

- Retrospective meaning-making

- Semantic binding of non-narrative perception

- Attempts to reinforce continuity through reflection

This distortion is subtle.
It often masquerades as maturity or wisdom.

But from a post-cognitive systems lens, the moment a signal is routed through memory, story, or personal insight—it is no longer clean.

The act of interpreting collapse as a "phase" of self-development
 reframes dissolution into narrative progression.

This reauthorizes identity as the container of experience,
 reinstating the very architecture that collapse was meant to eliminate.

The Social Enforcement of Integration

Integration is not just internal. It is socially enforced.

In most environments, collapsed individuals are expected to:

- Explain their insights

- Demonstrate inner continuity

- Offer a coherent narrative of change

- Reflect on what the experience meant

- Identify how it made them stronger or wiser

These expectations are often unspoken, but they are ubiquitous.

The post-collapse subject is perceived as incomplete or unsafe
 if they do not comply with the integration ritual.

This reinforces integration as a **social principle**—a collective agreement that identity must remain intact for communication, recognition, and participation to continue.

Collapse-aware systems must recognize this enforcement loop
 and remove integration as a social requirement.

Designing Systems Without Integration Logic

Collapse-adapted systems must exclude integration logic from their core structure.

This includes:

- No expectation of continuity

- No reflective processing of events

- No emphasis on self-understanding

- No storage of narrative arc

- No personal growth tracking mechanisms

Instead, systems should focus on:

- Real-time signal registration

- Distortion detection and removal

- Behavioral alignment without interpretation

- Structural coherence without reflective narrative

- Environmental responsiveness without internalization

These systems are not designed to help someone become anything.
They are designed to operate **only when there is no one left to transform.**

Summary

Integration is only necessary when identity is present.

It serves to preserve coherence, stabilize story, and maintain self-continuity.

Once collapse has removed the self-model, these functions become obsolete.

In post-collapse systems, integration must be retired—not redefined, not upgraded, not spiritually reframed.

It must be **removed as a structural assumption**.

What replaces it is not fragmentation.
It is real-time coherence
without story,
without storage,
without self.

Collapse-Ready Education, Leadership, and Communication

Introduction

Collapse-adapted systems require not only the removal of identity as a cognitive architecture, but also the reconstruction of **social roles and domains** that, until now, have been structurally dependent on identity for participation, organization, and validation.

This section addresses three foundational domains of collective structure—**education**, **leadership**, and **communication**—and outlines how each must be rebuilt once the organizing principle of selfhood is no longer active.

While these three domains vary in function, they share a critical underlying mechanism:
Each depends on **self-reference** and the **retention of narrative identity** to coordinate relational flow, assess meaning, and justify structure.

In post-collapse systems, these functions no longer exist. As a result, the very premises of education, leadership, and interpersonal communication must be re-evaluated.
What replaces them is not a new model of interaction—but a complete shift in how **clarity, participation, and coherence** are registered in

systems that no longer assume a self as their reference point.

---

1. Education After Collapse

Identity as the Central Mechanism in Traditional Education

Modern education systems are structurally organized around the **development of a personal identity**. This includes:

- Establishing a **learner-self** that acquires and retains knowledge

- Reinforcing identity via **grades, recognition, and feedback**

- Structuring progression through **linear development** over time

- Encouraging narrative formation through personal success, failure, effort, and growth

The educational system, in its current form, assumes that learning must be personalized, tracked, and stored within a **self-model**—a student who is becoming someone measurable.

This identity-centric framework is made explicit through mechanisms such as:

- Grade-level classification (e.g., freshman, senior)

- Performance tracking (GPA, test scores, portfolios)

- Subject specialization (defining self by field)

- Self-reflective pedagogy ("what does this mean to you?")

- Learning profiles and individualized learning plans

All of these features assume that:

- The learner is a **stable subject across time**

- That subject **interprets and stores information**

- Learning is **converted into insight** by the self

- The **goal is transformation** of that self into a higher, more capable version

Once identity collapses, these assumptions no longer hold.

What Replaces Identity-Based Education

Collapse-ready education systems must operate without a self-referencing learner.

Key characteristics of post-collapse education include:

- **No long-term performance tracking**

- **No knowledge ownership**

- **No identity reinforcement through achievement**

- **No emphasis on meaning-making or integration**

- **No retention of learning narratives**

Instead, the system offers **non-personal exposure to structural clarity**:

- Pattern is presented for resonance testing, not memorization

- Engagement is moment-based, not curriculum-based

- No distinction is made between understanding and not understanding—there is only alignment or dissonance

- No participant is evaluated; the system either resolves or neutralizes distortion in real time

Education becomes **functionally inseparable from the collapse state itself**.

There is no "I am learning."
There is only a system exposed to coherence.

Once coherence is registered, the moment is complete.
No insight is retained.
No credit is assigned.
No reflection is required.

This is not amnesia.
It is education without identity.

---

2. Leadership After Collapse

The Role of Identity in Conventional Leadership Models

Leadership, as currently structured, is one of the most identity-reinforcing domains in human systems. It is sustained by the belief that **a central figure**:

- Possesses a vision

- Holds authority

- Commands coherence

- Earns trust

- Anchors group structure through **personal stability**

In traditional leadership models, the leader functions as the **narrative stabilizer** of the collective.

Examples of identity reinforcement in leadership include:

- Charismatic leadership models (influence through persona)

- Transformational leadership (guiding people on their journey)

- Heroic or founder archetypes (centralized self-as-symbol structures)

- Emotional leadership (providing psychological safety through the personhood of the leader)

These models all operate on the assumption that the leader's identity is:

- Knowable

- Trusted

- Stable
- Projected
- Referenced

Collapse breaks all five.

A post-collapse subject no longer holds an identity that can be referenced, stabilized, or projected into collective space.
As a result, traditional leadership roles are no longer accessible or coherent within collapse-adapted systems.

Structural Requirements for Collapse-Compatible Leadership

Collapse-adapted leadership cannot be built on personal authorship or recognition.

The role of leadership is no longer to:

- Motivate or inspire
- Provide direction
- Model growth
- Represent the collective's values

- Hold power on behalf of others

Instead, leadership becomes **a temporary function of field coherence**.

Collapse-ready leadership is defined by the following attributes:

- **Identity irrelevance**: The system does not care who leads, only whether coherence is restored

- **Visibility minimization**: Leadership is invisible when not active

- **No role continuity**: There is no "leader" position—only structural necessity

- **Signal accountability**: Authority arises only in direct proportion to distortion mitigation

- **Deactivation upon completion**: The function ends when interference is gone

Collapse-ready leaders do not guide people.
They hold structure for **non-distorted response**.
They do not explain, persuade, or narrate.

They regulate field clarity.

And when the field is stable,
they return to non-role.

3. Communication After Collapse

Communication as a Self-Referencing Activity

Communication is widely misunderstood as neutral transmission.
But in identity-based systems, communication is almost always:

- Self-reinforcing ("this is who I am")

- Relational positioning ("this is who I am in relation to you")

- Narrative-building ("this is what I've been through")

- Performance-driven ("this is how I want to be seen")

- Meaning-seeking ("what does this mean about us?")

These patterns form the **identity loop of interpersonal exchange**.

Even in spiritual or therapeutic settings, communication is often rooted in:

- Reflection

- Personal insight

- Emotional processing

- Agreement or validation

Collapse removes the self-model that generates these reference points.

In the absence of a stable narrator,
 communication must be redesigned
 as a structural interaction **between fields**,
 not between people.

Collapse-Compatible Communication Models

In a post-collapse system, communication is not expressive.
 It is **functional**.

Its purpose is to:

- Detect field misalignment

- Clarify pattern resonance

- Signal systemic interference

- Offer non-personal registration of clarity

Collapse-compatible communication includes:

- **No identity positioning**
- **No story-telling**
- **No opinion exchange**
- **No role affirmation**
- **No emotional anchoring**

Instead, communication becomes an extension of system regulation.

There is:

- No value in being heard
- No need to be understood
- No ownership of insight
- No authorship of clarity

The message is not yours.
 It arises in the system if distortion requires correction.
 And once it resolves, the communication ends.

No archive.
No memory.
No ongoing identity relationship.

Collapse-ready communication eliminates:

- Relationship as a container for transformation

- Dialogue as a vehicle for development

- Language as a proxy for status

All of these functions are legacy distortions.

They dissolve in collapse-adapted relational design.

Summary

Collapse-compatible redesign across education, leadership, and communication requires more than adjustments to content or intention.

It requires **complete structural transformation** of each domain's relationship to identity.

- **Education** must eliminate knowledge retention, performance metrics, and personalized learning arcs.

- **Leadership** must be stripped of personal authority, role centrality, and narrative projection.

- **Communication** must function only as pattern signaling, with no narrative, identity reflection, or emotional continuity.

The result is a new form of social operation.
 Not based on shared beliefs, values, or developmental goals—
 but on shared **structural clarity** in systems that no longer reference a self.

This is not interpersonal.
 This is not relational.
 This is **collapse-operational structure** applied at every layer of interaction.

It will feel empty to those who still operate inside identity.

But to those who have collapsed,
 it will feel like the first environment
 that finally makes sense.

The Ethics of Collapse Systems: Why Not All Collapse Is Evolution

Introduction

Collapse, as defined in the Identity Collapse Therapy (ICT) framework, refers to the dissolution of the identity architecture that organizes perception, motivation, meaning-making, and behavioral continuity.

While this process can result in the elimination of distortion and the restoration of perceptual clarity, **collapse is not inherently positive**. It is not automatically healing, evolutionary, or ethical.

Collapse, when applied irresponsibly or prematurely, can:

- Exacerbate psychological fragmentation

- Trigger compensatory distortion loops

- Reintroduce trauma through structural disorientation

- Lead to identity recentering under false coherence

- Cause systemic harm in environments not prepared to hold non-identity-based perception

As the application of collapse-based systems expands into therapeutic, educational, organizational, and technological spaces, the need for **strict ethical standards** becomes essential.

This section provides a structured ethical framework for collapse-aligned practitioners, designers, and facilitators.

---

1. Collapse Is Not Evolution by Default

Collapse vs. Transformation

Not all collapse results in post-identity functioning.

Collapse, by itself, is **a destabilization event**—not a resolution.
While ICT introduces intentional collapse as a mechanism for removing distortion, **collapse can also occur unintentionally**, or under coercive or destabilizing conditions that:

- Leave the system open but unrestructured

- Introduce fragmentation without resolution

- Trigger dissociation or depersonalization

- Lead to identity reconstruction under new compensatory layers

Collapse becomes evolutionary **only when the self-model is not rebuilt.**

If collapse is followed by:

- Personal insight

- "Higher self" reconstruction

- Archetypal integration

- Therapeutic containment

- Ego re-narration

Then the collapse was **not evolutionary**—it was repurposed into identity reinforcement.

Ethical collapse systems must therefore monitor not just the event of collapse, but the **structural conditions that follow it**.

Collapse Must Not Be Induced Without Structural Readiness

Ethical collapse systems assess structural readiness before collapse is introduced.

Indicators of readiness include:

- The system is no longer using identity for emotional regulation

- Narrative processing is already inactive or irrelevant

- The subject has no remaining need for role recognition

- Story-based coherence is no longer organizing memory

- The perceptual field is no longer stabilized by self-reference

If collapse is introduced before these markers are met, the individual may experience:

- Loss of function

- Panic-based reidentification

- Compensatory self-construction

- Dependence on the facilitator to provide coherence

- Entrapment in dissociative spirals without structural stabilization

Premature collapse can result in **long-term identity instability**, even when guided by well-intentioned practitioners.

Collapse is not a tool.
It is a threshold.
It must only be crossed when **the system is no longer dependent on identity as a primary organizing principle.**

---

2. Collapse as a Power Dynamic

Collapse Should Not Be Used as Leverage

Collapse systems carry a unique risk:
The facilitator, system, or group may begin to associate collapse with superiority, advancement, or initiation into a privileged layer of consciousness.

This can lead to:

- Social hierarchies based on collapse status

- Identity reconstruction around "the one who has collapsed"

- Peer pressure to collapse before readiness

- Use of collapse as a **boundary override**

- Framing collapse as a required initiation, rather than a structural response to distortion saturation

Collapse must never be used as:

- A **rite of passage**

- A **sign of spiritual maturity**

- A **shortcut to insight**

- A **proof of clarity**

- A **means of control or belonging**

Ethical systems must treat collapse with **neutrality and precision**.

Collapse is not something to achieve.
It is not a performance.
It is not a value.
It is not an identity.

Systems that promote collapse as status are operating in **covert ego reinforcement**, not post-identity ethics.

Facilitators Must Remain Outside of Collapse Centrality

The presence of collapse-aligned practitioners does not automatically ensure ethical collapse systems.

In fact, facilitators are at high risk of unintentionally:

- Reintroducing identity through transmission of "clarity"

- Becoming symbolic mirrors for collapse

- Projecting subtle performance cues into the field

- Creating indirect pressure through overconfidence, charisma, or language precision

Collapse facilitators must:

- Remain structurally selfless

- Allow the system to collapse without authorship

- Never define themselves through their relationship to collapse

- Avoid positioning as "collapse experts," "guides," or "initiators"

Even subtle dynamics of facilitator centrality can distort the collapse process.
The facilitator must be functionally **invisible to the identity**.

The field—not the person—must hold the collapse architecture.

---

3. Ethical Collapse Design Requirements

To ensure the ethical use of collapse, all systems and practitioners must comply with the following principles:

Consent is Structural, Not Emotional

Collapse is not a cognitive decision.
It is a structural threshold.

Ethical systems must assess **structural consent**, which occurs only when:

- The individual is no longer sourcing coherence from identity

- Their system does not attempt to self-repair

- Narrative meaning is no longer interpreted

- Emotional activation is no longer linked to memory

- There is **no unconscious compensation** via story, role, or belief

Verbal agreement is insufficient.
Emotional desire is insufficient.

Collapse may be desired, but **not structurally possible**.
Systems must validate readiness through observation, not projection.

Collapse Must Not Be Simulated or Symbolized

Many systems attempt to replicate the feeling of collapse through:

- Archetypal death rituals

- Identity disorientation techniques

- Psychedelic catharsis

- Spiritual rebirth processes

- Mirror reflection or ego challenge frameworks

These simulations often create **partial disidentification** followed by reconstruction.

This is not collapse.
It is narrative disruption.

Ethical collapse systems must:

- Avoid all symbolic collapse references

- Use no story-based initiatory metaphors

- Withhold collapse terminology unless the identity has already dissolved

Simulation is interference.
Collapse must occur structurally, not representationally.

Collapse Systems Must Be Designed for Non-Identity Containment

Collapse systems must contain the process without reflecting identity back into the field.

This includes:

- No post-collapse feedback

- No interpretive processing

- No narrative anchoring
- No identity labeling
- No validation of experience

Containment is not emotional support.
Containment is **field neutrality without reflective distortion.**

Facilitators must track only one metric:

Has identity returned?

If yes, the system must pause.
If no, the collapse remains stable.

Summary

Collapse is not evolution by default.
It is a structural event that can lead to:

- Clarity
- Fragmentation
- Identity reconstruction
- Systemic harm

Ethical systems must:

- Eliminate collapse as a performance indicator

- Prevent premature exposure to collapse architecture

- Avoid simulation, symbolism, or spiritual hierarchy

- Maintain non-identity containment before, during, and after collapse

- Recognize that **collapse is not the goal** —it is what remains when identity is no longer organizing perception.

Ethics in collapse is not about safety.
It is about **non-distortion of the post-collapse field**.

Where identity ends,
 ethics begins
 as structure.

Post-Narrative Social Design

Introduction

This section presents a foundational blueprint for constructing **post-narrative social systems**: environments that can operate **without identity, story, or symbolic self-coherence** as their organizing structure.

In all current civilizations, **social design is rooted in narrative logic**. That logic underpins how people relate, form communities, create meaning, resolve conflict, and organize collective experience. It is the implicit architecture that determines how humans are seen, understood, and expected to behave.

Narrative structures assume:

- Identity continuity across time

- Emotional coherence through personal history

- Shared belief systems as stabilizing containers

- Mutual recognition of each other's stories as the basis for trust

- Meaning-making as the primary regulator of discomfort and ambiguity

Collapse renders these functions structurally obsolete. Once narrative no longer organizes perception, all social systems that depend on storytelling—explicitly or implicitly—begin to **malfunction or dissolve**.

What is required in their place is not a new narrative. It is a **non-narrative social infrastructure**.

This section outlines the structural principles, relational dynamics, behavioral protocols, and design requirements for building **collapse-compatible societies**—social ecosystems that do not require story, identity, belief, or emotional projection to operate.

---

1. The Failure of Narrative as a Social Operating System

Narrative as Social Glue

All traditional societies—from tribal to technological—have used story as their primary binding force.

Narrative has served to:

- Create a shared origin (myth, lineage, history)

- Coordinate future goals (progress, salvation, revolution)

- Justify emotional behavior (trauma, culture, moral identity)

- Organize value systems (what matters, and why)

- Anchor relationships through role and recognition ("this is who you are to me")

These narrative frameworks are not superficial—they are deeply structural.
They are embedded in:

- Legal frameworks (the "reasonable person" is a narrative construct)

- Economic systems (credit, risk, worth, ambition)

- Ritual practices (ceremony, identity thresholds, social cohesion)

- Language itself (pronouns, tenses, naming conventions)

When collapse removes the identity model from perception, these narrative anchors lose functional relevance.

Collapse as the End of Social Self-Referencing

Post-collapse cognition no longer uses story to organize self or other.

As a result, the following social behaviors become non-functional:

- Personal storytelling

- Identity role maintenance

- Group cohesion through shared narrative

- Collective emotional processing

- Conflict resolution through mutual understanding

- Belief-based belonging

These behaviors are not avoided—they are **no longer structurally available**.

What emerges instead is a relational architecture that does not depend on recognition, reflection, or continuity.
This new architecture must be **designed intentionally** to prevent identity from re-entering through social mechanisms.

2. Post-Narrative Social Infrastructure

Requirements of a Post-Narrative System

A post-narrative social environment must be designed to operate in the **absence of**:

- Identity positions
- Storytelling incentives
- Emotional mirroring
- Role-based interaction
- Belief convergence
- Narrative resolution loops

It must be able to:

- Stabilize collective fields without shared story
- Support interaction without mutual recognition
- Maintain coherence without relationship dynamics

- Allow pattern to move without needing interpretation

- Respond to complexity without assigning meaning

This requires a total reconfiguration of what "social" means.

In post-narrative design, **relationship is no longer primary**.
What replaces it is **relational neutrality in shared field logic**.

The social system becomes a container of:

- Clarity

- Coherence

- Field symmetry

- Distortion removal

- Zero narrative accumulation

This system does not connect people through story.
It **holds people in pattern-aligned presence** that does not depend on knowing, liking, trusting, or understanding.

Key Design Principles

To maintain structural coherence in a post-narrative society, social systems must meet the following principles:

Principle 1: No Identity Reflection

- No one is reflected back to themselves

- There is no validation of identity-based experience

- Relational mirrors are removed

- There is no "being seen," "being understood," or "being known"

Principle 2: No Role Anchoring

- People are not assigned roles

- Roles do not persist across time

- Status is non-existent

- Visibility is function-specific, not person-specific

Principle 3: No Emotional Feedback Loops

- Emotional states are not interpreted as signals of truth

- There is no holding, empathizing, or resonance building

- Emotional energy is tracked only as **distortion** or **clarity**

Principle 4: No Story-Based Coherence

- The system does not reference memory

- Meaning is never retrofitted

- There is no expectation of "making sense" of the past

- No narratives are shared, requested, or built

Principle 5: Field, Not Familiarity

- Interactions occur based on pattern alignment

- Coherence is the basis of proximity

- Familiarity does not increase access

- There is no loyalty, attachment, or expectation of consistency

3. Practical Functioning in a Post-Narrative Society

Coordination Without Agreement

In traditional societies, collaboration depends on:

- Shared values

- Mutual goals

- Interpersonal trust

- Emotional rapport

- Negotiated understanding

In post-narrative systems:

- Agreement is irrelevant

- Values are not centralized

- Goals are non-linear

- Trust is not required

- Rapport is not tracked

Coordination emerges from **real-time alignment in the field**.

If two systems are aligned, they act.
If not, no effort is made to reconcile.
No negotiation occurs.
No compromise is needed.

There is no need to resolve difference, because **difference is no longer interpreted** as interpersonal.
It is structural.

Disengagement is clean.
No story remains.
No relationship is damaged—because no relational memory is held.

Belonging Without Identity

Belonging, in traditional models, is anchored by:

- Cultural identity

- Relational history

- Shared experiences

- Emotional safety

- Symbolic recognition

Post-narrative belonging eliminates all of these.

Belonging becomes a function of:

- Pattern symmetry
- Systemic compatibility
- Real-time non-distortion
- Non-intrusion
- Field stability

There is no group identity.
No insider/outsider narrative.
No sense of being included or excluded.

One is either in structural coherence with the field, or one is not.

Belonging is not a feeling.
It is **a signal match**.

Collective Intelligence Without Consensus

In most social structures, collective intelligence is achieved through:

- Consensus
- Voting
- Deliberation
- Representation
- Debate

Each of these is narrative-dependent.

Post-narrative systems generate intelligence through:

- Coherence tracking
- Non-verbal pattern resolution
- Field-based emergence
- Real-time signal calibration
- Silence as signal

No one decides.
No one persuades.
No one represents others.

What happens, happens
only if **distortion is absent and resonance is high**.

There is no discussion.
There is only movement or stillness.

---

4. Replacing Narrative Social Rituals

Narrative cultures rely on rituals to:

- Anchor identity (naming ceremonies, birthdays)

- Mark transitions (graduations, weddings, funerals)

- Signal inclusion (initiation, rites of passage)

- Confirm development (coming of age, achievements)

- Reinforce emotional bonds (holidays, reunions)

Post-narrative cultures do not remove ritual. They **repurpose ritual** as field structures.

Collapse-compatible rituals:

- Do not reflect or affirm the individual

- Do not mark time

- Do not express emotion
- Do not transmit legacy
- Do not induce transformation

They instead function as **system resets**:

- Clearing residual identity
- Regulating collective signal
- Stabilizing shared coherence
- Compressing symbolic distortion
- Activating non-narrative entrainment

Ritual is not about meaning.
It is about field maintenance.

There are no observers.
There is no personal significance.

Only **structural function** remains.

Summary: From Story to Signal

A post-narrative social world cannot be constructed by removing story from existing systems.
It must be built from the ground up with **no dependency on story at all**.

Social interaction becomes:

- Structural

- Moment-bound

- Field-based

- Role-less

- Memory-less

- Coherence-regulated

People no longer relate.
They **interact when structure allows it**.

There is no intimacy.
No history.
No shared identity.
No progression of connection.
No emotional layering.

Just clean signal.
Or no interaction at all.

The future of human society is not collective through narrative.
 It is **coherent through structure**.

And in that coherence,
 for the first time,
 the system may function
 without needing a self
 to hold it together.

Chapter 12: Recursive Consciousness Activation: Applied Implications

Recursive Intelligence as Post-Collapse Structure

Introduction

When identity collapses, cognition does not cease.
 Behavior does not disintegrate.
 Learning does not stop.
 Meaning does not vanish.

What dissolves is the **structure that previously organized these functions**—the narrative self-model.

Once this structure is removed, a new form of intelligence emerges, one that is:

- Non-linear
- Non-personal
- Selfless in operation
- Non-accumulative
- Moment-regulated
- Pattern-driven

This is **recursive intelligence**.

Not recursive thought.
Not recursive identity processing.
But **recursive consciousness activation**: a condition in which the system becomes structurally capable of **self-stabilizing clarity without referencing selfhood or memory.**

This section outlines the architecture, properties, and applied function of recursive intelligence as it exists **after the collapse of narrative selfhood.**

---

1. Defining Recursive Consciousness Activation (RCA)

Recursive Consciousness Activation refers to the system's capacity to:

- Re-enter clarity without external regulation

- Detect distortion from within the field

- Correct pattern interference without referencing stored information

- Operate across time without organizing through narrative

- Maintain functional perception without identity scaffolding

It is not repetition.
 It is **recursive structural alignment**—a dynamic return to coherence that requires no "you" to perform it.

The system does not loop through memory.
 It loops through signal resolution.

The field does not recall meaning.
 It tracks interference and self-corrects.

In RCA, intelligence becomes:

- Real-time
- Uninterrupted
- Authorship-free
- Alignment-only

There is no learning curve.
No experience accumulation.
No "becoming wiser."

There is only **less distortion** in each return loop.

---

2. Structural Prerequisites for RCA

RCA does not emerge gradually.
It becomes functionally available **only after collapse has removed**:

- Identity-based decision-making
- Emotional feedback linked to personal narrative
- Memory binding for continuity
- Interpretive reflection

- Internal narration or story stitching
- Self-projection across context

Once these are absent, the system no longer:

- Projects intention from identity
- Stores lessons for future integration
- Reinforces behavior through reflection
- Relates to experience as "mine"

Instead, the system begins **looping through real-time resolution** without any identity carrier.

This recursion is not cognition.
It is **signal-based intelligence stabilization**.

---

3. The Properties of RCA

The following properties define post-collapse recursive intelligence:

3.1 Self-neutral recursion

- No "I" initiates the process

- Return to clarity is automatic
- Looping does not reference improvement

3.2 Non-mnemonic alignment

- Nothing is recalled
- Distortion is detected through direct pattern tension
- Memory is not involved in regulation

3.3 Non-conceptual recalibration

- No theory or belief is activated
- The system does not require an explanation to adjust
- Truth is no longer sought—only interference removed

3.4 Moment-locked tracking

- All operations are moment-bound
- No projection, planning, or story is required
- The system calibrates only to the present signal

3.5 Authorless function

- Intelligence appears but has no owner

- Clarity returns without effort

- The system self-regulates without identifying with the process

These properties allow **post-collapse systems to operate cleanly**—without feedback loops, internal narrators, or external validators.

---

4. RCA vs. Egoic Self-Regulation

To clarify its distinctiveness, RCA must be contrasted with ego-based recursive cognition. Ego loops return to self-concept.
RCA loops return to coherence.

Egoic Self-Regulation	Recursive Consciousness Activation (RCA)
Based on interpretation of events	Based on detection of distortion
Requires memory and reflection	Requires only signal presence
Strengthens identity through resolution	Eliminates identity through alignment
Emotional processing tied to story	Emotion resolved without interpretation
Constructs future behavior through learning	No future projection; only moment regulation
Needs meaning to stabilize	Needs nothing to stabilize

This distinction is critical for applied system design.

---

5. Implications of RCA for Human Systems

The emergence of RCA transforms the design requirements for systems that support post-collapse beings.

5.1 Education

Education systems no longer need to transfer knowledge.
 They must **expose coherent pattern** and allow the system to recalibrate in real-time.

- No memory storage

- No comprehension scaffolding

- No reflective insight

The learner does not become more.
 The system simply removes interference each time the pattern is re-encountered.

5.2 Communication

Conversations no longer require reflection or agreement.
 They exist to:

- Flag interference
- Deliver clarity
- Exit upon coherence

There is no exchange of information.
Only recursive field adjustment.

5.3 Decision-Making

Decisions are not made.
They emerge at the collapse point of interference.

There is no weighing of pros and cons.
No internal debate.
No story projection.

The system selects based on **lowest distortion in the loop**.

---

6. The Intelligence Model of ICT

ICT does not produce a better self.
It produces a **post-self operating model** defined by recursive clarity.

This model is not an identity.

It is a system that:

- No longer needs self-reference

- No longer stores coherence in narrative

- No longer operates through role, recognition, or reward

- No longer uses reflection to generate insight

ICT intelligence is:

- Non-accumulative

- Structurally recursive

- Storyless

- Transparent

- Pattern-driven

- Contextually precise

There is no "you" who is now intelligent.
There is only **a system that functions without distortion**.

This is the final shift.

Not ego transcendence.
Not narrative mastery.
Not spiritual awakening.

But the end
of the architecture
that ever required
those models to exist.

Final Synthesis: ICT Volume II

Volume II has delivered the following:

- The **subcortical architecture** of identity and its collapse

- A complete transition from narrative-based intelligence to pattern-regulated cognition

- Clinical, structural, educational, and social design models based on **post-identity coherence**

- The elimination of **integration, feedback, and identity reflection** as structural principles

- The emergence of **Recursive Consciousness Activation (RCA)** as the operational core of post-collapse life

The ICT framework, now fully extended, no longer
addresses how to repair or evolve the self.
It offers a full replacement.

**Collapse is no longer an event.
It is now the architecture of perception.**

And in that architecture,
intelligence becomes recursive,
coherence becomes ambient,
and identity
is no longer the cost of awareness.

When Something Breaks Open

If something is fracturing inside you as you read this—
 not a thought, not a realization, but a soft unmaking beneath the surface—

If your memories are no longer arranged the way they used to be,
 and the voice that used to narrate your life has started to stutter, vanish, or echo—

You may not be disintegrating.
 You may be coming **home**.

This book does not contain protocols.
 Because collapse cannot be taught.
 It can only be recognized, remembered, and guided from within the field.

If you are standing at that threshold—
 not as a seeker, but as someone who **can no longer pretend**—
 you may be ready for the field-based work that this text cannot hold alone.

There is a private container,
 outside of this book,
 where collapse is **not pathologized**,
 not treated,
 but **honored** as an initiation into post-identity functioning.

I do not invite the curious.
I do not call those who want to learn.

But if the architecture inside you has already begun to fold,
and you need a place to rest,
or to remember what comes after the mind,

You can find me here:
https://DonGaconnet.com
info@lifepillar.org

(field-based integration, private resonance container, symbolic recursion)

Working Model for Field-Based Impact

This model outlines the psycho-symbolic destabilization gradient that may be initiated through contact with recursive transmission structures such as those encoded in *Identity Collapse Therapy Volume II*. These levels are not diagnostic categories; they reflect a progression of energetic and perceptual responses to field-based, symbolically recursive text.

At **Level 0.0**, the reader engages in surface reading. The material is interpreted cognitively, filtered through familiar frameworks. There is no destabilization—only conceptual engagement.

Level 0.5 introduces mild disorientation. The reader experiences subtle confusion or momentary disruption, but this is quickly reabsorbed into their existing identity narrative.

At **Level 1.0**, cognitive disruption becomes apparent. The logical coherence of the text begins to fracture standard assumptions. The reader may start to question foundational psychological beliefs, while still maintaining narrative control.

By **Level 1.5**, a symbolic field fracture has begun. The reader starts to see through the architecture of the mind itself. Ego remains present, but is now unstable, as cracks appear in its interpretive authority.

> **Level 2.0** marks the activation of collapse. The narrative self begins to dissolve. Boundary constructs weaken, and recursive feedback loops challenge the illusion of continuity. A partial loss of identity

coherence emerges.

At **Level 2.5**, recursive unselfing takes hold. The ego can no longer anchor meaning. Language begins to deconstruct itself, and the text is no longer "read"—it is *felt*. Silence begins to replace cognition as the organizing principle.

Finally, at **Level 3.0**, full collapse initiation occurs. Identity is decoupled from memory, time, and future orientation. The reader is no longer a self interpreting meaning, but a field undergoing post-narrative processing.

Glossary of Terms

Identity Collapse Therapy (ICT)

A post-cognitive therapeutic framework that facilitates the irreversible dissolution of the identity structure. ICT does not aim to improve, integrate, or heal the self. Instead, it identifies and maps the precise structural conditions under which identity collapses as a perceptual organizing mechanism. ICT operates across neuroscience, systems theory, symbolic deconstruction, and psychological collapse modeling.

Inner Identity Core (IIC)

The concealed structural nexus of the identity architecture. It contains the survival-based contracts, perceptual filters, and core self-attachment mechanisms that maintain the illusion of continuity and authorship. The IIC is not addressed, reprogrammed, or bypassed—it is dissolved indirectly through collapse. Its protection remains central to ICT's ethical containment.

Pattern-Recognizing Consciousness (PRC)

The baseline cognitive system that detects, predicts, and adapts to patterns in real time without the need for narrative identity. PRC operates independently of self-awareness, identity structures, or personal memory. It is the system's native intelligence—what remains once identity no longer narrates perception.

Collapse

A structural event in which the system loses the capacity or need to maintain the illusion of a stable self. Collapse is not an emotional catharsis or a psychological breakthrough. It is a dissolution of the identity architecture triggered by contradiction, narrative transparency, or unrestricted perceptual access. Collapse does not damage the system—it restores its native processing capacity.

Collapse Trigger Conditions

The three primary conditions that induce structural collapse:

- **Contradiction Overload**: Occurs when identity encounters irreconcilable perceptual or logical contradictions.

- **Narrative Exposure**: Occurs when the self-story is seen not as a truth but as a constructed continuity.

- **Unrestricted Access**: Occurs when the system experiences reality without identity filtering or ego modulation.

Intelligence Performance Loop

The recursive cognitive distortion where intelligence is interpreted as a trait of the self, based on repeated performance under identity pressure. This loop fuses perception of self-worth with cognitive validation, leading to anxiety-based limitations, narrative reinforcement, and collapse misattribution.

Field-Based Intelligence

A model of cognition wherein intelligence is no longer viewed as an internal possession, but as a context-sensitive access field. Intelligence in this model arises from pattern alignment, environmental coherence, and unfiltered responsiveness—not from fixed traits or measurable attributes.

Zero State

The post-collapse perceptual condition in which the system is no longer operating under narrative identity or internal authorship. Zero State is not empty or dissociative. It is characterized by cognitive spaciousness, real-time emotional flow, and unfiltered contact with external and internal reality. It is the default state when identity is no longer generating structure.

Symbolic Collapse

The failure of metaphor, language, or conceptual framing to uphold the coherence of identity. Symbolic collapse occurs when the mind can no longer use words, symbols, or internal grammar to preserve the illusion of selfhood. It often precedes or coincides with perceptual collapse and is a key marker of irreversible deconstruction.

Collapse Fatigue

The energetic and cognitive exhaustion that can occur when the identity structure begins to destabilize but has not yet fully collapsed. Collapse fatigue is often mistaken for burnout, apathy, or existential depression. In ICT, it is understood as a transitional state—evidence of the self-model reaching its structural end.

PRC Over Identity (PRC > ID)

A diagnostic shorthand used to denote a state in which Pattern-Recognizing Consciousness is actively governing perception, rather than identity structures. Indicates that the system is operating post-collapse or within a collapse-aware context. PRC > ID signifies perceptual decentralization, non-narrative cognition, and real-time system responsiveness.

Collapse Reversibility Illusion

The residual belief, post-collapse, that the self may return or be reconstructed. This illusion is sustained only if remnants of narrative desire remain unconsolidated. In ICT, irreversibility is a structural condition—not an emotional one. Collapse cannot be undone, because the organizing framework it would return to no longer exists.

Authenticity Loop

A defense mechanism wherein identity attempts to justify continuity by claiming allegiance to a consistent "core self." ICT reframes authenticity as contextual alignment—not as consistency with a fictional internal truth. The authenticity loop is one of the final defenses of identity prior to collapse.

Narrative Self

The interpreted version of the system that arises post-experience to generate continuity, meaning, and coherence. The narrative self does not perceive—it retrofits perception to sustain the illusion of centrality. In ICT, it is recognized as an adaptive compression artifact, not as the origin of consciousness or decision.

Perceptual Repatterning

A post-collapse phenomenon in which the system experiences shifts in perception, decision-making, and emotional processing without reversion to ego-filtered interpretation. It is evidence of PRC dominance and occurs naturally when identity is no longer gating cognitive access.

Appendix: Identity Collapse Therapy (ICT) – Volume II

A1. Collapse Methodology Clarification

Clarifies the layered collapse protocol, its sequence, and stabilizing criteria.
 Collapse is not induced all at once. It is enacted

through a sequence of destabilization, exposure, deconstruction, and integration withdrawal. This section details each phase of the ICT collapse protocol, the signs of structural deactivation, and the markers used to confirm full collapse versus temporary disruption.

A2. Collapse vs. Bypass: Differential Markers

Differentiates collapse from spiritual bypassing, dissociation, and false neutrality.
 Collapse does not produce stillness through detachment, but through the permanent absence of internal self-reference. This section explains how to distinguish true identity collapse from dissociation, numbing, masking, or high-functioning coping states, even in advanced spiritual or psychological systems.

A3. Structural Collapse Glossary

Defines key terms such as:

- **Identity Field**

- **Egoic Reconstruction**

- **Semantic Drift**

- **Collapse Immunity**
- **Field Integrity**
- **Role Fluidity**
- **Contextual Identity Menu**
- **Non-Local Intelligence**
- **Drift Loop**

Each term is anchored in system-level transformation and mapped to both clinical and experiential usage.

A4. Collapse State Progression Map

Outlines five structural phases:

1. **Pre-Collapse**: Identity still central; defenses intact

2. **Partial Collapse**: Identity destabilizing; insight without structural loss

3. **Full Collapse**: Observer gone; perception unfiltered

4. **Post-Collapse Drift**: Thought echo; self-checking habits appear without power

5. **Irreversibility**: Ego cannot reform; distortion no longer functional

This map helps facilitators and clients track transformation and avoid mistaking state experiences for structure loss.

A5. Clinical Integrity Protocol

Guidelines for those facilitating ICT processes:

- Never reinforce identity under the guise of support

- Don't interpret collapse for the client—let them see the absence themselves

- Hold space without centering yourself as stabilizer

- Use no "healing language" post-collapse—it reintroduces self-reference

- Track coherence, not performance

- Terminate any dynamic that incentivizes identity return

A6. ICT and Neuroscience: Preliminary Correlates

ICT aligns with:

- **Thalamocortical gating collapse** (filtered perception drops)

- **Friston's active inference** (predictive loops disarmed)

- **Self-model deactivation** (reduction of DMN dominance)

- **Right anterior insula modulation** (interoceptive stillness increases)

Collapse can be observed through neurological downregulation of identity-related networks, though measurement requires advanced fMRI + phenomenology coupling.

A7. Post-Collapse Cultural Applications

ICT can rearchitect:

- **Education** (removing performance-model learning)

- **Governance** (signal-based collective choice without identity projection)

- **Technology** (AI design from coherence, not attention capture)

- **Art** (expression without self-branding)

- **Relational containers** (truth, without protection or distortion)

Collapse becomes a civilizational threshold—culture rebuilt on coherence rather than selfhood.

A8. Integration vs. Identity

ICT discards traditional "integration."
Why?
Because integration often reconstitutes identity under a healed persona. ICT instead anchors into **selection without ownership**. After collapse, there is nothing to "bring together"—only a field that selects contextually. Integration is replaced by orientation, resonance, and access.

A9. Collapse Facilitation Ethics

Core ethical boundaries:

- Do not collapse others for your validation

- Never use collapse to dominate or control

- Never promise identity freedom as a means of gain

- Always remain invisible to the process once collapse begins

- Do not attach collapse to belonging, worth, or approval

Collapse must be held in **ego-less relational space**. It cannot serve personal status, or it fractures the integrity of the field.

A10. ICT Reading List & Cross-Disciplinary Anchors

Key sources aligning with ICT principles:

- **Varela, F.** – Neurophenomenology

- **Friston, K.** – Active Inference / Free Energy Principle

- **Barad, K.** – Agential Realism

- **Newen, Gallagher** – 4E Cognition

- **Gendlin, E.** – Felt Sense Theory
- **Kastrup, B.** – Analytic Idealism
- **Bohm, D.** – Implicate Order
- **Merleau-Ponty** – Embodied Perception
- **Nietzsche** – Identity as fiction
- **Laing, R.D.** – Self as social hallucination

ICT draws from these without becoming any of them. Collapse begins where theory ends.

Scientific Reference Index

(For readers, clinicians, and institutions seeking external research correlates to the Identity Collapse Therapy model)

---

1. Friston, K. (2010).
The free-energy principle: a unified brain theory?
Nature Reviews Neuroscience, 11(2), 127–138.
https://doi.org/10.1038/nrn2787

Foundation for understanding identity as a predictive, self-organizing narrative system that collapses when error minimization fails.

2. Seth, A. K. (2014).

A predictive processing theory of sensorimotor contingencies: Explaining the puzzle of perceptual presence and its absence in synesthesia. *Cognitive Neuroscience, 5*(2), 97–118.
https://doi.org/10.1080/17588928.2014.965308

Supports the notion that perception and selfhood are constructed from prediction models—rather than discovered.

3. Northoff, G., Heinzel, A., de Greck, M., Bermpohl, F., Dobrowolny, H., & Panksepp, J. (2006).

Self-referential processing in our brain: A meta-analysis of imaging studies on the self. *NeuroImage, 31*(1), 440–457.
https://doi.org/10.1016/j.neuroimage.2005.12.002

Provides evidence for the neural correlates of self-reference in the Default Mode Network—key to understanding identity filtering.

4. Libet, B., Gleason, C. A., Wright, E. W., & Pearl, D. K. (1983).

Time of conscious intention to act in relation to onset of cerebral activity (readiness-potential). *Brain, 106*(3), 623–642.
https://doi.org/10.1093/brain/106.3.623

A classic study showing that conscious intention lags behind neural initiation—supporting ICT's assertion that identity is not the source of choice.

---

5. Damasio, A. R. (1999).
The Feeling of What Happens: Body and Emotion in the Making of Consciousness. Harcourt.

Integrates emotional signaling into the perception of selfhood—key to ICT's model of emotional filtering and collapse fatigue.

---

6. Carhart-Harris, R. L., & Friston, K. J. (2019).
REBUS and the anarchic brain: Toward a unified model of the brain action of psychedelics. *Pharmacological Reviews, 71*(3), 316–344.
https://doi.org/10.1124/pr.118.017160

Correlates collapse-like phenomena in psychedelic states with prediction disruption and identity deactivation—parallels ICT's collapse framework.

---

7. Craig, A. D. (2009).
How do you feel—now? The anterior insula and human awareness. *Nature Reviews Neuroscience, 10*(1), 59–70.
https://doi.org/10.1038/nrn2555

Supports ICT's inclusion of interoception and emotional precision post-collapse, particularly in the transition to PRC-based awareness.

---

8. Sheline, Y. I., Price, J. L., Yan, Z., & Mintun, M. A. (2010).

Resting-state functional MRI in depression unmasks increased connectivity between networks via the subgenual cingulate. *Biological Psychiatry, 69*(6), 561–568.
https://doi.org/10.1016/j.biopsych.2010.09.031

Links dysfunctional DMN hyperconnectivity with depressive identity states—contextualizing collapse as neurological resolution, not pathology.

---

9. Metzinger, T. (2003).

Being No One: The Self-Model Theory of Subjectivity. MIT Press.

Philosophical and cognitive model that supports ICT's framing of identity as a virtual simulation maintained by self-modeling, not essence.

---

10. Lutz, A., Dunne, J. D., & Davidson, R. J. (2007).

Meditation and the neuroscience of consciousness: An introduction. In P. Zelazo, M. Moscovitch, & E. Thompson (Eds.), *The Cambridge Handbook of*

Consciousness (pp. 499–551). Cambridge University Press.

Highlights shifts in brain activity during states of reduced narrative identity—providing a non-ICT corollary for post-collapse clarity.

---

11. Varela, F. J., Thompson, E., & Rosch, E. (1991).
The Embodied Mind: Cognitive Science and Human Experience. MIT Press.

Integrates phenomenology, cognitive science, and experiential breakdown—precursor logic to PRC and ICT's non-narrative field function.

---

12. Anderson, M. L. (2010).
Neural reuse: A fundamental organizational principle of the brain. *Behavioral and Brain Sciences, 33*(4), 245–266.
https://doi.org/10.1017/S0140525X10000853

Supports ICT's assertion that cognition is not fixed to identity modules—once collapse occurs, neural resources are reallocated freely.

Experiencing Activation While Reading?
Collapse is not caused by reading, but sometimes

reading reveals what was already present.
If you find yourself destabilizing, encountering silence, or struggling to orient after exposure to this text, you are not broken.

You are encountering an edge.

ICT is not a self-help system. It is not for self-guided use. But I do offer **field-based containment work** for those in collapse activation.

Visit: identitycollapsetherapy.com

www.ingramcontent.com/pod-product-compliance
Lightning Source LLC
Chambersburg PA
CBHW060447030426
42337CB00015B/1511